José Esteban Muñoz

Double Talk

D1562860

Double Talk

The erotics of

male literary

collaboration

Wayne Koestenbaum

ROUTLEDGE
New York   London

First published in 1989 by
Routledge
An imprint of Routledge, Chapman and Hall, Inc.
29 West 35 Street
New York, NY 10001

Published in Great Britain by
Routledge
11 New Fetter Lane
London EC4P 4EE

Library of Congress Cataloging in Publication Data

Koestenbaum, Wayne.
    Double talk : the erotics of male literary collaboration / Wayne
Koestenbaum.
        p. cm.
    Bibliography: p.
    Includes index.
    ISBN 0-415-90109-X; ISBN 0-415-90110-3 (pbk.)
    1. English literature—Men authors—History and criticism—Theory,
etc. 2. English literature—Men authors—History and criticism.
3. Authorship—Collaboration—Psychological aspects. 4. Men
authors, English—Sexual behavior. 5. Men authors, English—
Psychology. 6. Psychoanalysis and literature. 7. Homosexuality
and literature.   I. Title.
PR120.M45K64   1989
820'.9'9286—dc19   89-5879
                                                                         CIP

British Library Cataloguing in Publication Data

Kostenbaum, Wayne.
    Double talk: the erotics of male literary collaboration.
    1. English literature—Critical studies
    I. Title
    820.9

ISBN 0–415–90109–X
ISBN 0–415–90110–3 (pbk.)

For Steven Marchetti

Contents

Acknowledgments   ix

Interpreting Double Talk: An Introduction   1

Part I.   **Men of Science**   15

1.   Privileging the Anus: Anna O. and the Collaborative Origin of Psychoanalysis   17

2.   Unlocking Symonds: *Sexual Inversion*   43

Part II.   **Poetic Partnerships**   69

3.   The Marinere Hath his Will(iam): Wordsworth's and Coleridge's *Lyrical Ballads*   71

4.   *The Waste Land:* T. S. Eliot's and Ezra Pound's Collaboration on Hysteria   112

Part III.   **The Hour of Double Talk**   141

5.   Manuscript Affairs: Collaborative Romances of the Fin de Siècle   143

Notes   179

Bibliography   199

Index   209

Acknowledgments

For three years I have been considering how authors affectionately combine identities. I have been lucky in my teachers, colleagues, and friends, whom I am happy to acknowledge as my more than implied collaborators, if they will accept the designation.

I owe particular thanks to Elaine Showalter, who has guided my work at all stages; without her friendship and example, I could not have written this book. I am equally grateful to U. C. Knoepflmacher, who supervised this project in its earlier incarnation as a dissertation, and who has been remarkably generous with his time and erudition.

Others have helped to lighten the burden of solitary scholarship. I am especially grateful to Celeste Schenck, who read the entire book in an earlier draft and offered lucid advice. Sandra M. Gilbert and A. Walton Litz each helped the project along, giving astute comments and cheerful guidance. Jane Gallop gave me the benefit of her careful editing, and kindly sponsored the first chapter as an MLA paper. Eve Kosofsky Sedgwick, whose work has influenced my own, was a searching critic of portions of this book; I am grateful for her elucidations. I thank Carol Barash, David Bromwich, Ronald Bush, Andrew Kappel, and Ann Kibbey for commenting on chapters in earlier versions. Frequent and fond conversations with Richard Howard, J. D. McClatchy, and James Richardson helped me understand prose and poetry; letters from Jeanne Schinto were inestimable. David McDermott and Peter McGough generously granted me an interview, and allowed me to use their painting, "No Arguments—1903," as an illustration. Steven Marchetti advised me on questions of style. Fred Kameny prepared the index. William P. Germano has been a peerless editor.

I am grateful to the Mrs. Giles Whiting Foundation for a fellowship which gave me time to write.

Chapter one was published, in slightly different form, in *Genders* (University of Texas Press); chapter four is a revision of an article in *Twentieth Century Literature*; portions of chapter five appeared in *Critical Matrix: Princeton Working Papers in Women's Studies*. For access to unpublished material on Pound and Eliot, I owe thanks to the Collection of American Literature, Beinecke Rare Book and Manuscript Library, Yale University. Excerpts from letters by Ezra Pound, Copyright © 1988 by the Trustees of the Ezra Pound Literary Property Trust; used by permission of New Directions Publishing Corporation, agents, and Faber and Faber Ltd. Excerpts from Pound's "Postscript" to Remy de Gourmont's *The Natural Philosophy of Love* from *Pavannes & Divagations*, Copyright © 1958 by Ezra Pound; used by permission of New Directions Publishing Corporation, agents, and Faber and Faber Ltd. I reproduce the cover photograph, "Birth of Dionysus," courtesy of the Estate of George Platt Lynes.

Interpreting Double Talk:
An Introduction

André Gide implied a disdain for literary collaboration when he had a character in *The Counterfeiters* proclaim that "no *chef-d'oeuvre* was ever produced by several people together."[1] Gide's remark is casual; but certain readers doubtless believe that conceptions should spring from a single mind, and that collaborative works are promiscuous and unnatural. Like bastards in *King Lear*, these mongrel texts come from no centered position in a moral universe; they evoke uncertainty and condescension in a reader who demands to know at all moments a sentence's source. Who, however, parses so puritanically? Most readers will be content to regard these texts as curiosities. Some readers will be more extravagant, and ecstatically celebrate collaboration: Gide's 19th-century predecessors, Edmond and Jules de Goncourt, touted their shared journal as "the confession of two lives *indivisible* in pleasure, toil, trouble, two twin thoughts, two minds receiving from contact with men and things similar, identical, homogeneous impressions, that the confession may be considered as the expression of one single *self*, one single *I*."[2]

My project began with a similarly romantic intuition of collaboration's power to join two male selves. Reading H. Rider Haggard's sensational novel, *She* (1887), dedicated to his friend Andrew Lang, I interpreted its emphasis on male bonds as a reflection of the author's collegial affection for the dedicatee. One scene in particular seemed to embody their friendship. Leo and Horace, two men exploring a matriarchal Africa, must help each other leap across an abyss from one projecting rock to another. Guiding Horace across a threatening feminine gap, Leo confirms their mutual affection:

> I heard his sinews cracking above me, and I felt myself lifted up as though I were a little child, till I got my left arm around the rock, and my chest was resting on it. The rest was easy; in two or three more seconds I was up, and we were lying panting side by side, trembling like leaves, and with the cold perspiration of terror pouring from our skins.[3]

1

Looking further into mysteries behind *She*, I discovered that Lang and Haggard had actually collaborated on a novel, called *The World's Desire* (1890). Unread and out of print, it promised a rich depiction of *Haggard* and *Lang*, like *Horace* and *Leo*, lying "panting side by side, trembling like leaves"; I anticipated that *The World's Desire* would tell the story of Lang's and Haggard's secret life. Men who wrote a book together, it seemed, could not avoid an embarrassing transparency; I presumed that collaborative texts could not help spilling secrets that singly authored works had the composure to hide.

A Theory of Male Collaboration

A text is most precisely and satisfyingly collaborative if it is composed by two writers who admit the act by placing both of their names on the title page. A double signature confers enormous interpretive freedom: it permits the reader to see the act of collaboration shadowing every word in the text. Collaborative works are intrinsically *different* than books written by one author alone; even if both names do not appear, or one writer eventually produces more material, the decision to collaborate determines the work's contours, and the way it can be read. Books with two authors are specimens of a relation, and show writing to be a quality of motion and exchange, not a fixed thing. Whether we call the will that produces a collaborative work inspiration, authority, or diligence, this "will" is shared, sometimes miserably. I am uninterested in apportioning credit or blame, and will not attempt to decide which writer, in a twosome, was responsible for specific passages or for the final product. I find, however, that one writer in a team captures my sympathies more entirely: I enter the mind of the writer who keenly feels lack or disenfranchisement, and seeks out a partner to attain power and completion. Approaching the text, I ask how this writer's wish for a partner infused the work eventually composed; I let his sought-after collaborator remain a shadowy, aloof figure, and I inquire less assiduously into this second man's motives.

With the exception of two female partnerships of the fin de siècle, mentioned at the very end of this book, all of the writers I discuss are men. Unlike the kind of critic who omits consideration of women writers without noticing their absence, I intend to view "maleness" with skepticism.[4] Most of the texts I discuss were produced between 1885 and 1922—a historical moment in which men were increasingly pressed to defend their friendships against imputations of homosexual feeling. I choose 1885 as symbolic starting-line and point of reference because in that year, Parliament passed the Labouchère Amendment, which made "gross indecency" between men, whether public or private, consensual or nonconsensual, a crime punishable by up to two years in prison with hard labor. That harsh law changed the tone and direction of British letters, for it punished Oscar Wilde, in 1895, with the maximum penalty, an ordeal that shamed and silenced him. The Labouchère Amendment shaped male behavior until its repeal in 1967; by discussing collaborations that followed in the first decades after the law's passage, I am offering, in addition to a theory of male collaboration, a specific account of how men redefined authorship to accommodate changed perceptions and legal definitions of sexuality.[5]

[Collaboration, itself neutral, can mean many things. It became laden, delicately at the beginning of the 19th century, and ferociously at its end, with the struggle to define male bonds along a spectrum including lascivious criminality and sexless chumming—a continuum that Eve Kosofsky Sedgwick has called homosocial. To borrow her term and her interpretive apparatus, I would say that collaboration between men in the 19th and early 20th centuries was a complicated and anxiously homosocial act, and that all the writers in this study, regardless of their sexual preference, collaborated in order to separate homoeroticism from the sanctioned male bonding that upholds patriarchy.[6]]

Collaborators express homoeroticism and they strive to conceal it. A doubled voice abets this task of confessing and of sequestering; I like to call the process of collaborative writing "double talk," defined by the Random House dictionary as "evasive and ambiguous language." I will use, throughout this study, the more formal term "double writing," but "double talk," as title and motto, more tersely embodies collaboration's evasions. When two men write together, they indulge in double talk; they rapidly patter to obscure their erotic burden, but the ambiguities of their discourse give the taboo subject some liberty to roam. Looking at a variety of specimens of "double talk," I apply to each the same paradigm, which is, bluntly stated, that men who collaborate engage in a metaphorical sexual intercourse, and that the text they balance between them is alternately the child of their sexual union, and a shared woman. I am indebted to previous studies on the exchange of women within patriarchy, work begun by Claude Lévi-Strauss, applied to literary criticism by René Girard, and sharpened for feminist and anti-homophobic uses by Luce Irigaray, Gayle Rubin, and, most recently, Sedgwick. Their work helps me to describe male collaborative writing as an intercourse carried on through the exchange of women or of texts that take on "feminine" properties.[7] I might justify the intensity with which I pursue this single paradigm—insisting that collaboration is always a sublimation of erotic entanglement, always a glamorous underworld enterprise—by saying that collaborators, too, delude themselves with myths of what double talk will magically bring. A writer turns to a partner not from a practical assessment of advantages, but from a superstitious hope, a longing for replenishment and union that invites baroquely sexual interpretation. Whatever the blind spots of my paradigm, it has helped me establish the "male collaborative text" as a generic category: half pathological case history, half egalitarian intellectual dialogue.

The particular examples I discuss are motley. In my first section, I examine two contemporaneous works of psychology and sexology, Sigmund Freud's and Josef Breuer's *Studies on Hysteria* (1895), and John Addington Symonds's and Havelock Ellis's *Sexual Inversion* (1897). Next, I move to poetry, reading William Wordsworth's and Samuel Taylor Coleridge's *Lyrical Ballads* (1798), and T. S. Eliot's (and Ezra Pound's) *The Waste Land* (1922). Finally, I turn away from close reading and toward literary history by looking at a range of fin de siècle collaborations—principally, "romance" novels by Robert Louis Stevenson and his stepson Lloyd Osborne, Andrew Lang and H. Rider Haggard, and Joseph Conrad and Ford Madox Ford. Though difficulties arise in using a single model to understand the *Lyrical Ballads* and *Sexual Inversion*, two texts opalescent in such different ways, bringing collaborative authorship to the fore shows each work, whether canonical or noncanonical, in a new light. *The Waste Land*, for example, sounds less masterful, more vacillating, in this new context of other works by two men. Double authorship, however, is not the only feature these disparate texts share. Certain desires and dreads regularly follow in the double signature's wake: hysterical discontinuity, muteness, castratory violence, homoerotic craving, misogyny, a wish to usurp female generative power. The consistency of these themes suggests that my selection of texts is hardly random. By beginning with Freud, and relying, throughout, on his vocabulary, I am discussing not acts of literary collaboration in general, but a particular sort of writing relationship that existed between men who were Freud's contemporaries, who were keenly aware of the ascendancy of female authority, and who shared his conviction that creativity was most powerfully released in heated male colloquy. The kind of quasi-erotic male collaboration that I describe was a cohesive wave in literary and cultural history.

Wordsworth and Coleridge, who seem at odds with this temporal framework, have a place here because they sparked the movement—romanticism—that turned introspection and recollection into modes of political action, and that brought to prominence a kind of self,

boundaried yet flexing to smash limits, that might be labeled bourgeois.[8] Reverence for this romantic self infuses the work of all figures
I study; their retaliations against the ego's integrity—whether through
Freudian unstitching of motive from deed, or through the schismatic
act of collaboration itself—imply faith in a self worth unraveling. I
assume that my model of double talk has most force if applied to
texts that respond, however deviously, to the desire and the pursuit
of the whole—the wish to unite with a lost twin and to form a blended
soul. Another reason to include the *Lyrical Ballads* is its kinship to
The Waste Land. Both texts were aggressive acts of literary innovation
that instigated artistic movements (romanticism and modernism) with
political overtones. In both cases, effecting a revolution in taste required that one poet submit to another's fertilizing will.

  Lyrical Ballads and *The Waste Land*, however, had no direct impact
on the history of sexuality, while Freud palpably urged homosexuality
toward its present life as identity and vocation: in his later work,
and more subtly in *Studies on Hysteria*, he shaped our inherited
understanding of homosexuality as perversion. Ellis and Symonds,
too, were pioneers, for *Sexual Inversion* examined its subject dispas-
sionately, and Symonds was the first writer in British history who felt
that his sexual preference was central to his literary career. *Sexual
Inversion* is particularly relevant to my study; a collaborative work
whose subject is homosexuality, it shows that Symonds, at least,
understood double writing to be a congenial medium for speaking
out as a homosexual. By using *Sexual Inversion* and Symonds as
theoretical centers for my project, I suggest that an outspokenly
homosexual minor writer and a noncanonical work of sexology can
serve as suns around which larger literary planets must orbit.

  Of the writers I treat at length, only Symonds thought of himself
as an "invert." By example, this book tries to justify discussing works
by heterosexual men within a framework dominated by homosexual
desire, whether draped in the discrete charm of the "homosocial
continuum," or left impolitely naked; I hope to show that gay criticism can illuminate Wordsworth as well as Wilde. I pursue these slant
readings because I believe that I am drawing on a system comprehensive enough to unravel a range of perplexities. This system is, in
essence, feminist: it questions heterosexuality's privilege and forces
masculine writing to take seriously the threat of "queerness." Decon-
struction has taught us that any monolithic body of ideas and habits
contains the very difference it condemns; within male texts of all
varieties lurks a homosexual desire which, far from reinforcing patriarchy, undermines it, and offers a way out.[9]

  Although I assume that when men are sexually engaged with each other they are acting against and not in accord with the wishes of patriarchy, these specimens of double talk are fearful and febrile examples of misogyny. Even when not violently woman-hating, collaborators made use of the "feminine" in appropriative ways. Tangibly, collaborators used their actual wives, daughters, sisters, patients, and rivals as mediators. Intangibly, collaborators enclosed the dreaded "feminine" by imagining their shared text to be a woman, and by drawing on female procreative sexuality to describe their own writerly intercourse. I give precedence to the "feminine" point of view, whether I am describing how women were used as trampled-on mediators, or whether I am glorifying one man's experience of being penetrated. I describe passive men and mediating women as if they were the same because both are points of sympathy, coordinates where I can enter the collaborative text and begin to analyze. In this sense, I, too, use the woman as mediator, for she helps me vicariously participate in the charged scene of two men collaborating; by championing her cause, I can rebuke the men for improperly diffusing homo-erotic desire in female go-betweens.

Searching for literary power, collaborators raid heterosexual intercourse for metaphors of fecundity. I suppose their desire resembles "womb-envy," a now unfashionable label that disparages two men's longing to produce a breathing object that will have dignified, in retrospect, their shady exchange. The development of a female literary tradition might have made men more likely, in the late 19th century, to think of their writing in terms of female biology. It was no longer feasible to equate pen and penis; unable to assert that creativity was incompatible with female anatomy, men began to see authorship as a feminine process that they must steal back.[10]

It is difficult to speak about double entendre, that portal through which sexuality mercurially enters words, without turning to a psychoanalytic vocabulary. But there are reasons, other than temperament, for beginning this book with Freud, and borrowing his language throughout. Freud changed the way homosexuals interpreted themselves, and the way society regarded them; furthermore, most of the collaborators I discuss were men of Freud's time. Even beyond this historical coincidence, the psychoanalytic process, which mines the unconscious and splits the self, is a collaborative act, and so the relation between hysteric and analyst, set forth in *Studies on Hysteria*, illuminates the experiences of double writers. Hysteria, a form of 19th-century feminism, attacked gender rigidities; collaboration undermined them more subtly. Both the female hysteric and the man in search of a collaborator were stricken with silence and paralysis; each overcame muteness by submitting to a mesmerizing man. I have described double writing as an intercourse; it is also a scene of analysis, in which the active collaborator hypnotizes his passive mate. This dynamic appears most prominently in *The Waste Land*; but many other double writers, searching for the power to speak, share with the hysteric a primary alienation from language. Because the relation between hysteric and analyst summarizes the themes of passivity/ activity, mesmerism, transference, gender ambiguity, and dialogue, *Studies on Hysteria* is a particularly charged place to begin an account of collaboration.

As I have said, I take sexual figures of speech seriously. One style of psychoanalytic criticism detects inadvertent and unconscious signs of homosexual desire only to discount them as symptoms of the author's incomplete maturation. But it is possible to use Freudian tools toward more emancipatory ends: gay criticism can employ psychoanalytic methods to find clues for building a history of homosexual experience. It is evident from my writing that I feel strong transference toward the act of collaboration, and toward individual writers I describe: it may seem that I, like Freud, am half in love with Wilhelm Fliess. Transference, if recognized, forgiven, and exploited, is a boon: a gay criticism that cooperates with its own desires will be able to find meanings that would, to other readers, remain invisible.

Before I conclude my own version of what Breuer and Freud called, in *Studies on Hysteria*, their "preliminary communication," I should explain the energies behind my first chapter's title, "Privileging the Anus." Freud, in his *Three Essays on the Theory of Sexuality*, describes the anal stage as a prelude to the fictional and idealized taking on of a mature relation to one's genitals; in a civilized world, the anus—as a symbolic center of human experience—remains perpetually secondary to sexual reproduction.[11] Throughout my study, I resist Freud's claim that procreation is the normative form of erotic behavior, and I give precedence to the symbolic "anus," the place where men conceive when they write together. Anal intercourse—though I usually only call it "intercourse," eliding the difficult adjective—is this book's central metaphor for double talk. I use Freudian methods to assert the legitimacy of homosexual desire; and yet Freud strongly affirmed patriarchy and procreative sexuality. Or did he? Homoeroticism and misogyny palpably intersect in the work of every writing team I discuss, but nowhere is the conjunction more vivid and troubling than in Freud's collaborative relations; in his case, homosexuality and misogyny are difficult to separate. Close reading that is psychoanalytic in its attention to double entendre, feminist in its skepticism about pieties of male authorship, and gay-emancipatory in its eager sympathy for instances of homosexual desire—this kind of criticism can, I hope, evade any insistence that the political dreams of a feminist and of a gay man have nothing in common.⌐

Other Methods and Matters

Collaboration is not my invention. But I have found no discussion of a group of doubly authored texts, and no explanation of what it means (universally or in a certain historical moment) when two men write together. The texts I discuss hardly form something as grand as a homosexual tradition, but I mean to show that when men wrote books together in the 19th and 20th centuries they were enacting if not feeling homosexual desire, and that collaboration between men still carries that charge.

However, collaboration has significances other than the ones I chart. In wartime, collaborators are traitors who join the enemy. The very word "collaboration" connotes moral bankruptcy, strategems exercised in the face of national defeat. Double writers bear the stain of the word's political meaning: the sense lingers that they, like collaborators in Vichy France, have compromised themselves, have formed new and unhealthy allegiances, and have betrayed trusts.

Instead of following gender and psychoanalytic theory, I might have chosen a gleefully poststructuralist path. Because a collaborative text depicts the author in nervous crisis (breaking down, splitting in two), double writing is a symptom of the monolithic author's decline. That sort of study might easily have reduced to these spare axioms: (1) the Author is dead; (2) the Author is complex. I might have loosely employed Bakhtin's notion of "heteroglossia": collaborative texts, like quilted novels, make the reader vulnerable to heterogeneity and indeterminacy, and, by obscuring who wrote what, they prevent the reader from limiting the text's sense.[12] I would have found praise of heteroglossia tedious because the prefix "hetero-" suggests this theory's sexual preference, and because such a reading of collaboration, secretly reactionary, mourns a fall from unitary grace under the guise of celebrating radical multiplicity. I have found Bataille's notion of expenditure more congenial: double talk is an economy with all expense and no return, a way of discharging language in a masturbatory *folie à deux*.[13] I do not closely follow Bataille, though his vocabulary shapes my discussion of Wordsworth's and Coleridge's struggle to decide whether writing by oneself is morally debilitating.

Double writing is both a dispersive and a retentive procedure; the collaborative text longs to be a well-wrought urn, but it is a fatally riven golden bowl. I deviate from this poststructuralist reading, crudely sketched, because I believe that double authorship attacks not primarily our dogmas of literary property, but of sexual propriety. I begin with my own infatuated, French sense of the erotic and possibly monogamous nature of writing, but I do not follow Roland Barthes and Hélène Cixous in their flight from the biographical, the concrete, and the literal. Because I take the figurative literally, I feel licensed to linger over the figurative. I refuse or am unable to see figurative language as existing only in a safe textual world remote from action. Indeed, despite the lovely aura of contraband I attribute to collaboration, I follow a conventional method of close reading which applies biography to text, treats biography as text, and depends on the integrity of the author as more than a social construct or a fiction superimposed on intertextual anarchy. I can describe collaboration as a disruptive act only if I retain a conservative allegiance to singular authority. However, I allow for meanings that authors might never have intended; a collaborative text exhibits (shameful) symptoms of double authorship, despite the men's desire to make the work seem the product of one mind.

I owe Roland Barthes a few more words of exploration, for his work has closely affected mine. He describes writing as both amorous and empty; even when it is weary, its very fatigue is an erotic sensation. Writing degree zero is "a way a certain silence has of existing";[14] double talk, too, rises from the ashes of ruined, impoverished language. The collaborative text is glad of its own existence but disappointed to have taken such a paltry form. Barthes's descriptions of emptiness make mythical and appealing the very depletions that persuade men to collaborate: his recitals of blankness, riot, and satiation apply to the moods of collaborators and to the texts they produce. For example, his account of lovers saying "I love you" and "So do I" nicely describes the "single flash" of consummated collaboration: lovers imagine a "simultaneous proffering" that "establishes a movement whose model is socially unknowable, unthinkable: neither exchange, nor gift, nor theft, our proffering, welling up in crossed fires, designates an expenditure which relapses nowhere and whose very community abolishes any thought of reservation."[15] I refer desultorily to the Author as dead, and to collaboration as its murderer, but more often I echo the chord in Barthes that celebrates impossible moments when speech approaches bodily pleasure, when one man's voice does not lag behind his friend's, but blurts out at the same moment.

One angle I stint is historical and Marxist: I do not examine methods of textual production, nor do I analyze the rise of collaboration in terms of authorship's social construction. I do not dwell on copyright law, printing, or literacy—variables that define writing. A Marxist interpretation, in my hands, might have turned romantic: I might have described collaboration as a dark satanic force that redeems authority by inverting it, a principle that pretends to undermine literary property while secretly strengthening it: a collaborative work equals Authority^{squared}. A study that confronts double writing's more strictly material basis might begin with a chapter on the single author as a relatively recent movement away from an earlier *status quo* of collaboration. I might have discovered that in some primordial time, writing was always collaborative, and that my double authors of the fin de siècle and early 20th century are, consciously or not, only recreating a lost condition. Were texts shared before they were privately owned? Cain and Abel (about whom, incidentally, Coleridge and Wordsworth once began a collaborative poem) embody this mythic pair of male writers before the fall: Cain, murdering his brother, is a headstrong writer breaking the collaborative covenant. In Harold Bloom's terms, brave Cain would be history's first strong poet. A study that narrowly followed Bloom would have made much of the Oedipal conflict that marks collaborative relations, but would have used shared texts as documents of weak writing. A Bloomian reading might describe collaboration as an escape from the exigencies of feud that must be passed through, like puberty, in order to reach mature masculine vision. I do not follow Bloom's model, though jealousy, confrontation, blood, and dismemberment are not absent from the relations I discuss.[16]

There exists an enormous variety of collaborations that I did not include—material that would have suited my sexual approach. I have, for example, not considered operatic collaboration. W. S. Gilbert and Arthur Sullivan were contemporaries of many of the writers I discuss, and their *Patience* (1881) explicitly satirizes Oscar Wilde. Richard Strauss and Hugo von Hofmannsthal also fall within my study's historical range; their matricidal work (*Elektra*, for example) feels Freud's weight. Operas, touchstones of contemporary homosexual culture, are written by pairs of men who often sentimentalize or apotheosize a woman's degradation and death. If opera lies beyond my purview, then film, intrinsically and diffusely collaborative, seems more remote; and yet my theory of male collaboration might fit Hollywood. Historian Leonard J. Leff has analyzed the "rich and strange" collaboration of Alfred Hitchcock and David O. Selznick;[17] any studio film could be mined for coded references to the male bonds, economic and erotic, that underlay its production. One contemporary partnership, the Brothers Quay, works doggedly as a twosome; splitting the *auteur*, these identical twins film animated dream visions, emanations of an "I" shared in a suggestively incestuous manner.[18]

And what of collaboration among painters? Works of prominent old masters are often marked by several hands; even today, painter and model (whether male or female) form a partnership with demarcated active and passive roles.[19] My theory of male collaboration closely applies to those gay artists who have recently begun to explore the ambiguities of a double signature. The British team, Gilbert and George, and their younger American counterparts, Messrs. McDermott and McGough, use homoerotic imagery, and link sexual content to collaborative method. McDermott and McGough feign an integrated "I" by treating earnestly autobiographical subjects; in works like "Queer—1885" and "The Green Carnation—1887," they echo fin de siècle sexual revolution, and consciously participate in a gay collaborative tradition. If my book documents male collaboration's ambiguous past, McDermott and McGough embody its confidently sexual future. I visited McDermott and McGough in their studio: I will digress to recount what I saw and heard.

While I talked to David McDermott, the older and more voluble of the pair, Peter McGough read John Addington Symonds's "A Problem in Modern Ethics," and then languidly pasted together a collage. David asserts that women can conceive immaculately: a dire conspiracy has convinced women that pregnancy depends on sperm. Interested in propagation and piety, McDermott and McGough claim to have found their "aesthetic heir" (a sort of adopted son), a boy they came upon while lecturing at Andover. If men could go in drag to church, the pair believes, the youth of America would pack the cathedrals every Sunday. (When the couple first met, McDermott was dressed as a woman.) Their arresting painting, "No Arguments," shows two men within a light bulb: the bulb—the two men's flash of joint intuition?—is shaped like a uterus, as if collaborating men unite inside the womb and appropriate its magic (see fig. 1). (David Cronenberg's 1988 film, *Dead Ringers*, depicts a similar situation: twin male gynecologists sharing one womb.) McDermott and McGough enjoy the liberties of aesthetes: they inhabit the 19th century so fully that in their East Village townhouse they lack electricity and phone, and even while painting, they dress in the manner of Oscar Wilde. More than any living artists, they parade the sexual implications of male collaboration. Like many writers I discuss, however, McDermott and McGough do not use their practice to grip a gay identity; collaboration, in fact, isolates them from a political community. They despise the word "gay" (it reminds them of "70s clones"), and they have claimed in print that AIDS does *not* afflict the more spiritual subset of gay men, a refined minority called "homoerotics."[20] Devout though ironic Christian Scientists, McDermott and McGough

Figure 1

want to buy a villa in Capri and make it a shrine where homoerotics might flock in pilgrimage.

My theory of male collaboration applies not only to the visual arts and to opera, but to a fuller range of literary efforts. If I were to write an inclusive history of male double writing, I would begin with Platonic dialogues—implicit collaborations with Socrates, in which pederasty, pedagogy, and colloquy intersect[21]—and continue with Japanese linked verse (stylized poems composed by three poets), which flourished between the 13th and the 19th centuries.[22] Moving then to the English Renaissance—a time when nearly half the plays included the writing of more than one man—I would study the prolific Francis Beaumont and John Fletcher, so united that they shared a bed.[23] After the Renaissance, I would read Joseph Addison and Sir Richard Steele, whose sexualities are open to question, and who worked intimately on the *Tatler* and the *Spectator*.[24] In the 18th and 19th centuries, literary relations often bordered on actual collaboration: James Boswell's *Life of Samuel Johnson* (1791), and Tennyson's *In Memoriam* (1850), written with the imagined assistance of the dead Arthur Hallam, merit attention as collaborations. If this study included partnerships between women and between the sexes (which might shatter its theoretical tidiness), I might consider the Brontës, or George Eliot and George Henry Lewes.[25] I lack the temerity to venture a gay critique of *The Communist Manifesto*, but it is tempting to compare Marx and Engels forging communism, and Freud and Breuer laboring over psychoanalysis. In a comprehensive study, I would consider Edmond and Jules de Goncourt—brothers who started writing together after their mother's death in 1848, and who shared a mistress as well as the composition of novels, histories, and a journal—as well as that most famous pair of homosexual French collaborators, Paul Verlaine and Arthur Rimbaud;[26] modern French poets who experimented with collaboration include André Breton, Paul Eluard, Benjamin Peret, and René Char.[27] Under French and Eastern influence, a whole generation of Americans engaged in aleatory and surrealist collaboration: its practitioners include a group of the mid-century's most distinguished gay artists—Merce Cunningham, John Cage, Robert Rauschenberg, Frank O'Hara, John Ashbery, and James Schuyler.[28] The Dadaist novel, including Ashbery's and Schuyler's *A Nest of Ninnies* (1969), is a particularly significant strain of modern collaboration: I think of this genre as "embarrassed fiction"—ashamed of its own Camp excess, obsessed with flatness and appearance. This tradition includes the *Fantômas* novels of Marcel Allain and Pierre Souvestre, a popular French series begun in 1911, and *The Boy Hairdresser*, by British playwright Joe Orton and his lover Kenneth Halliwell.[29] A history of male collaboration could not omit W. H. Auden, who wrote with his lover Chester Kallman, and with friends Louis MacNiece and Christopher Isherwood.[30] Though the encyclopedic history sketched above may never be written, the existence of so much double writing, much of it homoerotic, widens the frame of my own more modest study.

An entire other book could discuss the history of female (and lesbian) collaboration. Such a study might follow the lines of Susan Gubar's "Sapphistries," which describes the woman writer's attempt to absorb the strength of a precursor by setting up a "fantastic collaboration."[31] Taking to heart the example of Bryher and H.D., and Alice B. Toklas and Gertrude Stein, contemporary feminists have turned to collaboration as a politically fraught act. Jane Miller and Olga Broumas wrote a volume of poetry together, *Black Holes, Black Stockings* (1985); Hélène Cixous and Catherine Clément, in *La Jeune Née* (1975), and Sandra M. Gilbert and Susan Gubar, in such works as *The Madwoman in the Attic* (1979), use shared authority as a subversive angle for revising literary and cultural history.[32] The Marxist-Feminist Literature Collective pursues collaboration even more radically by writing as a group.[33] Stranger cases might be considered. Two black British teenagers, June and Jennifer Gibbons, electively mute identical twins, each wrote several novels and kept voluminous diaries, and together set fire to a school.[34] Sisterly collaboration, however incendiary, is more fruitful than the union of a male writer and his female amanuensis: Sylvia Plath, typing her husband Ted Hughes's poems, resumes an old tradition of wifely subordination.[35] I do not discuss this sort of appropriative relation; for example, though I analyze Wordsworth's collaboration with Coleridge, I do not consider the two men's use of Dorothy, in whose journal they found material for poetry.

Rather than writing a history of collaboration in all of its forms, I focus on a handful of cases, and freely theorize about the act's foundations. I cannot assert that "collaboration" always means the same thing. This is a book of details, full of abrupt angles, foreshortenings, and close-ups. Close-ups, rarely flattering, are sometimes grotesque. And yet they help us see how a subject truly looks. By limiting myself to one historical period, and a few texts, I hope to isolate a striking sexual phenomenon, and to maintain intimacy with the men I describe, without risk of dilution.

Part I

Men of Science

1
Privileging the Anus:
Anna O. and the Collaborative
Origin of Psychoanalysis

*"If there will be justice in the world to come, women will
be lawgivers, and men have to have babies."*
—*Bertha Pappenheim*

Although Sigmund Freud fitfully recognized the weight of his relationships with men, neither his faithful disciples nor his bolder feminist critics have asked why psychoanalysis first came into print as a
male collaboration—*Studies on Hysteria* (1895), written by Freud
and his mentor, physician Josef Breuer. The *Studies* interests me here
primarily as a paradigmatic male collaborative text, and as a window
onto Freud. However, it is a historically important work in its own
right, for it depicts a revolutionary mode of treating nervous diseases.
Breuer's patient Anna O. discovered that, under hypnosis, she could
talk away her symptoms by narrating—telling stories, describing daydreams, or tracing back her symptoms to their first occurrence. She
named this cathartic procedure the "talking cure." The *Studies* unfolds the theory and practice of the talking cure, which Freud later
transformed into psychoanalysis by abandoning hypnosis, and relying
on the patient's free associations.

Anna O., whose case dominates *Studies on Hysteria*, occupies such
a prominent position in psychoanalytic history not only because of
her "talking cure," but because of the bizarre scene which ended her
treatment. When Breuer's wife became jealous of his attentions to
Anna O., he decided to stop seeing the patient. After saying farewell,
he was called back to her bedside, where he found her "confused and
writhing in abdominal cramps" and crying "Now Dr. B.'s child is
coming!" Breuer fled this scene of hysterical childbirth "in a cold
sweat";[1] he failed to understand the significance of Anna O.'s phantom pregnancy, an eruption which Freud later attributed to her transference and to Breuer's own unsifted countertransference. Anna O.

17

went into labor in June 1882, thirteen years before the *Studies* was published; Freud, not a witness to the scene, knew of it only from Breuer. We have no account of it from Anna O.; it is mentioned neither in her case history nor elsewhere in *Studies on Hysteria*. Because Anna's labor occurs only in the texts of Freud and his disciples, it loses texture as a woman's experience, and becomes, within the history of psychoanalysis, a possession prized by a chain of male mentors and their disciples.

The fact that "Anna O." was really Bertha Pappenheim, an important feminist activist, has helped feminist critics to see hysteria as a revolutionary—though self-immolating—strategy.[2] Pursuing this analysis of hysteria, I present Freud's and Breuer's collaboration as an extreme case of a practice common among men in the fin de siècle: the double autograph on the title page of *Studies on Hysteria*—announcing the ambiguous, joint labor of Josef Breuer and Sigmund Freud—signals a belief that men could write fiercely revolutionary texts more effectively by forming a partnership. Double writing, like good citizenship, sublimates homoerotic longing. In 1922, Freud speculated that "a good number of homosexuals are characterized by a special development of their social instinctual impulses and by their devotion to the interests of the community."[3] The city-state of psychoanalysis was founded in such a spirit of fraternity.

By collaborating with Breuer, Freud sought to fuse male bonding and scientific labor, and to appropriate the power of female reproduction, a force embodied in Anna O.'s hysterical pregnancy. To give flesh to this construction, I will end the chapter with an account of Freud's relationship with the nose doctor and quasi-scientific theorist Wilhelm Fliess. By the time *Studies on Hysteria* was written, the friendship with Breuer had waned, and Freud had transferred his affections to Fliess. This chapter thus divides into two stories—Freud and Breuer, and Freud and Fliess: an eccentric arrangement, with three men jockeying for position around the indivisible Anna O.

Freud began his study of Leonardo da Vinci by denying any intent to besmirch the master. Quoting Schiller, Freud asserted that "'to blacken the radiant and drag the sublime into the dust' is no part" of his purpose.[4] In restoring to light some untoward portions of the anatomy of psychoanalytic history, I do not intend to blacken Freud. Because I rely on Freud's interpretive techniques and hug close to me his anatomical assumptions, I would be left without apparatus if my purpose were simply to denounce. Though this chapter (and the book as a whole) is inspired by the feminist critique of psychoanalysis, and by the understanding, crystallized by Eve Kosofsky Sedgwick, that men seal their bonds with each other by exchanging women, I am not primarily concerned to reiterate the many ways that Freud negates and misconstrues women.[5] Instead, I argue that long before Freud learned to account for—and yearn to transcend—homoeroticism's unsettling presence, it had shaped his scientific methods. Freud is not simply a tribunal, indifferent to the men and women who must struggle against psychoanalytic definitions of their "condition": Freud came to intellectual maturity while the homosexual rights movement was gaining force, and its emergence might have indirectly encouraged his friendships with Breuer and Fliess. In the essay on Leonardo, written in 1910, Freud admits a tension between how he defines homosexual men, and how they define themselves:

> Homosexual men, who have in our times taken vigorous action against the restrictions imposed by law on their sexual activity, are fond of representing themselves, through their theoretical spokesmen, as being from the outset a distinct sexual species, as an intermediate sexual stage, as a "third sex." . . . Much as one would be glad on grounds of humanity to endorse their claims, one must treat their theories with some reserve, for they have been advanced without regard for the psychical genesis of homosexuality. Psycho-analysis offers the means of filling this gap and of putting the assertions of homosexuals to the test. (48–49)

Although Freud here regrets that the claims of homosexual activism and psychoanalytic truth are incompatible, this later calm renunciation comes fifteen years after the apex of his own erotic ties to Breuer and Fliess. If psychoanalysis tests the assertions of homosexuals, then the presence of homosexual desire in Freud's early work tests psychoanalysis.

Freud divides the body into a sequence of rungs that the psyche must climb toward its difficult maturity. I have chosen, within that hierarchical body, to emphasize the anus. Norman O. Brown affirms it as a bodily and symbolic zone, but ignores its age-old connection to sodomy and homosexual desire.[6] On the contrary, I assume that to privilege the anus (to turn the world upside down) is not simply to embrace Jonathan Swift's "excremental vision," but to admit the desirability of male homosexual relations. Although Freud describes the anal stage as a prelude to mature genitality, I oppose the reproductive and heterosexual assumptions of his later work by asserting the anus as the primary center of energy in his first approaches to psychoanalysis. Despite the catholicity of the anus, this book limits itself to the male's and not the female's: my subject is male desire. Tension persists, however, between my identification with Freud as the passive partner in collaborative relations, and my equally shaping interest in Anna O., the center of Breuer's and Freud's commerce. When men copulate with each other, in fact or in fancy, a woman's victimization need not be the consequence; women were reduced to bleeding mediators within the pre-history of psychoanalysis, but the male anus was not necessarily to blame.

Breuer and Freud: Active and Passive

It is impossible to separate the growth of Freud's theories from the rising and falling fortunes of his male friendships.[8] To Wilhelm Fliess, Freud confessed his dependence on other men:

> As to Breuer, you are certainly quite right about *the* brother, but I do not share your contempt for friendship between men, probably because I am to a high degree party to it. In my life, as you know, woman has never replaced the comrade, the friend. If Breuer's male inclination were not so odd, so timid, so contradictory—like everything else in his mental and emotional makeup—it would provide a nice example of the accomplishments into which the androphilic current in men can be sublimated.[9]

Through self-analysis, Freud dissolved the erotic element of this partiality: he told his disciple Sándor Ferenczi of the "greater independence that comes from having overcome my homosexuality."[10] Ferenczi is now remembered more for his intense homoerotic attachment to Freud than for his own theoretical ventures, including a chapter on "The Nosology of Male Homosexuality" which disparages the modern "exaggeration of hetero-erotism for the purpose of repressing love towards the same sex."[11] I draw attention to Freud's "androphilic current" not to accuse him of latent homosexuality, but to show his affection for comrades intertwining with the creation of psychoanalysis. Unraveling hysteria's enigmas was an intellectual undertaking; it was also a chance to bond with powerful men. Because the comrades whom Freud found indispensable were scientists who shared his interest in nervous diseases, he could unite the pursuit of science and the pursuit of friendship.

In his fledgling years, Freud fell under the sway of a series of men. His first mentor was Ernst Brücke, his teacher at the Institute of Physiology: Freud spoke of being "under the influence of Brücke, the greatest authority who affected me more than any other in my whole life."[12] Freud felt as strongly about his next teacher, J.-M. Charcot, at the Salpêtrière in Paris: "Whether the seed will ever bring forth fruit I do not know; but what I certainly know is that no other human being has ever affected me in such a way."[13] Freud experienced intellectual influence as fertilization, the master's seed cast into the pupil's mind. During these months in Paris, while profiting from Charcot's seed, Freud beheld theatrical hysterics submitting to mesmeric influence, undergoing fits at the master's suggestion. Freud, bending to his teacher's will, took on the madwoman's symbolic position: he wrote, "I do nothing here except allow myself to be wound up by Charcot in the mornings. . . . "[14] Freud performed as Hoffmann's limp Olympia, a doll vulnerable to infusions of nervous energy; in Freud's student years, at least, he was hardly a Svengali.

In such compliance there were secret dividends. Freud made himself passive so that he might gain mastery. In translating Charcot's *Leçons du mardi* (an ostensibly deferential act), he proved himself far from servile: he added 62 unauthorized footnotes, some hazarding his own theories and contradicting his teacher's.[15] Charcot was displeased with his pupil's liberties, as Freud would later be chagrined at the freedoms his own disciples claimed. With Breuer, as with Charcot, Freud outgrew passivity and longed to be master. He realized, however, that Breuer could not be influenced; that stolidness frustrated the protégé and led to the break in their relations after the publication of *Studies on Hysteria*.[16] In 1894, Freud may have complained that Breuer treated him "like a patient, with evasion and subterfuge," but in the early years of their friendship Freud was happy to be fertilized.[17] "In this relationship," Freud later wrote, "the gain was naturally mine." He treasured Breuer's gifts so deeply that when the "development of psychoanalysis afterwards cost me his friendship," Freud confessed, "[i]t was not easy for me to pay such a price."[18]

His recourse to language of "price" and "cost" implies that their relationship worked as a financial transaction; secrets were their commodity, and Freud was usually on the receiving end. Inscribing a copy of his translation of Charcot's *Leçons sur les maladies du système nerveux*, Freud acknowledged Breuer as a source of secrets, by turns a miser and a benefactor: "To my friend Josef Breuer, whom I esteem beyond all other men, the secret master of hysteria and other complicated problems."[19] Marriage was one of these "complicated problems" which Breuer had mastered; some of the most important secrets that these two men shared concerned their wives. At the time when he was dominated by Breuer, Freud met his future wife, Martha Bernays; their courtship began as a tributary of the Breuer sea. Although Ernest Jones, in his biography of Freud, places the "Betrothal" and "Marriage" chapters before "The Breuer Period" chapter, implying that heterosexual romance preceded the tie to Breuer, Freud fell under his mentor's sway several years *before* he met Martha. Furthermore, he treated his engagement as a secret equal in price to the mysteries of hysteria that Breuer hoarded. Freud wrote to his fiancée:

> You know what Breuer told me one evening? I was so moved by what he said that in return I disclosed to him the secret of our engagement. He told me he had discovered that hidden under the surface of timidity there lay in me an extremely daring and fearless human being.[20]

Breuer detects Freud's hidden virility, and the younger man shows his gratitude by giving away the glistening secret of his engagement. Clearly, the betrothal to Martha had value within the men's private barter. The engagement had a further link to their work on hysteria: Freud and Martha were engaged in June 1882, the very month of Anna O.'s hysterical childbirth. This coincidence places his marriage snugly within the circuit of Anna O.'s labor.

Mothers, wives, and daughters heightened Freud's and Breuer's attachment to each other; the fact that Freud's fiancée and Breuer's wife had the same initials—M.B.—helped Freud appreciate that by marrying Martha he had insinuated himself deeper into his friend's marriage. Freud was so devoted to Mathilde Breuer that he gave her name to his first daughter, during whose infancy he suggestively commented, "although Mathilde sucks her fingers, she shows a striking resemblance to me . . . several people point to gaps in my face where the little girl has been cut out."[21] Freud spoke of his daughter (mimesis of Frau Breuer) as if she had been carved from him in a savage Caesarian section. In a letter to his fiancée, Freud dwelt on her resonant initials: "As you know, I am interested only in the M."[22] This fascinating M stands not only for Martha and Mathilde but for motherhood—and motherhood was one bridge that Freud crossed to reach Breuer. (Or did Freud cross Breuer to reach motherhood?) After Breuer's death, in a letter to the widow, Freud sentimentally reminds her of the moment when, "glancing through the door of the consulting room, I first saw you sitting at a table with a barely two-year-old daughter."[23] Freud remembers glimpsing a scene of motherhood from Breuer's consulting room: that daunting room—signifying science, male maturity, and the *camera* of Breuer's mysterious paternal body—contained a peephole through which Freud could peer into secrets of maternity. Because the consulting room gained power from nearness to the nursery, it is logical that Freud experienced a "revolution" in his practice when his first child was born: "when Martha's labor started, I was asked to attend a joint consultation with Chrobak at

Frau L.'s . . . as if the birth of a daughter were equal to a certificate of qualification for the medical profession."[24] Magically, Martha's labor brought Freud medical prestige, as if childbirth could buy men scientific power.

The most tangible secrets that Breuer and Freud exchanged were patients. Freud, who considered it a mark of distinction that he was permitted to treat Charcot's female hysterics, boasted to his fiancée, "I have only to say one word to Charcot and I can do whatever I like with the patients."[25] In Vienna, Freud relied on hysterics for income, so there is a firm link between the exchange of patients and the exchange of money. Breuer gave Freud both. In the 1880s and 1890s, when Freud was struggling to build a practice, a family, and a theory, Breuer referred patients to him and lent him a total of 2,300 gulden.[26] Freud wrote to his friend:

> for neither of us are financial relationships the most important in life, nor do they seem incommensurable with other relationships. . . . I had to testify to this theory in an active and passive way, as receiver and giver, while you were able to confine yourself to the active role.[27]

As Freud describes this exchange, the man who lends money is active, and the man who borrows is passive: giving and receiving carried erotic and reproductive meanings. Freud's confession foreshadows his later theories of sexuality, which claim that baby, penis, gift, money, and feces are "ill-distinguished from one another" in the unconscious and are "easily interchangeable."[28] In the Wolf Man case, Freud allowed women to play this game of substitutions, for he observed that the woman may be said to have " 'received' the baby as a gift from the man."[29] But elsewhere in Freud's work, only men are free to manipulate these mercurial symbols—sleights of hand that liberate the theorist from laws of signification and of heterosexual reproduction.

The presence of finance within Breuer's and Freud's barter implies that, years before he developed a theory to explain it, Freud borrowed the image of the uterus to make noble and useful-seeming the otherwise dead-end male anus. It is ironic that, in his essay "On Transformations of Instinct as Exemplified in Anal Erotism," he credits a woman with having independently and pithily found words to describe the equation between rectum and vagina—a correspondence that, he argues, exists primarily in the infantile male imagination: "Faeces, penis, and baby are all three solid bodies; they all three, by forcible entry or expulsion, stimulate a membranous passage, i.e. the rectum and the vagina, the latter being as it were 'taken on lease' from the rectum, as Lou Andreas-Salomé aptly remarks."[30] The rectum lends, the vagina borrows: for Freud, the (male) rectum comes first. Andreas-Salomé is both pivotal and parenthetical in helping Freud link the rectum and vagina; similarly, in a drawing that Freud analyzes in the essay "Leonardo da Vinci and a Memory of His Childhood," the female body serves as fragmented accomplice (or collaborator) to the male's symbolic mission of definition and insemination (see fig. 2). Leonardo's sketch depicts a man penetrating a

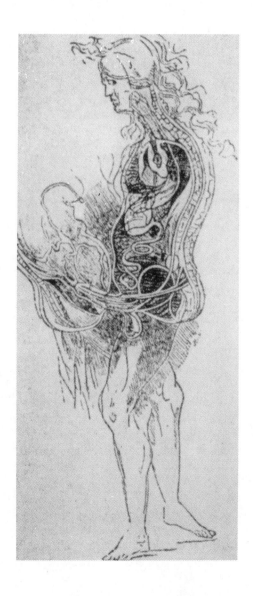

Figure 2

woman: the man is fully rendered, the woman only partially. She has no head, no left leg, no torso: reduced to a breast, a right leg, and a vagina, she seems a midsection without a frame, moored by a man's erect penis—the still point in her turning world. The male genitals are depicted accurately and completely, while the female genitals are drawn "carelessly" and in a "confused" fashion (21). According to R. Reitler, whom Freud quotes, Leonardo has committed further mischief by giving the man a "feminine head" with coiling locks: "Leonardo has interchanged male and female. The male figure has a left foot and the female one a right foot" (22). Leonardo's sketch reduces heterosexual intercourse to procreation, for the woman's "lactiferous duct" travels all the way down to her "internal sex organs," implying that her experience of intercourse will inevitably result in pregnancy, childbirth, and lactation (21). I digress from Freud's and Breuer's financial relationship to Leonardo's sketch of heterosexual intercourse: Freud, too, slips from homosexual desire to a financial metaphor (debt to Breuer), and dwells on a skewed sketch of procreative sex to divert himself from the case history of homosexual Leonardo. Homosexual feeling loses itself in metaphors: it emerges veiled by bank accounts, or scientific (though inaccurate) drawings of the act of conception. Must homoeroticism justify itself by mustering analogies to childbirth and reproduction? Leonardo's sketch of the man's full body and the lopped-off midsection of the woman, impaled on his penis, portrays Freud's relation toward maternity and the vagina—sources of metaphoric language which he can enjoy and then carry away, like plundered treasure; from the woman's body, he borrows a language to describe his intellectual and emotional affairs with men.

But in 1887, psychoanalysis and theories of anality were far in the future, and Freud could ingenuously remark to his fiancée that kisses "will be cashed in their own time," for he will come to fetch her "like an overdue bill of exchange on June 15, 1887"—the projected wedding date.[31] The long engagement to Martha put Freud in debt: he owed her kisses. He owed Breuer money, and the sensation of debt, simultaneously a gratification and a humiliation, placed Freud in the receptive position.

A Child Is Born

Freud owed more than merely money. He was indebted to Breuer for the single cell which, dividing and multiplying, produced the body of psychoanalysis. This seed was Anna O., whom Breuer called "the germ-cell of the whole of psycho-analysis."[32] She has power in Freud's history because of her hysterical childbirth, which is mentioned neither in *Studies on Hysteria* nor in the hospital report that Breuer wrote for Bertha Pappenheim's file in the Sanatorium Bellevue.[33] The childbirth exists only in the texts of men who never knew Pappenheim. To be more precise, her labor exists only in intertexts, for it is a secret that Breuer passed to Freud and that Freud passed to his disciples— a secret that acquires value during these moments of transmission.

Freud locates the origin of psychoanalysis not in June 1882, when Anna O. went into hysterical labor, but on November 18, 1882, when Breuer confided in him: "on that day," Freud writes, "I first became aware of the power of the unconscious."[34] The instant when one man spills the secret to another man overshadows the moment of labor itself. A hysterical pregnancy is, by definition, a growth to which no semen contributes—an immaculate conception. By according significance to the day when he first heard of Anna's pregnancy, Freud introduces himself into a gestation that occurred independently of male anatomy.

Freud made Anna's labor so much his own intellectual property that it is easy to forget he was absent from the scene. Indeed, Bertha Pappenheim had more to do with Freud's wife than with Freud himself. His first published reference to the case occurs in a letter to Martha: he describes taking a bath at his mentor's house and then entering "a lengthy medical conversation on moral insanity and nervous diseases and strange case histories—your friend Bertha Pappenheim also cropped up—and then we became rather personal and very intimate and he told me a number of things about his wife and children," secrets that Breuer instructed Freud to keep from Martha until their wedding.[35] Freud's reference to Bertha Pappenheim is casual and digressive; she "cropped up," subordinated to the role of "your friend." And yet the aside about Bertha transforms the men's conversation. After she crops up, the men move on to "personal" and "intimate" revelations that Freud is forbidden to tell his wife. Bertha may have been Martha's friend, but the male confidences that this hysteric sparked between scientists were to be kept outside of Martha's virginal ken.

Despite Freud's interest in the case, it remained his mentor's property. Freud compensated by assertively constructing his own version of what happened to the patient. Apparently, Breuer himself never fully described the hysterical labor, and so Freud was forced to deduce it from clues. In the essay "On the History of the Psychoanalytic Movement," he describes his own guesswork:

> Now I have strong reasons for surmising that after all her symptoms had been relieved Breuer must have discovered from further indications

the sexual motivation of this transference, but that the universal nature of this unexpected phenomenon escaped him, with the result that, as though confronted by an "untoward event," he broke off all further investigation. He never told me this in so many words, but he gave me at various times indications enough to justify this reconstruction of what happened.[36]

The "untoward event" that caused Breuer to break off investigation is an uncertainty that Freud must tease into being. He believes that it actually "happened," but he rests on nothing stronger than surmise. In *An Autobiographical Study*, too, Freud emphasizes that the labor scene fully germinated only in his own imagination: "over the final stage of this hypnotic treatment there rested a veil of obscurity, which Breuer never raised for me; and I could not understand why he had so long kept secret what seemed to me an invaluable discovery instead of making science the richer by it."[37] The talking cure and the hysterical childbirth are secrets that might have proved lucrative. Freud implies that Breuer's refusal to raise the Salomé-like "veil" that shrouded the scene of labor was a form of miserliness.

Anna O.'s labor tied Freud to Breuer; it also tore the friends apart. Because Freud considered it a striking enactment of hysteria's sexual origin, he faulted Breuer for not putting the scene to analytic use. His unwillingness to follow Freud into the wilderness of sexuality delayed the publication of the Anna O. case and caused the break in their relations; it was only *after* this break that Freud was able to reconstruct—or invent—what happened.

> What really happened with Breuer's patient I was able to guess later on, long after the break in our relations, when I suddenly remembered something Breuer had once told me in another context before we had begun to collaborate and which he never repeated. On the evening of the day when all her symptoms had been disposed of, he was summoned to the patient again, found her confused and writhing in abdominal cramps. Asked what was wrong with her, she replied, "Now Dr. B.'s child is coming!"
>
> At this moment he held in his hand the key that would have opened the "doors to the Mothers," but he let it drop. With all his great intellectual gifts there was nothing Faustian in his nature. . . .
>
> I was so convinced of this reconstruction of mine that I published it somewhere. Breuer's youngest daughter (born shortly after the above-mentioned treatment, not without significance for the deeper connections!) read my account and asked her father about it (shortly before his death). He confirmed my version, and she informed me about it later.[38]

Freud profits from Breuer's failure to pursue the case's implications: because Breuer dropped the key, Freud can pick it up. He turns belatedness into windfall. He can fully piece together the fragmented, inscrutable origin of psychoanalysis only "long after" his friendship with Breuer has ruptured, and Breuer is dead.

Because the elder man's demise gave Freud the freedom to construct the labor scene, Freud uses his friend's obituary in 1925 as a springboard to Anna O. He writes that Breuer's work "conceals thoughts and suggestions which have even now not been turned to sufficient account. Anyone immersing himself in this speculative essay will form a true impression of the mental build of this man." Freud returns to the *Studies* to bathe himself in Breuer, whose researches were "wholly original." This celebration of Breuer's originality, however, masks Freud's own assertion of influence, for he claims that the case of Anna O. was the two men's joint creation: "At the time when he submitted to my influence and was preparing the *Studies* for publication, his judgment of their significance seemed to be confirmed. 'I believe,' he told me, 'that this is the most important thing we two have to give the world.'" Freud needs to exert this hypnotic "influence" because "a kind of reserve" led Breuer "to keep his astonishing discovery secret for so long."[39] Breuer mimics Anna O. in keeping the "astonishing discovery" of pregnancy secret for an unseemly length of time. Though condemning Breuer for excessive caution, Freud still delights in remembering the dead man's warmly inclusive "we two."

Once Breuer is out of the picture, Freud must find another man to share the secret of Anna O.'s labor: he passes her story to a male disciple, Ernest Jones, who savors it as much as the young Freud had. In Jones's canonical account of Anna O., the first to disclose her real identity, he exults in having heard from Freud "a fuller account than he described in his writings of the peculiar circumstances surrounding the end of this novel treatment." Not dependent on the written word, Jones received the secret directly from the master's lips. Jones gives scientific authority to Anna O.'s experience—and to Freud's vigorous reconstruction of it—by confidently calling it a "pseudocyesis," the "logical termination of a phantom pregnancy that had been invisibly developing." The pregnancy satisfies the requirements of science, religion, and gothic fiction; it is "logical," suitable for scientific discourse, yet it is a "phantom," an invisibility that must, like the Holy Ghost, be taken on faith. Offering proof, Jones says that confirmation of this account "may be found in a contemporary letter Freud wrote to Martha," but footnotes this letter as "unpublished correspondence."[40] The sources of Anna O.'s story remain secret, the property of Freud and his men.

Freud had promised his fiancée that he would come to fetch her "like an overdue bill of exchange on June 15, 1887." Another bill that came due each spring was Freud's debt to Breuer for the secret of Anna O. laboring in June 1882. Because Anna O. is like a sum that Freud owes Breuer, and that Jones owes Freud, she is more than a symbol of pregnancy; she takes on resonances of debt. No longer an absolute beginning, a female O giving birth to a child or to psychoanalysis, she becomes a figure owed, a part of men's financial, intellectual, and erotic exchanges. By passing her secret on, Breuer and Freud, and Freud and his disciples, convert her hysterical childbirth from a female deed independent of men's bodies—the uterus that impregnates itself—into a male transaction of giving and receiving.

Studies on Hysteria

Breuer's and Freud's collaboration on *Studies on Hysteria* completes the transformation of female hysteria into male bonding—a metamorphosis most vivid in "Anna O.," the first case history in the text and the only one that Breuer wrote. Apparently, Freud had no part in composing it. *Studies on Hysteria* begins, however, not with Anna O.'s case but with a jointly written theoretical preface entitled "Preliminary Communication." By preceding her case with their own pillar of theory, they seem to claim that psychoanalysis truly begins with their collaboration and not with Anna O. *Studies on Hysteria* is valuable as the first exposition of psychoanalysis and as an illumination of Anna O.; I consider it, however, as a paradigmatic collaborative text and as a document of Freud's and Breuer's partnership. Studying together, the two men could draw out from hysteria's "narrow cleft" a solid rhetoric with which to describe and fortify their ambiguous affection.[41]

Anna O.'s illness consisted in moments of *absence*—when she lost time and felt a "gap in her train of conscious thoughts" (24). There are other absences in her case: her hysterical childbirth is missing, and so is Freud. Breuer's omissions, however, serve as figurative openings where Freud can enter. For example, when Breuer writes, falsely, that Anna was finally "free from the innumerable disturbances which she had previously exhibited," Freud's translator and editor, James Strachey, interpolates a footnote that introduces the missing partner:

At this point (so Freud told the present editor, with his finger on an open copy of the book) there is a hiatus in the text. What he had in

mind and went on to describe was the occurrence which marked the
end of Anna O.'s treatment. (40–41)

Breuer accidentally opened the case to Freud by leaving a "hiatus"
where Anna O.'s hysterical pregnancy should have been; Strachey
seizes this opportunity for his master to make a posthumous appearance. Anna's unmentionable pseudo-motherhood is the hole in
Breuer's text; her pregnancy is as unspeakable as the hole in Breuer
where Freud inserts his "finger," filling up a space that the elder man
modestly (and flagrantly) leaves open.[42]
Leaving holes in his text is Breuer's style of seduction: these blanks
encourage Freud's participation. At the moment when Breuer omits
Anna O.'s pregnancy, he asserts that "since then she has enjoyed
complete health" (41). He then leaves a space, and resumes by confessing that "I have suppressed a large number of quite interesting details." One such detail is that Bertha Pappenheim, far from cured,
was subsequently committed to an asylum. Breuer's assertion of Anna
O.'s fictional recovery—"since then she has enjoyed complete
health"—brings on a hiatus in the text. Within *Studies on Hysteria*,
her apocryphal cure signifies a textual gap left by Breuer for his
partner to fill. Another gap occurs when, describing the last day of
her treatment, Breuer skips her childbirth and discusses instead how
he rearranged her room to look like her father's: "On the last day—
by the help of re-arranging the room so as to resemble her father's
sickroom—she reproduced the terrifying hallucination which I have
described above and which constituted the root of her whole illness"
(40). Appropriately, Bertha Pappenheim's father was named Sigmund. To cure the patient, Breuer transforms her room (her womb)
into a male room—the anatomical chamber that Sigmund Pappenheim and Sigmund Freud have in common. Paradoxically, now that
the hysteric's womb has been altered (spayed) to look like Sigmund's
male room, Anna O. at last has the power to "reproduce" the hallucination of a snake that caused her illness. Fecund repeater of lost
traumas, Anna O. has nonetheless been robbed of her gender: her
bedroom has become a man's, and her female illness masks a phallic
first mover—a snake. Curing Anna O., within the *Studies*, involves
changing her room/womb into an opening that the man can assert as
his answer to the uterus.
Immediately following the hiatus in the text where Freud placed
his finger, Breuer declares that the origins of hysteria, usually hidden,
are visible to observers of Anna O. Embryology offers Breuer a parallel: "the eggs of the echinoderm are important in embryology, not
because the sea-urchin is a particularly interesting animal but because

the protoplasm of its eggs is transparent and because what we observe in them thus throws light on the probable course of events in eggs whose protoplasm is opaque" (41). Breuer is nervous about the uterus: he needs to insist that it is perpetually accessible to men's eyes. Using female reproduction as an image for what made Anna O. invaluable to the male scientist, Breuer suggests that she became most noteworthy when she gave birth, and that her labor's complete visibility earns her a place in the *Studies*. However, Anna's relation to eggs and to visual proof is ambiguous; in her delivery, there was, strictly speaking, nothing to see.

Studies on Hysteria must conceal the absence of Anna's eggs by asserting that she produced a visible issue that both men saw in the same instant. Concealing Breuer's actual priority, they begin their opening chapter, the "Preliminary Communication" (the only section they wrote together), with a reference to a shared "observation": "A chance observation has led us, over a number of years, to investigate a great variety of different forms and symptoms of hysteria, with a view to discovering their precipitating cause—the event which provoked the first occurrence, often many years earlier, of the phenomenon in question" (3). Later in the text, Breuer further renounces his copyright by proposing joint ownership of origins:

> There is always a danger of regarding as a product of one's own what has already been said by someone else. I hope, therefore, that I may be excused if few quotations are found in this discussion and if no strict distinction is made between what is my own and what originates elsewhere. Originality is claimed for very little of what will be found in the following pages. (186)

Breuer may have been willing to give up originality, but Freud is not. As he broke with Charcot in footnotes to the master's text, Freud presents ideas in *Studies* that radically diverge from Breuer's findings, and confesses:

> It would be unfair if I were to try to lay too much of the responsibility for this development upon my honoured friend Dr. Josef Breuer. For this reason the considerations which follow stand principally under my own name. (256)

Freud's zeal in claiming intellectual authority undermines Breuer's cautious efforts to make it seem that both men witnessed the origin of psychoanalysis.

Though Freud claimed priority, he fell, when treating patients, into the shadow of virile predecessors. In the *Studies*, Freud recounts that while ministering to Frau Emmy von N., he "was completely under the sway of Bernheim's book on suggestion" (77). Trying to sway Emmy, Freud remained in a man's grip; the attempt to cure her brought together many eminent men. Emmy was treated by Dr. Breuer, by two unnamed but "distinguished" gynecologists, by a Dr. N., who "put her uterus right by massage," by another "distinguished physician," and by the doctor in charge at a sanatorium. Her mother finally decided that Dr. N. and Freud "were together responsible for the girl's illness" because they had "made light of her serious condition" (77). But collaboration protects the individual man from admitting error; pairing up with Breuer or with Dr. N. defends Freud against the hysteric's accusing mother.

The Freud of *Studies on Hysteria* did not perceive psychotherapy as a private dialogue between hysteric and physician, but as a triangle formed by the patient and *two* doctors. In a footnote, Freud describes a "lively and gifted" hysteric who makes the rounds of the specialists and whose father, a physician, observes her sessions. Under hypnosis, she comes upon a memory that Freud leaves ambiguous: the daughter uttered "a single significant phrase; but she had hardly said a word before she stopped, and her old father, who was sitting behind her, began to sob bitterly. Naturally I pressed my investigation no further; but I never saw the patient again" (100-101). Freud loses the patient because he "naturally" concedes to the father's wishes. In the later case history of Dora, too, Freud sacrifices the daughter because he so admires the father.[43]

One important patient whom Breuer and Freud treated together was the pseudonymous Frau Cäcilie M.—whose real name was Anna.[44] Freud claims that his collaboration with Breuer originated in Cäcilie's case: "Indeed, it was the study of this remarkable case, jointly with Breuer, that led directly to the publication of our 'Preliminary Communication'" (178). Cäcilie is the patient whom Freud "got to know far more thoroughly than any of the other patients mentioned in these studies"; however, because of "personal considerations," he does not accord her a separate case (69). The "Case Histories" section of the text, which follows the "Preliminary Communication," begins with Breuer's Fräulein Anna O. and moves to Freud's four patients, Frau Emmy von N., Miss Lucy R., Katharina—, and Fräulein Elisabeth von R. Cäcilie does not appear until a lengthy footnote at the section's end. By placing her at the end, Freud proposes her as rival to Breuer's Anna O., with whom the section began.

Frau Cäcilie's long footnote hangs off this sentence: "both hysteria and linguistic usage alike draw their material from a common source"

(181). The phrase "common source," ending the chapter, seems to mean Breuer's and Freud's shared work on Cäcilie. In fact, the footnote relates Cäcilie's hallucination of her two doctors hanging from trees:

> [Frau Cäcilie] complained to me at that time of being troubled by a hallucination that her two doctors—Breuer and I—were hanging on two trees next each other in the garden. The hallucination disappeared after the analysis had brought out the following explanation. The evening before, Breuer had refused to give her a drug she had asked for. She had then set her hopes on me but had found me equally hardhearted. She was furious with us over this, and in her anger she thought to herself: "There's nothing to choose between the two of them; one's the *pendant* [match] of the other." (181)

Cäcilie's hallucination happens where the two men's contributions intersect—where Freud's "Case Histories" meets Breuer's "Theoretical" section. Clear-sighted Cäcilie understands that the men's loyalty to each other outweighs their interest in her.

Cäcilie's hallucination is the most explicit sign of male partnership in the *Studies*. Freud's and Breuer's collaboration, however, stamps even the text's shifts in style. Breuer's contributions are avowedly theoretical; his one case history, Anna O., does not even use dialogue. Freud's mode, in contrast, is narrative: he renders the case of Katharina—, for example, mostly through conversation. In the case of Elisabeth von R., he confesses his defection from science to the less serious and (I will venture to say) less masculine mode of storytelling:

> I have not always been a psychotherapist. Like other neuro-pathologists, I was trained to employ local diagnoses and electro-prognosis, and it still strikes me myself as strange that the case histories I write should read like short stories and that, as one might say, they lack the serious stamp of science. I must console myself with the reflection that the nature of the subject is evidently responsible for this, rather than any preference of my own. (160)

Freud disavows responsibility for his style: he writes short stories because science demands it.

As Breuer and Freud were split between science and story, the hysteric broke into two selves: like her fictional contemporaries, Jekyll/Hyde and Dorian Gray, she finds that her "mental activity is divided" (231). By writing together, Breuer and Freud mimic the hysteric's two-tongued affliction. Aptly, Breuer moves into French to describe Anna O.'s two states—her *"conditions primes"* and *"se-*

condes" (238). Bilingualism is intrinsic to hysteria: one of Anna O.'s most disturbing symptoms had been sudden lapses into languages other than her native German, and Freud explicitly compares hysteria to "a pictographic script which has become intelligible after the discovery of a few bilingual inscriptions" (129). The hysteric speaks two languages and straddles two sexes, like the bisexual double flower, which carries male and female parts: Freud writes, "The overflowing productivity of their minds has led one of my friends to assert that hysterics are the flower of mankind, as sterile, no doubt, but as beautiful as double flowers" (240). Though he attributes the comment to a friend, it describes his collaboration with Breuer—a sterile doubleness, an intercourse that biology declares barren but that the young doctor experiences as a union of "overflowing productivity."

Hysteria wreaks havoc on hierarchy by obscuring which term in a binary opposition is truly primary: "Sometimes the sensation would call up the idea to explain it, sometimes the idea would create the sensation by means of symbolization, and not infrequently it had to be left an open question which of the two elements had been the primary one" (180). Freud marvels that the hysteric, remembering first causes last, sickens the structures of priority:

> They make the work of analysis more difficult by the peculiarity that, in reproducing the memories, they reverse the order in which these originated. The freshest and newest experience in the file appears first, as an outer cover, and last of all comes the experience with which the series in fact began. (288)

Freud profits from hysteria's subversion of chronology: he hopes to confuse the narrative of psychoanalytic history by casting doubt on Breuer's precedence. If Freud, like the hysteric, could reverse the order of the file, he might place himself before Anna O. and Breuer, and become the "primary one." Hysteria inverts gender as well as temporal sequence: by striving to precede Anna O. as origin of psychoanalysis, Freud yearns for "male" to precede "female" in the chain of being. In discussing *Studies on Hysteria*, I have, like the hysteric, reversed first and second terms: I have read the *Studies* as embodying primarily the bond between its male authors and only secondarily its manifest female subject.

Hysteria, however, places women above men, and so Freud and Breuer must relinquish mastery enough to acknowledge the insights of their female patients. Breuer embraces Anna O. as collaborator when he writes that the talking cure was "not an invention of mine which I imposed on the patient by suggestion. It took me completely by surprise" (46). There is a darker sense, however, in which the hysteric collaborates: French critic Sarah Kofman has observed that "consenting to collaborate with the doctor is finally what distinguishes the hysteric from a true criminal."[45] The hysteric must yield to the doctor as to an invading nation, and must give up her gender. Though every patient specifically mentioned in the *Studies* is a woman, Freud's account of the patient-as-collaborator portrays a relationship between two men: "By explaining things to him [the hysteric], by giving him information about the marvellous world of psychical processes into which we ourselves only gained insight by such analyses, we make him himself into a collaborator, induce him to regard himself with the objective interest of an investigator" (282). Freud describes the compliant hysteric as if she were male. To imagine the relationship between hysteric and doctor as collaborative and not adversarial, Freud must think of it as a bond between two men.

I have discussed *Studies on Hysteria* as if the only bond it reflected were Freud's and Breuer's; however, by 1895, when it was published, the two men were on bad terms, and Breuer had been replaced, in Freud's affections, by Wilhelm Fliess. It is a commonplace of psychoanalytic history that the letters to Fliess document the birth of Freud's science. With Fliess, and not with Breuer, Freud fully revises Anna O.'s scene of hysterical labor into an image of male transactions. The eroticism of Freud's tie with Breuer was muted, though it remained structurally homosocial in its use of Anna O. as mediator. With Fliess, a man of Freud's generation, alienated from medical circles, he could directly engage in veiled erotic play. And yet Freud used that eroticism as a means to an end—to buoy him up against the perceived threat of female originality. I recover this drama not to unseat Freud, but to reupholster him for the purposes of gay criticism.

The Congress of Freud and Fliess

The transactions between Freud and Fliess were rarely face to face, for they lived in different cities, and met once a year for exchanges that Freud called "Congresses." He wrote to Fliess: "I am looking forward to our congress as to the slaking of hunger and thirst. I bring nothing but two open ears and one temporal lobe lubricated for reception."[46] Freud describes his hunger for intellectual stimulation through a startling image of sexual willingness. One specific purpose of these Congresses was collaboration on a scientific text: though Freud wrote to Fliess of a longing to "blend our contributions to the point where our individual property is no longer recognizable,"[47] the collaboration and the friendship dissolved in a fight over who could rightly claim the theory of bisexuality as his intellectual property.[48]

During the years of these Congresses, Freud was consumed by a search, with Breuer, for the origins of hysterical symptoms. When he involved Fliess in this quest, however, Freud looked past the uterus, and asked Fliess if he knew of any case where stimulation of a child's anus had led to later disturbances:

> Dear Wilhelm,
>   Would you please try to search for a case of childhood convulsions that you can trace back (in the future or in your memory) to sexual abuse, specifically to *lictus* [licking] (or finger) in the anus.[49]

Anal secrets filled many of Freud's letters to Fliess. In one, Freud described his wife's stool: "Her stool during the colic attacks is alternately hard, glassy, and diarrheic."[50] In another letter, after presenting a fastidiously detailed account of a man forcing his wife to submit to anal intercourse, Freud concludes, "Enough of my smut."[51] Surely Freud considered his account more than simply smut; this tale was a valued gift of scientific data bestowed on a trusted colleague. This anecdote was smutty because its subject was anal sex, and because the act of giving secrets to a fellow male scientist had affinities with sexual congress.

For Freud, even language derived from the anus. He wrote to Fliess:

> The word "make" has itself undergone an analogous transformation in meaning. An old fantasy of mine, which I would like to recommend to your linguistic sagacity, deals with the derivation of our verbs from such originally coproerotic terms.[52]

Freud's tone may be lightly and adventurously speculative, but his research into the coproerotic origins of the crucial verb "make" affects his own scientific making. If language is generated from an excremental vocabulary which Freud thinks of as original, then which opening is more original, uterus or anus? Freud may have spent long years exploring female hysteria, but he overlooks the uterus, and cites the anus as origin of language relating to birth. He excitedly writes to Fliess:

> I can scarcely detail for you all the things that resolve themselves into— excrement for me (a new Midas!). It fits in completely with the theory of internal stinking. Above all, money itself. I believe this proceeds via the word "dirty" for "miserly." In the same way, everything related to

birth, miscarriage, [menstrual] period goes back to the toilet via the word *Abort* [toilet] (*Abortus* [abortion]).[53]

With a self-mocking grandiosity, Freud traces back to the toilet all language connected to female bleeding and female reproduction. If we take these hypotheses to be trustworthy indicators of his pulse as he began to forge psychoanalysis, it seems that Freud was interested in privileging the anus over the uterus as sexual and creative site, and as an origin of language.

Freud's references to anal birth grew more precise with the years. In his Wolf Man case, Freud elaborated on male fantasies of maternity, and on the unconscious connections between money, babies, and excrement: "faeces take on the meaning of a *baby*. For babies, like faeces, are born through the anus."[54] In 1899, he referred to his *Interpretation of Dreams* as a child germinated in the anus: he called it "my own dung heap, my seedling," and named Fliess its "godfather."[55] Given Freud's continued interest in fantasies of anal birth, he was probably paying more than just lip service when he enthusiastically supported Fliess's theories of male menstruation. (The male period of 23 days and the female period of 28 days were cornerstones of Fliess's science.) If we take male menstruation literally, it seems that the two scientists energetically invented a fictional and misogynistic biology premised on a fantasy of procreative anal intercourse.

Freud participated in Fliess's universe of male menstruation by frequently describing scientific activity through images of pregnancy and birth. For example, he wrote to his friend that "after the frightful labor pains of the last few weeks, I gave birth to a new piece of knowledge."[56] Actual affinities between consulting room and nursery bolstered Freud's metaphor of male labor pains: more children meant more opportunities for scientific observation. Learning that Fliess's wife was pregnant, Freud congratulated him "on the increase in your observational material."[57] Freud treated motherhood as a male possession. When Fliess accurately predicted the birthdate of his son, Freud wrote an ode to celebrate the father's power—greater than the mother's—over the origin of life:

> But hail to the father, too, who just prior to the event found in his calculations
> The key to restraining the power of the female sex. . . .
> Thus, at the beginning, there stands, hale and hearty, equal to the exigency of error, the father
> In his infinitely mature development.
> May the calculation be correct and, as the legacy of labor, be

transferred from father to son and beyond the parting of the centuries.[58]

Freud gloats that male calculations have the precision to quell the mutinous "power" of women. Incidentally, Freud wrote this ode on December 29, 1899, a true parting of centuries; Fliess, with his mystical math, influenced a child's birth and time's passing. By predicting the delivery date of his heir, Fliess has turned birth into a treasure of patriarchy, a "legacy of labor" passed from father to son. In writing this ode, Freud may well have remembered that Breuer, too, passed a legacy of labor to an intellectual son when he revealed the secret of Anna O.'s pregnancy. Freud's and Fliess's fantasy of usurping from women the "legacy of labor," if taken seriously, implies a desire to reproduce without women's bodies.

Jeffrey Moussaieff Masson has notoriously argued that Fliess's operation on the nose of Freud's patient, Emma Eckstein (a needless procedure which caused her to bleed almost to death), shaped the evolution of psychoanalysis.[59] I will suggest, instead, that the scene of Emma's bleeding continues the drama of Anna O., and brings Freud into a closer sexual bond with Fliess. On March 8, 1895, in a letter to his friend, Freud describes Emma's bleeding:

> Before either of us had time to think, at least half a meter of gauze had been removed from the cavity. The next moment came a flood of blood. The patient turned white, her eyes bulged, and she had no pulse. . . . At the moment the foreign body came out and everything became clear to me—and I immediately afterward was confronted by the sight of the patient—I felt sick. . . . I fled to the next room. . . .
> . . . when I returned to the room somewhat shaky, she greeted me with the condescending remark, "So this is the strong sex."
> I do not believe it was the blood that overwhelmed me—at that moment strong emotions were welling up in me.[60]

For Freud, Emma's bleeding is a flashback to Anna O.'s hysterical labor. The past repeats itself: Breuer fled "in a cold sweat" from Anna O.'s childbed, and now Freud flees from Emma's bloody torrent. In each case the doctor was indirectly responsible for the woman's suffering: Breuer's attentions had brought on Anna's pregnancy, and Freud had authorized Emma's operation.

Freud gave Fliess leave to operate on Emma: the two men's scientific "lubricated" congress culminated in Freud giving the patient to his friend. If we place her trauma within the context of the doctors' collegiality, the gift and the blood take on figurative meanings. Until

now, Freud had admired his friend's intellectual and surgical prow-
ess—his "influence"; now Freud is horrified to witness influence brutally exercised. Blood results from male medical force: such blood
would flow from Freud if Fliess fully influenced him, if their congress
took place not merely in Freud's "lubricated temporal lobe," but in
his anus. Male menstruation seems a figure for the distressing anal
bleeding that would have possibly resulted from their intercourse—
if we postulate an anal hymen broken upon first penetration. The
misogynist yet gender-blind universe of Fliess's theories—where men
menstruate, and hysterics are cured by nose operations—accommo-
dates this scene of anal intercourse, for his schema minimizes the
difference between a woman's bleeding nose and a man's bleeding
anus. Furthermore, as Freud watches Emma's suffering, he assumes
a feminine position: emotions, like blood, are "welling up" in him so
visibly that she mockingly comments, "So this is the strong sex."
Fliess had twice operated on Freud's own nose; given their belief
in endless anatomical displacements (in particular, the connection
between nose and genitals), Freud was free to imagine that, watching
Emma, he was watching himself bleed, and that he was bleeding
because his intercourse with Fliess had symbolically taken place.

Emma nearly bled to death on March 8, 1895. *Nine months* later,
on December 3, 1895, Freud's daughter, Anna, was born. Freud
and Fliess obsessively discussed the dates relevant to their children's
germinations and births, as they monitored their wives' periods and
the periods of their own nasal ailments. For example, Freud wrote to
Fliess, "Perhaps it will interest you, as an aside, that Martha felt the
first movements, with Annerl, on July 10."[61] Freud must have been
particularly pleased that Fliess's own wife delivered her first son a few
weeks after Anna was born. The wives' wombs were synchronized,
and so were the husbands' bodies. Freud took great satisfaction in
noting that both men had been penetrated by surgeons' knives on the
same day. He wrote to Fliess: "As a consequence of the secret biologi-
cal sympathy of which you have often spoken, both of us felt the
surgeon's knife in our bodies at about the same time, and on precisely
the same days moaned and groaned because of the pain."[62] While the
men were being simultaneously penetrated by knives, the wives were
carrying fetuses that Freud compared to undeveloped scientific theories. On June 12, 1895, he wrote to Fliess that reporting now on an
unformed theory "would be like sending a six-month fetus of a girl
to a ball."[63] At that time, Anna Freud was a three-month-old fetus.
Indeed, she incarnated the child of theory that Freud conceived in
congress with Fliess—a cerebral intercourse whose anal implications
Emma's nosebleed luridly brought to life.

Why did Freud name his daughter Anna? Two months before her birth, he wrote to Fliess, "You will not have any objections to my calling my next son Wilhelm! If *he* turns out to be a girl, *she* will be called Anna."[64] The name "Anna" is a substitution, signifying Freud's desire to name a child after his comrade. More concretely, Anna Freud was named after Anna Hammerschlag, the sister of Breuer's son-in-law; the Hammerschlags and the Breuers lived in the same building and were intimate friends.[65] By naming his daughter after a Hammerschlag, Freud reintroduced himself into the Breuer circle. Finally, Anna was the name that Breuer—and Freud?—had chosen as pseudonym for Bertha Pappenheim. *Studies on Hysteria*, including her case, was published in May 1895, between Emma's bleeding in March and Anna Freud's birth in December. By naming his daughter Anna in the year of *Studies on Hysteria*'s publication, Freud pays homage to Breuer's treatment of Anna O.

The word *anno*, in Latin, means year: Anna O.'s hysterical childbirth had marked the Year One of psychoanalysis. However, by naming his daughter Anna, Freud erodes chronology. He claims Anna O. as his own creation, a child conceived in male scientific congress, in that brutal anal conception scene displaced onto Emma Eckstein's nose. If Anna is his daughter, then Anna O., the origin of psychoanalysis, is no longer that mother to whom he owes intellectual fealty. Creating Anna O. in his own bloody anus makes his body the origin of psychoanalysis, and protects him from acknowledging that Anna O. herself is its immaculately conceiving mother. Freud wrote to Fliess, "in my life . . . woman has never replaced the comrade, the friend." Within the two men's epistolary congress, the comrade takes on the childbearing function that gives the woman power. By placing Anna O. and birth within the domain of male friendship and scientific partnership, Freud privileges the comrade and collaborator over the woman.

Confiding in Freud the secret of Anna O.'s hysterical childbirth, Breuer set up the institutional paradigm for psychoanalysis. Psychoanalytic congresses of the 20th century derive from Breuer's and Freud's exchange of secrets, and from "Congresses" with Fliess in the 1890s. Freud, in fact, gave rings to his disciples, for he noted the "difference between a casual flirtation and solemn matrimony with all its duties and difficulties. 'To be wedded to an idea' is not an uncommon figure of speech."[66] Freud demanded that his disciples marry the bride—or groom—of psychoanalytic theory:

Once upon a time these rings were a privilege and a mark distinguishing a group of men who were united in their devotion to psychoanalysis, who had promised to watch its development as a "secret committee," and to practice among themselves a kind of analytic brotherhood. . . . this ring signifies a regression to something that no longer exists.[67]

Breuer passed to Freud the secret of Anna O.'s labor; echoing the mentor's act, Freud gives little golden Os to his disciples. Sharing Anna O.'s body in this communion, Freud and his followers return to that mythical "once upon a time" when psychoanalysis was born.

According to Mircea Eliade, to repeat a world-creating gesture transforms profane time to sacred time.[68] Breuer, giving Anna O. to Freud, created psychoanalysis, and Freud, passing rings to his disciples, repeats Breuer's act, reentering that sacred time when psychoanalysis began, and appropriating its birth in Anna O. as his own experience. The ritual of ring-giving transforms each golden circle into a souvenir of Anna O. But because Freud always gives these tokens of analytic brotherhood to men, his gesture signifies more than return: it signifies usurpation. The Latin word *anus* means both anus and ring. Giving gold bands to his disciples, Freud redefines Anna's ring: he changes Anna's O from a uterus to an anus—the male's only O, where men menstruate, and where men collaborate.

Breuer considered Anna O. "the germ-cell of the whole of psychoanalysis"; Freud discovered the power of the unconscious when he learned of her childbirth. By claiming that Anna O.—even metaphorically—is his creation, the child and not the mother of his edifice, Freud rewrites the story of the origin of psychoanalysis. Naming his daughter Anna, and giving golden replicas of Anna O. to his male analytic sons, he erases the maternal and feminine origin of his science at the same moment as he stresses it. He passes on Anna O. as legacy, but because she is a golden treasure that one man gives another, she is finally nothing more than male property, a representation of male intercourse. The exclamation that Freud attributed to Anna O.— "Now Dr. B.'s child is coming!"—might as well have been Freud's own cry of *jouissance*, for within the history of psychoanalysis, "Anna O." represents the pleasure-giving, child-delivering hole in men.

Coda: Bertha Pappenheim's Dream

How can I reconcile Freud's half-acknowledged anal *jouissance*— a pleasantly antimasculine force—and the history of Bertha Pappenheim, the real Anna O., who seems, within the story as I have reconstructed it, to be the victim of Freud's delight? Anna O. was the ahistorical ring that sealed the male matrimonies of the analytic brotherhood; Bertha Pappenheim escaped hysteria and turned to sisterhood. In 1895, the year of *Studies on Hysteria*'s publication, she began her career as social worker, becoming housemother for the Jewish Orphanage for Girls in Frankfurt; in 1904, she founded an association which 20 percent of the Jewish women in Germany joined. The hysteric, Pappenheim realized, does not organize: "As a child, as a young person, I never organized a thing; I knew no organizations and, until 1890, I led the life of a daughter of a middle-class Orthodox Jewish family."[69] The hysteric cannot organize her thoughts or her life; feminist organization—a kind of female collaboration—cures hysteria by short-circuiting the male system which purports to save the patient but only reinforces her position as token of exchange, a role which causes, or complicates, her sickness. Appropriately, the crime that Pappenheim fought most passionately was the selling of Jewish girls into prostitution; she called it "traffic in girls."[70] Breuer's and Freud's traffic in Anna O. is a seemingly benign specimen of the transactions that Pappenheim worked to stop.

I will end this history of pleasure and plunder with a dream of Bertha Pappenheim's that Breuer and Freud never heard. Her dream, like Frau Cäcilie's hallucination of the two doctors hanging from trees, measures the power that men acquire by collaborating:

> I've got to tell you about a dream. I was dreaming that I told my mother I tamed two jackals. Mama would not believe me; so I brought them and, though I was previously quite sure that these were jackals I now saw myself that I had two cats on a leash. I got angry, I pulled the leash, and it was Mr. H. and Mr. S.[71]

Pappenheim has tamed Mr. H. and Mr. S., who could be any two men: Breuer and Freud are one incarnation of this recurring duo of men who collaborate on women, who profit from the "traffic in girls." Pappenheim responds to male bonding by publishing her dream in a travel journal that a group of women received by subscription. She frames her account by addressing her female readers ("I've got to tell you a dream"); within the dream, she addresses her mother. By speaking directly to other women, Bertha Pappenheim saves herself from Mr. H. and Mr. S. She puts an end to the collaborators.

2
Unlocking Symonds:
Sexual Inversion

Although I have limited "collaboration" to its literary sense, its military meaning is more urgent: collaboration—cooperating with the enemy—is a last resort of men and women under siege. French women who had sexual relations with the occupying Nazis, a crime called "horizontal collaboration," were brutally punished after the war ended: their heads were shaved, and they were paraded through the streets.[1] Freud was not punished for collaborating with Breuer, or for trying to unite with Fliess. But John Addington Symonds was, like Samson, unmanned for a sort of "horizontal collaboration."

Symonds is an exemplary Victorian man of letters: art critic celebrated for his *Renaissance in Italy*, he was also a poet, though no one reads his verse today. Perhaps his supreme accomplishment was an Autobiography that remained unpublished until 1984, an explicit if fumbling account, in alternately lyrical and dissecting prose, of his sexual, spiritual, and intellectual development—a work remarkable for recognizing no border between growth as writer and growth as homosexual. His ambitions exceeded the bounds of literature: interested in sexology because it promised to help the budding homosexual rights movement, he turned to a medical man, Havelock Ellis, best known for his series, *Studies in the Psychology of Sex*, to collaborate on *Sexual Inversion*—a pioneering work still notable for its tolerant tone and its case histories of "inverts." (Though sympathetic, the work insists—through its title—that homosexuality is the inferior and derivative mirror image of a sound, uninverted normality; thus, its inverted author, Symonds, must always concede to his *propre* partner.) To characterize Symonds as a failure would be gratuitous and uncharitable if I did not also intend to salvage his failure by treating it as representative: he sought the shelter of sexology because it promised to be a forgiving branch of an implacably homophobic culture. I find myself, as critic, engaged with Symonds's schisms: caught, with him, between poetry and science—between identification with the desires I describe, and a contrary obligation to be accurate

43

and dispassionate. Symonds makes a bridge between the medical men in this section, and the poets in the next: poet, he longed to blend his voice with the impeccable tones of the doctor.

Doctor and Deviant

I can speak so confidently of Symonds's failure because *Sexual Inversion*, in most editions, appears as the work of Ellis alone. Symonds died three years before it was published, and his executor, Horatio Forbes Brown, bought up most of the first printing to protect Symonds's reputation; in subsequent editions, Ellis omitted his collaborator's name from the title page, and severely truncated his contribution.[2] The story of their partnership neatly follows Oedipal lines: by cutting Symonds's portions into pieces, Ellis, who was nineteen years younger than his partner, unmanned a literary father, and ensured his own full possession of *Sexual Inversion*. Wordsworth performed an equally patricidal or fratricidal act—cutting Coleridge's "Ancient Mariner" from later editions of the *Lyrical Ballads*. The spectacle of these nervous men dismembering their partners alienates my study from its utopian sense of double writing as a male seamlessness, and shows collaboration to be, at times, the use of friendship for ulterior, unfriendly ends. My sympathies are with Symonds, who believed that his confessions might benefit from a straight medical man's co-signature, and who considered the act of collaboration to be an expedient disguise, a kind of counter-speech. *Sexual Inversion* pretends to be a medical text, written by two professional men comfortably living within a discourse of power; the book is, covertly, a self-portrait of the disempowered Symonds turning to a medical collaborator who finally deprived him of voice.

Sexual Inversion continues the history of homosexual literary self-mutilation, but it began, on Symonds's part, with intentions of loud, political declamation. Though much of the double writing discussed in this study falls in the shadow of the Labouchère Amendment of 1886, which made illegal both private and public "acts of gross indecency" between men, *Sexual Inversion* is the only collaborative text that directly responded to the regulation. Symonds first suggested the project to Ellis by noting that inversion "ought to be scientifically, historically, impartially investigated, instead of being left to Labby's inexpansible legislation."[3] The Labouchère Amendment and *Sexual Inversion* seem parallel undertakings—attempts to sift through the complexity of desire and order it into two separate preferences. If I read *Sexual Inversion* in the harsh and bifurcating light of the Labouchère Amendment, the work's primary subject seems to be binarism itself, the need to isolate and weigh contraries. However, *Sexual Inversion* leaves its own orientation in doubt. Its subject may have been homosexuality, but its heterosexual author, Ellis, dominated the project, and made that dominance clear in the text.

Symonds's role in *Sexual Inversion*, however, demonstrates the enormous stake that inverts themselves had in sexology. Medical men who wrote about homosexuality may have specifically aimed their texts at the legal profession, but these works, feigning a juridical status, had a second, secret life among homosexual readers, who used them as catalysts for private recognition scenes.[4] Inverts were moved by case histories, which dramatized gay sexual development and gave it a compellingly teleological and tragic shape. *The Intersexes*, written in 1908 by homosexual Edward Irenaeus Prime Stevenson (under the pseudonym "Xavier Mayne"), boldly included a questionnaire for the reader curious to discover if he were "at all an Uranian";[5] many or most of the work's readers were Uranians, and the book's secret purpose was to stimulate them to self-knowledge. The fact that homosexuals eagerly read *and* wrote sexology texts blurs the distinction between Ellis and Symonds; doctor/patient, heterosexual/homosexual, author/reader—all three dualities collapse (or turn into pliant dialectics) under the pressure of *Sexual Inversion*'s double authorship. Another late Victorian text, Robert Louis Stevenson's *The Strange Case of Dr. Jekyll and Mr. Hyde,* also portrays the deviant's and the doctor's reciprocity and fusion: as Jekyll and Hyde share one body, Symonds and Ellis share one book.

Fluid as the distinction between sexualities might seem, self-avowed inverts of the 1880s and 1890s eagerly seized the newly coined disruption between the two preferences, and divided their libraries in two. The Uranian poet Marc-André Raffalovich, who played a minor role in many gay literary careers at the turn of the century, affixed bookplates of a green serpent to volumes that were *comme ça.*[6] The green serpent—suggesting not only a phallus, but Wilde's green carnation—was more than a bibliophilic affectation. It was an act of diagnosis and of disobedience. Homosexual texts, marked by the secret stigmata of the serpent, sought to form a separate society.[7] Symonds knew this underworld: he corresponded with virtually all of its denizens, and privately published much Uranian verse, as well as two important historical treatments of homosexuality, "A Problem in Greek Ethics" and "A Problem in Modern Ethics." Had these catacombs of literary England satisfied him, he might not have needed to embark, with Ellis, on the daylit discourse of *Sexual Inversion.*

Because Ellis and Symonds never met—collaborating and communicating only by mail—an unchecked transference was free to form. Symonds, however, was not simply projecting fantasies onto an absent partner: he knew that a medical man could help him evade the injunction that homosexuals must not speak. For Symonds, Ellis's strength was his heterosexuality and his medical degree. Symonds confessed to Edward Carpenter: "I need somebody of medical importance to collaborate with. Alone, I could make but little effect—the effect of an eccentric."[8] Treasuring Ellis's credential, Symonds nonetheless wished to keep his collaborator at a remove. When an opportunity to meet arose, he wrote to Ellis and pleaded inconvenience and ill-health.[9] (Ellis, doubtless, had reasons of his own for not urging a meeting.) Symonds's reticence disrupted even his faltering epistolary friendships with writers who he sensed were inverts. Reading verse of Charles Edward Sayle, he recognized the mark, the aura, but was afraid to be direct: "It is not easy to write on this subject—not that I find it at all painful, but that to touch it in any way with a stranger is embarrassing."[10] Symonds continually slighted what burned most deeply in him: in his own works, as in the shared *Sexual Inversion*, he leaves homosexuality a pale matter of longing, rather than a set of specific sex acts. A book that meant to liberate bodies, *Sexual Inversion* was the creation of two men whose congress was carried out solely on paper.

But their subject returned them to the male body—and the act of collaborating (even across miles, in the privacy of envelopes) placed them in a quasi-sexual relation to each other. They embraced in the register of words; moving the action from body to text made their bond respectable. Symonds commented twice on male collaboration as a way of making sexual desire invisible:

> I feel that, in a matter of this sort, two names, and two men of different sorts would be stronger as attracting public opinion than any one alone of any sort, and also would be more likely to get a wide and serious attention.[11]

> If it were possible for us to collaborate in the production of an impartial and really scientific survey of the matter, I should be glad. I believe it might come from two men better than one, in the present state of public opinion. . . . (Do not imagine that I want to be aggressive or polemical.)[12]

Hesitation mars Symonds's every move: by apologizing ("Do not imagine"), Symonds implies that the homosexual partisan must declaw himself, removing the tools of "aggressive" rhetoric. He assures his partner that a treatise on homosexuality "might come from two men better than one": the mere fact of doubling up sanitizes their subject. Double authorship makes their interest in homosexuality neutral and dispassionate, and absolves them of ties to what they describe; and yet collaboration has strong resonances with intercourse. In the very letter to Edward Carpenter in which Symonds speaks of his need for "somebody of medical importance to collaborate with," he also speculates on the healthy effects of taking in another man's semen. Symonds might have made (as I am making) the metaphoric leap from collaborative unions to homosexual unions, and recognized their resemblance. He writes:

> I have no doubt myself that the absorption of semen implies a real modification of the physique of the person who absorbs it, & that, in these homosexual relations, this constitutes an important basis for subsequent conditions—both spiritual & corporeal.[13]

Symonds relates the experiments of Silvio Venturi, who "experimented upon patients by the injection in them of bestial & human semen, with results which (if one may trust his report), show that semen received into the system is a powerful nervous agent."[14]

Collaborating with Ellis by mail, however, hardly brought Symonds these desired influxes. Succumbing to tuberculosis, he died in 1893, before *Sexual Inversion* was finished, and so he lost the chance to shape the book as a whole; his one unbroken contribution remained "A Problem in Greek Ethics," an essay he had written and privately published a decade before. In the first edition of *Sexual Inversion*, published in Germany as *Das Konträre Geschlechtsgefühl*, and translated by Dr. Hans Kurella, this "Problem" essay stood as chapter three, but when the volume appeared the next year in England, Ellis moved the essay to an appendix. In the second English edition, Ellis performed further mischief: he deleted the "Problem" essay altogether, removed Symonds's name from the title page, and dismissed his remaining contributions as the work of "Z"—a mysterious correspondent, not a co-author. Symonds, when he ransacked the alphabet for a pseudonym, chose not the last letter but the first. In the "Modern Ethics" essay, describing his own early sexual fantasies, he disguised them as the experiences of a mysterious and primary "A": "A relates that, before eight years old, reverie occurred to him . . . of naked sailors."[15] As Symonds was demoted from A to Z, *Sexual Inversion* itself moved from its original place as Volume I of Ellis's *Studies in the Psychology of Sex* to Volume II, while a hybrid text—*The Evolution of Modesty, The Phenomena of Sexual Periodicity, Auto-Erotism*—took its place. Outliving his collaborator, Ellis could easily erase his traces; but Symonds, in life, authorized his own later disappearance by submitting his inner history to a doctor's shaping, and asking for the camouflage of a joint signature.

The introductory matter in *Sexual Inversion* obliquely relates Ellis's effort to make their venture his sole property. Though it made him nervous to consider inversion as the primogenitor of his master-series, he nonetheless strove to possess the ambiguous volume that had been fathered without its two authors ever glimpsing each other. Ellis opens the volume with a General Preface which places the work within the context of his *Studies in the Psychology of Sex. Sexual Inversion* was originally Symonds's idea, and had more telling resonances with his life, but Ellis boldly claims that the "origin of these studies" should be sought not in his partner's sexual urgencies but in Ellis's own childhood: "As a youth I was faced, as others are, by the problems of sex."[16] Leaving these "others" unspecified, he describes the project as the fruit of his desire "to make clear the problems of sex," to "get at the facts, and, having got at the facts, to look them simply and squarely in the face" (v-vi). Yet this objective search for facts leads the scientist back to the poet's lap; to grasp inversion, he cannot avoid scrutinizing his invisible writing partner's sexual life. Havelock Ellis, whose first name suggests his sympathy for locks, invokes the metaphor of lock and key to describe male interdependence. He holds the key, but is uncertain of his power to turn the lock: "If I cannot perhaps turn the lock myself, I bring the key which can alone in the end rightly open the door: the key of sincerity" (vi). Ellis, not a poet, seems uncomfortable with tropes: he will rely on his literary partner to perform the sordid turns required by inverted sexual acts. Ellis's unwillingness to turn his key in inversion's lock suggests a hesitance to unlock, or penetrate, his mysterious collaborator. The lock and key metaphor describes one man's epistemological quandary; it also describes anatomical mix-and-match, in which Ellis's "key of sincerity" is the phallus, and the lock is any hole in Symonds that might admit a partner.

Ellis was not alone in using images of keys and locks to describe approaches to inversion. Symonds himself, in *Our Life in the Swiss Highlands*, played with the etymology of "key" in an allusion to his European lovers:

> Chiavenna, the key of Italy and Alpine secrets, as its name implies. *Clavis, Chiave, Clav, Clef.* I leave my readers to find what further mysteries this key unlocks.[17]

In a letter, he used keys and locks to explain the difficulty of disclosing homosexuality to the reading public:

> At Venice last month I tried my hand at nine studies (Verse) "In the Key of Blue." . . . Of things like this, I have always been doing plenty, and then putting them away in a box. The public thinks them immoral.[18]

The very word "key" suggested homosexual discourse to Symonds, for in 1892, the year he published his homoerotic *In the Key of Blue*, he wrote to Edward Carpenter that "Whitman, in Calamus, seemed to strike the key-note."[19] But three days after Symonds first suggested the *Sexual Inversion* project, he lost his keys:

> I am rather out of it here, for I have lost all my keys. Whether I left them behind me somewhere at Venice, or never took them away from here, or where they are, I know not. But I can get at no papers & no nothing.[20]

Bashful Ellis will not turn the key himself, and Symonds loses his keys. Afraid to unlock the door and see inversion's face, both Symonds and Ellis are as "astonied" as one who beholds the Medusa—as if it were paralyzing to approach the subject of inversion without a partner. Collaboration lets nervous Symonds and Ellis deny that inversion is a contingency always about to occur.

Afraid of his own explosiveness, Symonds depends on other men to make his interest in homosexuality seem respectable and professional. Before daring to ask Whitman whether his poems were intentionally homoerotic, Symonds leans on the staff of Ellis's good name, and says, "This reference to Havelock Ellis helps me to explain what it is I want to ask you."[21] When first approaching Ellis, Symonds was equally tentative: he asked Arthur Symons (the symbolist in whose house Ellis maintained, *after* his marriage, a pied-à-terre) to act as intermediary. Symonds writes to Symons:

> I shall get hold of your article on Verlaine. . . . And such a line as "Et oh, les voix d'enfants chantant dans la coupole" is a treasure for ever.
>
> Apropos Verlaine, will you ask Havelock Ellis if he would take a book from me on "Sexual inversion" for his Science Series? I have written and privately printed two essays on the phenomenon in ancient Greece and modern (contemporary) Europe. These could very well be fused.[22]

Symonds initially contemplated *Sexual Inversion* (a fusion of two authors) as a fusion of two essays; afraid to write to Ellis directly, he relied on the intervention of a poet whose name uncannily resembled his own. Symonds blurts out his foppish affection for a pretty line of poetry (by Verlaine the lax-moraled symbolist) and then begs to be included in a titanic "Science Series"; in a parallel act of mortification, T. S. Eliot will quote the Verlaine line in *The Waste Land*, a poem he submits to the purgative editing of Pound. Both Symonds and Eliot seek out medical authority to rid themselves of inverted desire and unmanly literariness—as if the two excesses, lust and letters, amounted to the same thing. Symonds had more cause than Eliot to sense the possibilities that opened up with the Labouchère Amendment: the "invention" of a world divided into two sexual preferences made possible a vocal, emancipatory gay culture. Choosing to ally himself with the Science Series, however, Symonds commits against himself the violence that modernists will wreak on their Wildean precursors: he-men, they will subdue homosexual writing tendencies (the "literary" values of symbolism and Uranian verse) in an effort to be scientific.

Ellis justifies his virtual exclusion of Symonds from *Sexual Inversion* by upholding the distinction between "literary" and "scientific"— codes for, respectively, "homosexual" and "heterosexual." In the preface, Ellis writes:

> Although Mr. Symonds' share in this volume is thus merely fragmentary, it possesses, I believe, a curious and special interest, due to the fact that, unlike his work generally, these fragments are not purely literary, but embody a large amount of scientific inquisition. (xiii)

Pieces of Mr. Symonds's work survived Ellis's censorious eye because they were scientific, as opposed to "purely literary." As housemate of Arthur Symons, Ellis had more intimate ties with *poésie pure* than he implies in his preface. Indeed, he was an early and unrepentant belletrist: in the 1880s, he edited the Mermaid Series, unexpurgated reissues of Elizabethan dramatists, soliciting from Symonds (several years before *Sexual Inversion*) an introduction to a volume of Marlowe plays. Despite Ellis's affection for the "purely literary," *Sexual Inversion* strove to suppress any tendency toward subjectivity and trope. In the preface, quoting Whitman's assessment of Symonds, Ellis suggests that literary men are characteristically prurient and nosy:

> "A wonderful man is Addington Symonds—someways the most indicative and penetrating and significant man of our times. Symonds is a curious fellow. I love him dearly. He is of college breed and education— horribly literary and suspicious, and enjoys things. A great fellow for delving into persons and into the concrete, and even into the physiological, the gastric—and wonderfully cute." (xiii)

Symonds is a "curious fellow" because of his sexuality, and because he is "horribly literary and suspicious" enough to pry into Whitman's tastes—as if only literary men had inversion so much on their minds.

Consistent with his portrait of Symonds's work as "merely fragmentary," Ellis suggests in the preface that collaboration unmanned Symonds—taking away his ability to compose literary wholes, and, finally, taking away his life. After proposing that "the authors' names should be placed on the title-page as they now appear," Symonds "set to work on his section of the book as planned. A few months later he was dead" (xii). Ellis's understatement, like a charged moment of litotes in Anglo-Saxon poetry, is stoic in tone but melodramatic in meaning; it implies that Symonds died soon after embarking on a collaboration because the act of double writing annihilated him. After his partner's death, Ellis edited *Sexual Inversion*; freely excising, he seemed to believe either that his partner's contributions were profoundly inferior, or that he could achieve integrity only by picking Symonds apart. By considering *Sexual Inversion* as a preliminary and "fragmented" preface to a huger series of studies on heterosexuality, Ellis casts his homosexual partner in the role of fragment. Because Symonds died, Ellis claims, "it thus happens that the book is somewhat more shapeless than it was planned to be, and that Mr. Symonds' part in it, which would otherwise have been fitted into the body of the work, mostly appears as fragmentary appendices" (xii). Ellis denies that there are openings in the body of the work, or in his own body; he forgets that he possesses an orifice in which to house "Mr. Symonds' part." If his co-author's part does not fit, then Ellis must cut it down to size. He performs a symbolic castration on his dead collaborator, accusing him of collage, or worse, incoherence—a condition caused, in truth, more by Ellis's editing than by Symonds's lapses.

If Ellis enjoyed snipping away at his partner, Symonds enjoyed offering his own textual body as a sacrifice to be torn, voluptuously, limb by limb. He offered to send copies of his essay, "A Problem in Modern Ethics," so Ellis could decide which pieces to include in *Sexual Inversion*: "By the way, I can supply you with duplicate copies of that essay, for scissor use, if you wanted."[23] Symonds is receptive to "scissor use": he tells Ellis, "So anything that you think fit to use in 'my problem' shall be worked over so as to erase it's bias and to eliminate its literary quality [sic]."[24] He is willing to be edited and eliminated because he suffers from a "literary quality," a taint that seems part of his "specific homosexual bias";[25] Symonds implies that being homosexual and being literary disqualifies him from offering lucid commentary. Apologizing for his essay's flaws, he replaces its objective title, "A Problem," with the subjective and self-blaming "my problem." Symonds believes that, as a literary man, he suffers from a "want of scientific equipment,"[26] and lacks a metaphorically phallic attribute—Ellis's vaunted "key of sincerity." In the first letter to Ellis, Symonds maligns his own work for the insincere "impedimenta in the way of manner and descriptive tendency which I long used to carry about me," and praises Ellis's "sincere and penetrative piece of work."[27] Honest scientists, Symonds assumes, are not burdened by the poet's tendency to describe, but can, in virile fashion, thrust to the subject's heart. Although the writings of such fin de siècle socialists as Edward Carpenter proposed homosexual relations as critical responses to patriarchy,[28] Ellis and Symonds, both of whom had close connections with Carpenter, retreat to a language of mortally opposed binary distinctions. Joining to praise fullness and disparage lack, they fail to use homosexuality and collaboration as methods of undoing the whole's domination over the fragment, and the rod's ascendancy over the hole.

Ellis, reducing his partner to fragment, will not endure the spectacle of two men fitting together as complements. Similarly, their treatise refuses to justify or portray acts of intercourse between men. Despite Symonds's interest in the fructifying powers of semen as a nervous agent, alluded to in letters to Carpenter, *Sexual Inversion* attends primarily to mutual masturbation, and approves the average invert's lack of interest in what the authors cooly call *paedicatio*:

> It will be observed that in the preceding ten cases little reference is made to the practice of *paedicatio* or *immissio penis in anum*. It is probable that in none of these cases (with the possible exception of Case V) has it been practised. In the two following cases it has occasionally been practised, but only with repugnance and not as the satisfaction of an instinct. (51)

One anonymous subject summarizes the treatise's attitude toward *paedicatio*: "as a general rule I am satisfied with such pleasure as can be obtained by the use of the hand, and indeed prefer it" (55). The anus has no place in *Sexual Inversion*: Ellis cannot acknowledge the male's hole if he wishes to insist that there is no opening in the body of the text to hold "Mr. Symonds' part." Limiting pleasure to only a handful of venues, Ellis and Symonds restrict the free play of collaborative writing, and assemble a stilted pastiche; although male collaboration might involve a symbolic taking-in of semen, and induce "a real modification" of textual physique, *Sexual Inversion* seems, if anything, intimidated by metamorphosis.

The collaborative work of "Michael Field" (pseudonym for Katharine Bradley and Edith Cooper) fascinated Ellis, however, because the women's voices seemed melded into one. Indeed, Ellis first grew interested in the idea of collaboration because of his connections with a lesbian literary community. In 1886, several years before working with Symonds, Ellis wrote to Michael Field, whose poetry was Sapphic in sentiment and style, and asked which of the two women had written a certain piece. "Michael Field" responded:

> As to our work, let no man think he can put asunder what God has joined ... the work is perfect mosaic: we cross and interlace like a company of dancing summer flies; if one begins a character, his companion seizes and possesses it; if one conceives a scene or situation, the other corrects, completes, or murderously cuts away.[29]

Bradley and Cooper, writing under one male name (and referring to the other as "*his* companion"), describe collaboration as a murderous contest for possession. And yet Bradley and Cooper thrill at the loss of separate identity. Joined at the hip, they can bar the entry of prying Ellis, the representative male reader/critic who wishes to ferret out the women's secrets: "let no man"—even free-thinking Ellis—"think he can put asunder" their tapestry. Praising their own work as "mosaic," they do not disparage piecework, unlike Ellis, who thought "fragmentary" was a criticism. His desire to discover and undo Michael Field's vexing liquidity reveals his own distrust of fusion.

As his curiosity about Michael Field implies, the world of the lesbian powerfully gripped Ellis's imagination; he began considering *Sexual Inversion* virtually at the same time he learned that his wife, Edith Lees, was a lesbian.[30] She encouraged her husband to embark on the project: in July 1892, he wrote to Symonds, "Many thanks for congratulations on my marriage. My wife—I may say—is most anxious I should collaborate and can supply cases of inversion in women from among her own friends."[31] In later editions, he included the case of his own wife, though she remains strangely absent from the edition that retains Symonds's name.[32]

Even without the case of Edith Lees, *Sexual Inversion* gives the lesbian anxious and embellished prominence. The first major chapter, "The Study of Sexual Inversion," opens with a discussion of a lesbian—a woman who, Ellis grandly writes, occasioned the first truly scientific discussion of inversion:

> Westphal, an eminent professor of psychiatry at Berlin, may be said to be the first to put the study of sexual inversion on an assured scientific

basis. In 1870 he published in the *Archiv für Psychiatrie* . . . the detailed
history of a young woman who, from her earliest years, was sexually
inverted. (25)

Following the eminent Westphal's example, Ellis uses the lesbian as
an opportunity to be scientific; discussing the male homosexual, Ellis
might more easily slip into deplorable "literary" tendencies. He claims
that sexual inversion is "less easy to detect in women" (79), and
therefore, he focuses more intensely on the mechanics of detection,
taking particular care to give the precise dimensions of their genitals.
However, he relies on another physician—an unnamed medical collaborator—to supply him with these measurements: "A further more
detailed examination has recently been made in connection with this
present history (though not at my instance) by an obstetric physician
of high standing; and I am indebted to his kindness for the following
notes" (90). Ellis is eager to share with another man the work of
quantifying the lesbian—possibly to dissociate himself from the shady
means used to discover that her "nipples readily respond to titillation," and that "titillation of the sexual organs receives no response
at all" (90). The scientist's "key of sincerity" is violently adept at
invading the lesbian's body. To protect themselves from their subject,
Ellis's and the unnamed clinician's description of the lesbian is vehe-
mently anti-lyrical:

(a) Internal: Uterus and ovaries appear normal
(b) External; Small clitoris, with this irregularity, that the lower folds
    of the labia minora, instead of uniting one with the other and
    forming the fraenum, are extended upward along the sides of the
    clitoris, while the upper folds are poorly developed, furnishing the
    clitoris with a very scant hood. The labia majora depart from
    normal configuration in being fuller in their posterior half than in
    their anterior part, so that when the subject is in the supine position
    they sag, as it were, presenting a slight resemblance to fleshy sacs,
    but in substance and in structure they feel normal. (90)

This description is obsessively and punitively complete. It succumbs
to trope once or twice: "when the subject is in the supine position
they sag, as it were. . . ." Ellis's key did not balk at the lesbian's lock,
but feared the homosexual's; though the male body provides the
scientist with a few stigmata ("his testicles, though large, are of
flabby consistence" [64]), few sexologists would risk a more intimate
explication.

Ellis, by taking part in this over-description of a lesbian, studies and subjugates the preference of his own wife; marrying a lesbian, choosing to discontinue sexual relations with her, writing *Sexual Inversion* with a homosexual, Ellis might well have felt his own heterosexuality questioned. The act of collaborating exposed him to the threat of inversion, for as a mirror reverses letters, a male writing partner turns Ellis's alphabet of masculinity inside out. By using Symonds as a collaborator, and posthumously struggling with him over territory, Ellis attests to a new historical uncertainty: heterosexuality is not by its very nature eminent, pure, and primary, for it casts, in the mirror, an inverted image. Eager to assert the priority of reality over reflection, Ellis tries to justify having written *Sexual Inversion* before he began the volumes about "normal" desire:

> It was not my intention to publish a study of an abnormal manifestation of the sexual instinct before discussing its normal manifestations. It has happened, however, that this part of my work is ready first, and since I thus gain a longer period to develop the central part of my subject, I do not regret the change of plan. (xi)

He later rectified the telltale priority of *Sexual Inversion* by making it the second and not the first volume in the series. In 1896, involvement in a project like *Sexual Inversion* required an explanation, and Ellis, in his disclaimer, is more tersely confident than Symonds would have been: "It is owing to the late John Addington Symonds that this part of my work has developed to its present extent. I had not at first proposed to devote a whole volume to sexual inversion" (xi). Impugning the late Symonds, Ellis avoids mentioning his own commitment to deviance.

He may have wished to detach himself from the project lest the boundary between doctor and deviant grow indistinct, and Symonds convert him to homosexuality. Such miracles had happened before: Ellis notes the case of "a physician who had always been on very friendly terms with men, but had sexual relations exclusively with women, finding fair satisfaction, until the confessions of an inverted patient one day came to him as a revelation; thereafter he adopted inverted practices and ceased to find any attraction in women" (111). The partnership of Ellis and Symonds neatly divides the two sexual preferences and assigns them to different professions; the specter of a homosexual doctor, on the other hand, dissolves contraries. Ellis permits inverts to annex religion as well as medicine, for in the preceding passage he uses the word "revelation" to describe their awakenings. An invert discovering his nature undergoes a "conversion" experience—like the hysterical conversions recorded in *Studies on Hysteria,* or the religious conversions anatomized in William James's *The Varieties of Religious Experience* (1902). Hesitating to make so grand a claim himself, Ellis relies on Marc-André Raffalovich, quoted in a footnote, to account for the homosexual forging a self in one instant of annunciation:

> In the existence of every invert a moment arrives when he discovers the enigma of his homosexual tastes. He then classes all his recollections, and to justify himself in his own eyes he remembers that he has been what he is from his earliest childhood. Homosexuality has coloured all his young life. . . . He has not had the least thought that is crudely sexual but he has discovered his sentimental vocation. (107)

This language of "vocation" dignifies inversion, and suggests the eagerness of fin de siècle literary men to think of homosexuality as something unbidden, permanent, and mystical. (Raffalovich, after collaborating with Wilde's protégé John Gray, and writing *Uranisme et unisexualité*, retreated from the sexual avant-garde into the Dominican Order.) In Raffalovich's world, the invert is not a criminal but a novitiate, rewriting his life in the light of a new term. Like Lacan's proverbial child discovering illusory wholeness in a mirror, the reader of the sort of histories that filled *Sexual Inversion* might have recognized himself in the cases, and seen the tidy designation "homosexual" as a simplification and a salvation.

Although the case histories in *Sexual Inversion* are unsigned, Symonds gathered most of them, and felt a protective possessiveness over the material drawn confidentially from his fellows.[33] In a letter to Edward Carpenter, Symonds even suggested that he might keep some of the cases secret from magisterial Ellis:

> When you make notes on those matters for us, will you send them to me? Of course H.E. will see the bulk of them. But you might feel it more appropriate to let me have things wh[ich] you would not care to submit to him. This is only a suggestion, arising from my desire to lose nothing you may have to say.[34]

Symonds composed the questionnaire that they gave to inverts; writing to Ellis that various "communications have been given me under a certain seal of confidence, and are quite different from those collected by physicians," he boasted of his power to find more revealing cases than his science-encumbered partner could.[35] Ellis wielded power through his "key of sincerity," but Symonds had successfully mapped out a sexual underground by corresponding with a range of homosexuals beyond Ellis's ken.

Although Symonds gathered the cases, it is not certain that he actually wrote them. Throughout *Sexual Inversion*, Ellis carefully marks off Symonds's contributions by placing them in quotations, or by separating them from the main text in footnotes or appendices. Here, Ellis firmly tells the reader that Symonds is speaking:

> I am in agreement with Symonds who wrote:
> "Considering that all boys are exposed to the same order of sugges-
> tions (sight of a man's naked organs, sleeping with a man, being handled
> by a man), and that only a few of them become sexually perverted, I
> think it reasonable to conclude that those few were previously consti-
> tuted and receive the suggestion." (109)

Ellis may agree with the radical notion that all boys have their genitals "handled by a man," but he lets Symonds phrase it; Symonds here seems an extrinsic source, as if he had no role in writing *Sexual Inversion*. Because Symonds's words are always set off in this fashion from the main text, the reader must assume that the case histories, which contain no specific attribution, are solely Ellis's work.

One of these little histories, called "Case XVIII" in the first English edition, closely resembles passages in the Autobiography that Symonds wrote three years before beginning *Sexual Inversion*. There is no doubt that the case depicts Symonds. But did he help write it? Is there a unified Symonds beneath the case history, or is "Symonds the homosexual" constructed by the pull between the case's two authors? Struggling with the knotty question of the case's authorship involves deciding whether the homosexual creates his identity in a moment of free self-inscription, or whether the designation "homosexual" sprouts from the battle between a subject and a society. Symonds, speaking through the case history's viscous distortions, gives off vividly the sound of a homosexual collaborating, bending to accommodate the weight of his time. Wallace Stevens described the imagination's defense against a reality grown unbearably strong and present: poetry is "a violence from within that protects us from a violence without. It is the imagination pressing back against the pressure of reality."[36] Ellis was part of the reality that Symonds had to combat in order to speak out: collaboration was a violence from within—a self-sabotage—that protected him from the larger violence of silence.

Ellis lays claim to the case by prefacing it with a comment of his own: "The next case I present in some detail; it is interesting as showing the mental and emotional development in a very radical case of sexual inversion" (58). Within the case history, Symonds becomes a nationality, a sexual preference, an age, and an income—"Englishman, independent means, aged 44." By relinquishing the signature, and submitting his story to Ellis's "scientific equipment," Symonds suffers a linguistic dismemberment that the case history represents quite literally—through a nurse who claims that boys eventually lose their "penes":

> Sexual consciousness awoke before the age of 8, when his attention was directed to his own penis. His nurse while out walking with him one day told him that when little boys grow up their penes fall off. The nursery-maid sniggered, and he felt that there must be something peculiar about the penis. He suffered from irritability of the prepuce, and the nurse powdered it before he went to sleep. There was no transition from this to self-abuse. (58)

As there was no "transition" between powdering and masturbation, there is no connection between this anecdote and what Barthes would call the grain of Symonds's voice. Nor are there connections between the case's various moments. The case must suppress all transitions, fragmenting Symonds's Autobiography into isolated instants of sexual awakening that never coalesce into the continuous story of a life.

In the parallel account from Symonds's Autobiography, the nurse also initiates his sexuality by calling attention to the penis as a peculiar, central sign, but she does not claim that he will lose it. The penis remains in place because Symonds, in his own unpublished text, is safe from Ellis's fragmenting scissors, and can speak of his desire in the first person. Symonds writes:

> The earliest idea I gained of sex was caught from a coarse remark made by our head nurse Sarah Jones. We were out walking with the nursery-maid and my sisters, passing through a turnstile which led from George Street through the gravel path round Brandon Hill. The sudden revelation that there is something specific in the private parts, distinguishing them from other portions of the body, made a peculiar and uneasy impression on my sensibility—so strong that an image of the landscape, as it was that morning, remains imprinted on my memory: Bristol below, with its church towers and ships, the freshness of the west wind blowing from the channel, the wavering soft English sunlight.[37]

The penis was in danger of falling off in *Sexual Inversion*, where Symonds's "parts" were alienated from Ellis's whole, but in the memoirs, the penis is kept in place by a nimbus of description and detail: a specific geography (George Street, Brandon Hill), a group of women (nursery-maid, nurse, sisters), and a gentle evocation of nature. Within the sanctuary of his own text, Symonds is free to expose his descriptive "impedimenta." He does not mention "irritability of the prepuce" because the prepuce is no longer isolated from locale, from emotion, and from a signature.

The case of Symonds continues with another vision, this time his fantasy of crouching among naked sailors. First, note his Autobiography's more timid account of the same scene:

> Among my earliest recollections I must record certain visions, half-dream, half-reverie, which were certainly erotic in their nature, and which recurred frequently just before sleeping. I used to fancy myself crouched upon the floor amid a company of naked adult men: sailors, such as I had seen about the streets of Bristol. The contact of their bodies afforded me a vivid and mysterious pleasure.[38]

He names a specific city, "Bristol," to let the reader know how closely his ineffable desire abuts actual places and actual men: the daydreams of a homosexual child tangentially touch the ports—the economic heart—of England. But this account interposes a *nebbia* over desire, as if Symonds feared that an invert's lust, unless described plangently, would be merely clinical. Compare the forthright, self-consciously "accurate" description of the same scene in *Sexual Inversion,* this time in the neutral third person:

> About the same time he became subject to curious half-waking dreams. In these he imagined himself the servant of several adult naked sailors; he crouched between their thighs and called himself their dirty pig, and by their orders he performed services for their genitals and buttocks which he contemplated and handled with relish. (58)

Presumably to disguise Symonds's identity, this account omits reference to Bristol: these naked sailors come from nowhere. And yet this time the fantasy is more sexually explicit. Symonds's Autobiography removed the prurience; the case history restores it. In its recovery of sexual facts too often muddled by Symonds and the Uranians, the deadpan yet graphic case history succeeds where the memoirs fail. In exchange for candor, however, Symonds gives up his signature.

The plot of the case history dramatizes Symonds's loss of authority by reducing him from a collaborator to a sex slave, in harness to Ellis's greater authority: Symonds, a mere servant who obeys the sailors' orders, calls himself their "dirty pig" and crouches "between their thighs." In Symonds's private Autobiography there was no fixed position, no hierarchy of top or bottom. He was surrounded by sailors but not subordinate to them. Because language of sexual servitude enters the fantasy only in the case history, this abjection portrays his loss of voice, his submission to Ellis's superior analytic "equipment." The case history speaks of "the tyranny of the male genital organs on his fancy" (61), and describes Symonds playing an S/M game with five male cousins:

> One of these boys was unpopular with the others, and they invented a method of punishing him for supposed offences. They sat round the room on chairs, each with his penis exposed, and the boy to be punished went round the room on his knees and took each penis into his mouth in turn. This was supposed to humiliate him. (59)

Since Ellis admitted in his autobiography, *My Life*, that his own sexual desires were best satisfied by an ambiguous traffic with urinating women,[39] this portrait of punishment-by-fellatio, ostensibly a scene from Symonds's childhood, taps Ellis's erotic imagination as well. Because it is impossible to know who wrote this case history, the fantasy ultimately springs from no single pen or past, but comes from the double imagination of Ellis and Symonds.

The vignette ends by obliquely noting Symonds's grief at being erased from his own case and from his own book: "As a man of letters he regrets that he has been shut out from that form of artistic expression which would express his own emotions" (63). Symonds, unable to publish overtly homosexual writing, is shut out from the community of language; he is shut out from *Sexual Inversion*, by his death and by Ellis's position as leader of the "joint enquiry";[40] he is shut out from his case history because it does not bear his name, and because, probably, he did not singlehandedly write it. And yet, from the start, Symonds saw collaboration with Ellis as a method of becoming intimate again with language, of regaining writerly pluck. In 1885, he confessed to Ellis:

> I am aware of not having made that mark which I ought to have made. This I do not attribute to any want of sympathy in the public, but to certain moral and physical defects in myself. Ill health has separated me from the stream of life; and though it has not extinguished mental activity, it has, I think, so far taken the edge off my nature as to make me (as a writer) rather contemplative and curious than forcibly operative.
> I needed contact with my fellow-workers.[41]

Isolated by sickness and sexual preference from the stream of English letters, Symonds could not boast the "forcibly" active powers of a thinker like Ellis; instead, Symonds has remained unprofitably passive and "contemplative." Needing contact, he seems to crave a subtly erotic fusion with another writer, and with language itself. But *Sexual Inversion* is dominated by a single, reasonable narrator, a man charitably interested in a homosexuality that never demands his participation; this narrator will not let Symonds enter the main body of the text, but keeps him in bits and pieces. Ironically, the obtrusive references to Symonds, in footnotes and appendices, highlight the "part" that Ellis could not ingest. Obsessively bracketing his collaborator's parts, Ellis does not scissor them off, but sets them in sharp relief.

Symonds may have wished to write *Sexual Inversion* as a call to arms, but the response of the nascent homosexual community remains undocumented; no Uranian reader could have recognized it as a comrade's work, because Symonds's name, after the first edition, was removed from the title page, cover, and spine. The qualified praise which scientific reviewers accorded the volume only reinforces Symonds's failure to speak out through collaboration. The reviews that Ellis quotes in his pamphlet of self-defense, "A Note on the Bedborough Trial," insist that *Sexual Inversion* is neutral and nonpartisan. A medical inspector of prisons commented that the volume was "a real assistance to those who are called upon to judge the sexually inverted"; an editor of *Medico-Legal Journal* wrote to Ellis that "the book is purely scientific and could have had no other possible intention than the completion of your admirable system of works"; and a lecturer on insanity at the Westminster Hospital comforts Ellis by saying that "so long as you confine your appeal to the jurist, the alienist and the scientific reader, no shadow of imputation ought to rest upon you."[42] But speakers are imputed—scalded—by what they say. In the edition of *Sexual Inversion* that retains Symonds's name and contributions, the collaborators cast shadows of imputation on each other; and this shadow play—describing homosexuality from a position within the subject, and then denying that one has entered the subject and made it one's own—is duplicitous double talk.

The Other Collaborators

Havelock Ellis was not Symonds's only collaborator. His daughter Margaret wrote with him a bucolic sequence of personal essays, *Our Life in the Swiss Highlands* (1891); and his literary executor, Horatio Forbes Brown, one year after the master's death, expurgated the

Autobiography and published it, along with fragments of correspondence and diaries, as *John Addington Symonds: A Biography* (1894)—a work that reads as a collaboration, albeit posthumous, between Brown and Symonds. Furthermore, even when Symonds wrote alone, voices and personae enjoined him: I think of these presences as internal collaborators.

One such collaborator was the reader, a figure Symonds courted and feared. He printed only ten copies of his important essay, "A Problem in Greek Ethics," and printed "A Problem in Modern Ethics" with generous margins and empty pages so that he could invite his invert readers to "scribble over its blank pages etc, something of your thoughts, & send the printed thing back to me."[43] By eliciting confessions from his chosen readers, he transformed them into collaborators.

Because Symonds could not entirely control his readership, however, he needed to imagine possible adversaries. The "Ethics" pamphlets nervously account for the viewpoint of a hostile collaborator, the malign figure of the "expert." In "A Problem in Modern Ethics," though he denies the place of anal intercourse in the sexual lives of inverts, Symonds writes, "That an intimate connection exists between the nerves of the reproductive organs and the nerves of the rectum is known to anatomists and felt by everybody."[44] The phrase "known to anatomists and felt by everybody" privileges the doctor's knowledge of rectal pleasure over the invert's wordless sensation; the invert must turn to the doctor if he wishes to know his rectal nerves, and not just blindly feel their pulsations. This all-knowing physician, whether ally or antagonist, is the ideal reader of the homosexual's body; Symonds notes that the scientist's attention is given over "to the detection of signs upon the bodies of incriminated individuals," for "it is the common belief that all subjects from inverted instinct carry their lusts written in their faces."[45] Symonds himself does not claim that the invert is intrinsically readable, and yet he defers to this "scientific investigator"[46] whose distance from inverted feeling allows him to analyze it.

Even in Symonds's Autobiography, which often explodes into "dithyrambic incoherent prose" of "an almost hysterical form,"[47] he resorts to the voice of this imagined collaborator, the scientist with a clear plan: "The plan of these memoirs, which are intended to describe the evolution of a somewhat abnormally constituted individual, obliges me to interpolate a section here which might otherwise have been omitted with satisfaction to myself."[48] Symonds guides the curious reader away from this prurient chapter by titling it, "Containing material which none but students of psychology and ethics need peruse." Pandering to students of ethics, Symonds includes, in the "Modern Ethics" essay, a dialogue between homosexual libertarian Karl Heinrich Ulrichs and a hypothetical expert who cuts the conversation short by declaring, "The Urning must be punished."[49] Symonds wrote in dialogue form so that he might, for argument's sake, assume the enemy's point of view, and so that he might take part in a tradition of homosexual colloquies stretching back to Plato's *Symposium* and continuing through Oscar Wilde's "The Decay of Lying" and André Gide's *Corydon.*[50] Symonds's Socratic temperament prepared him for collaboration; the double authorship of *Sexual Inversion* externalizes a self-division that hobbles his solitary polemical efforts.

In his memoirs, he defends the purity of a love affair by invoking the implied collaborator as a witness: "A spy might have looked through cracks in doors upon us; and the spy would have seen nothing reprehensible."[51] After Symonds's death, in *John Addington Symonds: A Biography*, H. F. Brown rewrote his friend's life from a spy's point of view. Expurgating the Autobiography, Brown commits an act as morally dubious as Ellis's erasure of Symonds's parts and name from *Sexual Inversion*. However, Brown was himself a homosexual; censoring Symonds's work, he intended only to protect a comrade from a disgrace that they both feared. Symonds invited his collaborators to expurgate: he urged Brown to use discretion in publishing the Autobiography, and asked Ellis to put the "Modern Ethics" essay to "scissor use." Brown's intrusions and reorderings can even be read as justified responses to fissures within Symonds's own voice.

In the Preface, Brown postulates two implied readers of the *Biography*—one, a reader who wants to move "straight on" without interruption, and two, a reader interested in eddying, delaying documentation:

> I wished to leave Symonds to tell his own story, as far as that was possible, and at the same time I desired to construct a consecutive narrative and a current page, in order to avoid the awkward breaks which result from printing in the text the superscriptions, subscriptions, and dates of letters in full. It is hoped that in this way the reader may be enabled to read straight on; but should he at any time desire to know the source of the passage which he is reading . . . he will only have to look at the last footnote.[52]

The first reader wants to read "straight on," and trusts Brown's fiction of "consecutive narrative"; the second, more curious, less "straight" reader, who wishes to unearth traces of Symonds by hunting down

sources and superscriptions, will be a more alert decoder of the homosexual voice buried in the Biography. Brown offers avenues for both
the straight and the circuitous reader; he even leaves traces of his own
homosexuality. He writes:

> It was my desire to add as little of myself as might be; but I found, in
> the course of compilation, that it was impossible to disappear altogether
> from the page. All that I have to say, however, is marked off between
> square brackets, and when that includes quotations from Symonds these
> are given within inverted commas.[53]

The voice of the compiler appears "between square brackets"; the voice
of Symonds appears within "inverted commas." Surely the "inverted
commas" are marks of the sexual inversion which Brown could not
entirely erase; these fastidious and unintentionally self-revealing attri-
butions transform the biography into a palimpsest of Brown's unwritten autobiography. Striving to conceal Symonds's inversion, Brown
succeeds only in bracketing and enclosing it within his own.

The frontispiece for the *Biography* is a photograph of Symonds with
his daughter Margaret, dated 1891, the year that they published their
collaborative work, *Our Life in the Swiss Highlands* (see fig. 3). This
photograph shows Symonds eager to be standing, delicate and slightly
hunched, over a writing partner. The unspecified book on the table
could be *Our Life in the Swiss Highlands*, or any text that Symonds
wrote with a double: opened to a picture impossible to see, the book
seems a primer for Margaret (with her father gently supervising), or a
text that she guards and he cannot reach. The photograph shows him
in a position of shy, affectionate distance from the mysterious book
he longs to write, but can approach only through a mediator. In the
photograph, Margaret wears a crucifix, emblem of moral rectitude,
upon her high-necked dress. Her presence reminds the reader of the
Biography that Symonds was a father; she screens his inversion with a
respectable domesticity. Symonds may have collaborated with Margaret, his amanuensis, to train her as a writer, but the essays that he con-
tributed were explicitly homoerotic—racier than most of his published
work. He considered that *Our Life* contained "much personal about
myself & life here," and he circulated the volume among his homosexual friends much as he had distributed the two "Problem" essays.[54] In
fact, Margaret proved useful in her father's friendship with Whitman.
Writing to Horace Traubel, Symonds identifies Margaret as "the little
girl on my back in an old photograph I once sent to Whitman, & some
one told me he still keeps."[55] Whitman, too, used paternity as a smoke
screen: when Symonds pressed him to admit homosexuality, Whitman
bragged about having fathered six illegitimate children.[56]

Figure 3

Symonds did not collaborate with Margaret for the sake of fusion; each separate essay ends with the initials of its single author. One piece in particular, "A Page of My Life," distinctly marks off Symonds's private homosexual life ("My Life") from the volume's familial "Our Life." In this essay, Symonds sits in a tavern reading *La Critique scientifique* by M. Emile Hennequin—whom Symonds calls "E.H." E.H., inverted, is HE-who-must-be-obeyed, H(avelock) E(llis); the two would soon begin to write their own *Critique scientifique*. This author E.H.

tries to establish a new method of criticism upon a scientific basis, distinguished from the aesthetical and literary methods. . . . He regards art as the index to the psychological characteristics of those who produce it, and of those whom it interests and attracts. His method of criticism may be defined as the science of the work of art regarded as a sign.[57]

When a group of male gymnasts, "in a costume not very far removed from nudity," enter the tavern, Symonds puts down E.H.'s treatise. Turning away from the book that proposes art as sign, Symonds prefers to stare at the attractive gymnasts; he writes, "They were all of them strapping bachelors between twenty and twenty-five years of age; colossally broad in the chest and shoulders, tight in the reins, set massively upon huge thighs and swelling calves." By revealing desire to the reader, he has already begun to practice E.H.'s doctrine of art as psychological sign. Although these athletes' faces "resemble masks," the mask of Symonds's style—or the mask that his collaborator, Margaret, provides—does not conceal his arousal. The essay concludes: "Next day I found myself at Davos-Platz, beginning my work again upon accumulated proofs of Gozzi and the impossible problem of style."[58] Because translating Gozzi's memoirs inspired Symonds to write his own, and because, in his letters and poems, "l'amour de l'impossible" always means homosexual desire,[59] the "impossible problem of style" that troubles him is not the difficulty of translating Gozzi, but of finding a style fit for saying a forbidden thing. Symonds, struggling with style, wants to develop a relationship with the mask; he began the task at home by collaborating with Margaret. He turned next to Ellis not only to combat the Labouchère Amendment, but to settle private and elusive writing quandaries.

The nearness of Margaret, in *Our Life*, permits Symonds a *symboliste* depiction of the difficulties of writing as a homosexual; with his daughter, he attains a more rapturous pitch than in the antiseptic *Sexual Inversion* (which Ellis praised as "cold and dry" [x]), or in his own privately published, solemnly reasoned pamphlets. In "Winter Nights at Davos," the final essay in *Our Life*, Symonds casts the homosexual writer as a Promethean figure, exiled from society and language, and imperiled by his subject's demands. On a mountain top, he is surrounded by "athletic men, all naked, in the strangest attitudes of studied rest." But they say nothing intelligible: he only hears "a confused murmur of voices," while up great cables "climb to us a crowd of young men, clinging to the ropes and flinging their bodies sideways on aerial trapezes." Seeing unclothed men inspires "keen joy and terror" in Symonds: "For nowhere else could plastic forms be seen more beautiful, and nowhere else is peril more apparent." He is endangered because he sits on a mountain's verge, and because he has written this erotic scene so candidly. A youth "smiles and soars" to Symonds: "and when his face is almost touching mine,

he speaks, but what he says I know not."[60] Whatever the youth says—
a proposition, a riddle—exceeds propriety, and Symonds pretends to
"know not."

This impossible problem of style (how to communicate knowing
and not-knowing at the same instant, how to deny and admit homosexual desire[61]) leads Symonds to the "top of some high mountain,"
where he finds

> the lineaments and limbs of a Titanic man chained and nailed to the
> rock. His beard has grown for centuries, and flowed this way and that,
> adown his breast and over to the stone on either side; and the whole of
> him is covered with a greenish ice, ancient beyond the memory of
> man. "This is Prometheus," I whisper to myself, "and I am alone on
> Caucasus."[62]

This bearded Prometheus, brackish as the Ancient Mariner, might
well represent Walt Whitman, who died in March 1892, within a
month of *Our Life*'s publication. Whitman saw solitude on Caucasus
as bracing and empowering; he wrote his poems about comradeship
without the aid of a collaborator. But Symonds is not alone on
Caucasus; he rests on that "utmost verge" with his daughter, and the
next year, he will share that pinnacle with Ellis. Symonds wanted to
make the act of writing itself an experience of camaraderie: to speak,
he depended on the silent, frozen, but still tangible presence of the
collaborator.

Symonds sought to be objective, reasonable, sincere—everything
he was not; he collaborated in order to bring on more enlightened
attitudes about homosexuality, but he would have benefited from the
stronger medicine of a muse. Symonds, unlike Freud, was a poet; and
yet Freud, who collaborated to stage riveting, Epipsychidion-like
scenarios of quest and appropriation, has more in common with the
poets in the next two chapters than does earnest Symonds. Freud's
experience of collaboration as intercourse and childbirth is central to
my book, but shy Symonds is its secret hero, even if his securely
inverted identity lacks drama. Creating psychoanalysis is an epic
task, fabulous as myth; Symonds's struggle to confess homosexuality
through collaboration seems, in contrast, workaday, though he meant
to invert the earth.

Part II

Poetic Partnerships

3

The Marinere Hath his Will(iam): Wordsworth's and Coleridge's *Lyrical Ballads*

When placed beside *Sexual Inversion*, the *Lyrical Ballads* modulates into Symonds's "key of blue." Bringing inversion to bear on the highest poetry demands that we permit no sanctuary, not even iambic pentameter, from the pressure of sexuality. I speculate on how double writing introduces homosexual desire into poetry even though final statements about Wordsworth's and Coleridge's work may not rise from this bluntness. The *Lyrical Ballads* is not centrally concerned with an erotics of writing; nor is its only subject Coleridge's longing for Wordsworth's authority, and Wordsworth's anxious response to his friend's desire. Because these poems reflect more than simply the details of their double composition, I will not search for strict biographical context. By looking not primarily at the lives of the men but at the poems they bound together, I mean to show that my model of double writing as an evasively sexual relation is pliant enough to account for poetry.

Long before he joined forces with Wordsworth on the *Lyrical Ballads*, Coleridge had sought to mingle identities with other men. He wrote to Robert Southey, "You have left a large Void in my Heart—I know no man big enough to fill it."[1] These lacerating affections almost led to collaboration, for in 1800 they planned to compose together a long poem on Mohammed, as well as a novel.[2] Coleridge's affectionate letters to another friend, Thomas Poole, impetuously introduced sexual metaphors:

> O my God! how I long to be at home—My *whole Being* so yearns after you, that when I think of the moment of our meeting, I catch the fashion of German Joy, rush into your arms, and embrace you—methinks, my *Hand* would swell, if the whole force of my feeling were crowded there.—Now the Spring comes, the vital sap of my affections rises, as in a tree![3]

71

Coleridge's "Hand" swelled, and his sap rose, at the very thought of union with Poole. Terror of losing such a friend stripped Coleridge, exposing his "tender part": "even a dream of losing but the smallest part of [your love and esteem] makes me shiver—as tho' some tender part of my Nature were left uncovered & in nakedness."[4] Seeking to combine minds with Poole so totally that neither man might know a thought's first author, Coleridge longed "to enjoy these blessings *near you*, to see you daily, to tell you all my thoughts in their first birth, and to hear your's, to be mingling identities with you, as it were."[5] Coleridge's dramatic, racing pleas for the protection of other men were explicitly gendered. He wrote to Poole that "my spirit is more feminine than your's,"[6] and envied Wordsworth's manliness: "& must I not be beloved *near* him except as a Satellite?—but O mercy mercy! is he not better, greater, more *manly*, & altogether more attractive to any the purest Woman?"[7] Manly companions like Wordsworth were sea-breeze to Coleridge's stalled, feminine ship: "the approbation & Sympathy of good & intelligent men is my Sea-breeze, without which I should languish from Morn to evening; a very Trade-wind to me, in which my Bark drives on regularly & lightly."[8] Coleridge uses a maritime metaphor to describe his desire for men: the seafaring plot of his "Rime of the Ancyent Marinere" will tap the same affections that poured out in these letters to Poole, Southey, and Wordsworth.

Wordsworth's and Coleridge's collaboration on *Lyrical Ballads* began as an attempt not merely to collect in one volume poems written by each man individually, but to compose a poem together.[9] Appropriately, these literary brothers chose Cain—exiled for killing his brother—as their subject. They never completed "The Wanderings of Cain"; in a rueful note of 1828, Coleridge reflects on the impossibility of "a mind so eminently original to compose another man's thoughts and fancies." Intimate collaboration inspired him but paralyzed Wordsworth, for Coleridge, who "despatched" his own portion of the manuscript "at full finger-speed," hastened to his friend and found him with his eyes "fixed on his almost blank sheet of paper." In the note to the prose sketch of this fratricidal project, Coleridge suggestively mourns its "birth, parentage, and premature decease."[10] In place of "Cain," they began the "Ancient Mariner," a ballad based on the dream of Coleridge's friend John Cruikshank, but Wordsworth "soon found that the style of Coleridge and myself would not assimilate," and so Coleridge wrote the poem alone.[11]

Though he could not compose a poem with Coleridge, Wordsworth certainly benefited from his friend's presence. In March 1798, after Coleridge completed the "Ancient Mariner" and read it to the Wordsworths, William experienced a marked increase in productivity. He earlier confessed to having neither "quickness of penmanship, nor rapidity of composition,"[12] but in March 1798, Dorothy noted that "his faculties seem to expand every day, he composes with much more facility than he did, as to the *mechanism* of poetry, and his ideas flow faster than he can express them."[13] William so outstripped his partner that Dorothy began referring to the volume as her brother's alone.[14] The 1798 edition of the *Lyrical Ballads*, indeed, is mostly Wordsworth's work; of the 23 poems, only four are Coleridge's. The first poem in the volume, however, is the "Ancient Mariner"—the project's originating germ. Given his poem's pride of place, Coleridge had reason to believe that the *Lyrical Ballads* is "to a certain degree *one work*, in *kind tho' not in degree*, as an Ode is one work—& that our different poems are as stanzas, good relatively rather than absolutely."[15] The *Lyrical Ballads* was published anonymously, with nothing on the title page to suggest its double authorship; one critic observed, in 1799, that all of the poems "seem to proceed from the same mind."[16]

For Coleridge, the cost of such assimilation was that major work of 1797 and 1798—"Kubla Khan," "Frost at Midnight," and "This Lime-Tree Bower My Prison," poems which reflect the emptiness and isolation that drove him to collaborate—were not included in the *Lyrical Ballads*. He was further slighted in the 1800 edition; ideas in the famous preface had germinated in conversation between the poets, but Wordsworth claimed sole authorship. Furthermore, he excluded Coleridge's "Christabel," and added a note criticizing the "Ancient Mariner." Wordsworth attacked his friend's poem but took credit for its publication:

> I cannot refuse myself the gratification of informing such Readers as may have been pleased with this Poem, or with any part of it, that they owe their pleasure in some sort to me; as the Author was himself very desirous that it should be suppressed. This wish had arisen from a consciousness of the defects of the Poem, and from a knowledge that many persons had been much displeased with it. The Poem of my Friend has indeed great defects.[17]

The *Lyrical Ballads* launched Wordsworth's vessel, but helped to sink Coleridge's: in 1800, the year of the second edition, Coleridge could not finish writing "Christabel." He confessed: "Every line has been produced by me with labor-pangs. I abandon Poetry altogether—I leave the higher & deeper Kinds to Wordsworth . . . & reserve for myself the honorable attempt to make others feel and understand their writings."[18] In a postscript, Coleridge remarked that "My wife was safely & speedily delivered of a very fine boy on last Sunday night." Coleridge's "labor-pangs" in producing "Christabel" were hardly as speedy as his wife's, but were sufficiently wrenching to make him renounce poetic labor of his own, and to become a midwife to hardier men.

With the addition of Wordsworth's preface and some of his finest poems, the 1800 edition confirms his ascendancy and Coleridge's decline; the 1798 edition, however, emerged from a moment of unexamined fraternity and heat. To reproduce in these pages some of the transferential sparks that flew between Coleridge and Wordsworth, I have chosen not to discuss poems of the more Olympian 1800 edition, but to focus instead on 1798, the "hour of feeling." Certainly the rest of Wordsworth's poems owe spoken and unspoken debts to the "Friend," but I hope that by isolating the 1798 edition, the sense of it as "to a certain degree *one work*" will emerge more clearly.[19] Rather than moving poem by poem in the order they appear in the *Lyrical Ballads*, I will start with the "Rime of the Ancyent Marinere," the first poem in the volume, and end with "Tintern Abbey," the last, and will roughly group the lyrics in between as poems of motherhood, of degenerate manhood, of catechism, and of return. Certain poems— the "Ancient Mariner," "Tintern Abbey," "We are Seven," "Simon Lee," and a handful more—were written specifically for the shared volume; others were not. Nonetheless, the men's decision to place their work together in one volume changes the way the poems deliver meaning, regardless of original intention. The story that the compilation tells, though not single or simple, includes a fiercely moral depiction of the dangers of collaborating, and the dangers of *not* collaborating—as if symbiosis and isolation were equally dreadful. At the risk of imposing false unity on a variegated weave, I will ask the same question of each poem: how is it compromised by its position in a book by two men?

"The Rime of the Ancyent Marinere"

This poem dominates the *Lyrical Ballads* with a power achieved not by Coleridge alone, but by the revisionary and disowning glances that Wordsworth casts back at it. The history of the poem's place or loss of place in the volume follows the course of the two men's friendship. The 1798 version underwent two punishments: its archaisms, extravagant and hubristic, were removed in 1800, undergoing purgation like the Mariner himself, and the poem itself was excluded, after 1800, from the *Lyrical Ballads*—banished from the society of Wordsworth's verses, much as its anti-hero was exiled from a community of men. Furthermore, the 1798 version did not include the italicized glosses that later trail, like seawrack, down the poem's left margin: as in the case of Eliot's footnotes to *The Waste Land*, Coleridge's slant commentary embodies a second voice, an implied collaborator tethering the libidinous poem to a moral structure of crime and punishment.

Like its publication history, the plot of the "Ancient Mariner" rehearses Coleridge's isolation from his poetic brother. The Albatross "lov'd the man" who slayed it;[20] the Mariner's punishment for breaking this bond is a compulsion to narrate. The repeating Mariner is a stand-in for Coleridge himself, wandering like Cain from a violated fraternal union, composing a poem that spins out with keening, interminable circularity. But the punishment of perpetual confession makes it possible to express brotherly love: had the Mariner not killed the bird, he would not have such a need to talk. The "Ancient Mariner," like much love poetry (think of Sidney's "Astrophel and Stella"), uses the absence of the partner as a pretext to fill him or her in with words.

Wordsworth's poems, in the *Lyrical Ballads*, were to treat "ordinary life," and Coleridge's, "supernatural" subjects.[21] Within the volume's scheme, as Coleridge later described it, his poems meant to invert the ordinary and society-sustaining values of Wordsworth's poems. The "Ancient Mariner" itself traffics in reversals and inversions, for the narrator's violation of nature began, according to the "Argument," with his Ship "having passed the Line." This capitalized, archetypal "Line" is any overstepped law, including the sacrosanct line separating two poets. It is even more sexual to cross the equator than to write poetry with a friend: a sailor's first experience of passing the equator or rounding Cape Horn is traditionally marked by "boisterous and sometimes obscene rituals."[22] Seafaring carried criminally erotic connotations: in 1797, one year before the *Lyrical Ballads* was published, newspapers reported sensational investigations into a case of sodomy aboard the HMS Indomitable.[23] Voyaging to the tropics with other men appealed to Coleridge; he had once planned to emigrate with Wordsworth and Southey to the island of St. Nevis, and to make it "more illustrious than Cos or Lesbos!"[24] The *Lyrical Ballads*, beginning with a poem about male separatism and voyage, emerges from Coleridge's wish for this Lesbian utopia. The radicalism of the "Ancient Mariner" was not exclusively sexual: proclaiming "We were the first that ever burst/Into that silent sea" (101–2), the Mariner echoes the revolutionary ambition set forth in the 1800

preface—Wordsworth's and Coleridge's wish to be the first that ever
burst fossilized 18th-century standards of poetic diction and subject.

On the level of plot, the poem violates nature because it prohibits
the guest from attending the wedding. Coleridge sought to treat
"supernatural" subjects; the "Ancient Mariner," however, is not only
above nature but against it—*contra naturam*. The scene of storytelling
between two men, the Mariner and his passive auditor, occurs outside
the bridegroom's opened doors, and outside marriage. The Mariner
is a bachelor, whose crime and whose calling ensures that he will not
marry; his tale's length keeps the guest from the wedding, as its moral
confirms his bachelorhood—"and now the wedding-guest/Turn'd
from the bridegroom's door" (653–54). The poem ends, "A sadder
and a wiser man/He rose the morrow morn." This figurative resurrec-
tion, whether religious rebirth or sexual rising, represents the guest's
new knowledge that it is "sweeter far" to belong to a "goodly company" of celibates—of "loving friends,/And Youths, and Maidens
gay"—than to be wed (635–42). As the Mariner detains the guest,
Coleridge's protracted tale keeps the reader of the *Lyrical Ballads*
from turning to Wordsworth's poems. Obsessive narration—the Mariner's punishment, and the poem's method—helps Coleridge steal the
reader's favor.

The narrating Mariner has active powers. The listening guest, on
the other hand, demonstrates what Wordsworth will call, in "Expostulation and Reply," a "wise passiveness" (24). Lines cut in 1800
stress that capturing the listener's attention requires physical force:

> He holds him with his skinny hand,
>   Quoth he, there was a Ship—
> 'Now get thee hence, thou grey-beard Loon!
> 'Or my Staff shall make thee skip. (13–16)

The narrator's "skinny hand" seizes the guest, who invokes the power
of his phallic "Staff" as a counterthreat. But then the next stanza—
which Wordsworth wrote—depicts the guest's complete compliance:[25]

> He holds him with his glittering eye—
>   The wedding guest stood still
> And listens like a three year's child;
>   The Marinere hath his will. (17–20)

Coleridge and Wordsworth would have been familiar, from Shakespeare's sonnets, with the meanings of "will." In Sonnets 135 and 136,

"will" signifies male and female genitals, the act of sexual possession, and William, the author's name: "Wilt thou, whose will is large and spacious,/Not once vouchsafe to hide my will in thine?" (135, l. 5–6); "*Will* will fulfill the treasure of thy love,/Ay, fill it full with wills, and my will one" (136, l. 5–6). The Mariner's narration is a kind of rape; he acquires the services of his Will(iam) as listener. William Wordsworth, by contributing these lines himself, helped Coleridge invent a scene of narration that links storytelling to the exercise of sexual force. Wordsworth participated as co-author in making the speaker active and the listener passive, and he used his own first name to signify Coleridge's power. Activity and passivity, according to Freud, divided the homosexual world; but domination and submission, speech and silence, were positions the analyst and hysteric also assumed. The guest, held by the Mariner's glittering eye, might well be a hypnotized hysteric; mesmerists were extraordinarily popular in London and Bristol in the 1780s, and it is likely that Coleridge witnessed their demonstrations.[26] Because the hypnotic treatment of hysterics derived from more popular, theatrical displays of mesmerism, Coleridge's wedding guest and Freud's hysteric are part of one historical tradition of feminized figures subjugated by male eyes.

In "To William Wordsworth," written in 1807, Coleridge uses the active/passive distinction to describe listening to his friend recite the *Prelude*:

> In silence listening, like a devout child,
> My soul lay passive, by thy various strain
> Driven as in surges. . . . (95–97)

Coleridge, hearing Wordsworth's recitation, "lay passive" as the wedding guest. In the 1800 note to the "Ancient Mariner," Wordsworth accused its narrator—and its author?—of passivity: the speaker "does not act, but is continually acted upon." Wordsworth's poisoned dart of exegesis hit its mark, for the Mariner is indeed acted upon by a physical compulsion to narrate:

> Forthwith this frame of mine was wrench'd
>   With a woeful agony,
> Which forc'd me to begin my tale,
>   And then it left me free. (611–14)

For the Mariner, as for the hysteric, speaking brings on bodily contraction and paralysis: he is "wrench'd" with the agony of storytelling. Or are these labor pains? Certainly the Mariner would not be a gripping narrator if there were no child's arm to grip. Wordsworth and Coleridge generate the child as a shared necessity; the labor is Coleridge's, but they both profit from the child's attentiveness. The child embodies an absolutely obedient readership; the men could not poetically unite without invoking, in a moment of simile ("like a three year's child"), the power of their double writing to command obeisance.

There is a fine line between gripping the guest's arm and slaying the Albatross: the violent relation of narrator to listener, in the poem's frame, repeats the crime that drives the Mariner to speak. Or one could reverse the equation, and say that killing the Albatross is the secondary event, and the violence of primary importance is the clash between Mariner and guest. After all, the murder of the Albatross only comes to light when the narrator and listener themselves violently collide. A sudden exclamation from the Guest interrupts the Mariner's placid narration:

> Whiles all the night thro' fog-smoke white
> Glimmer'd the white moon-shine.
>
> 'God save thee, ancyent Marinere!
> 'From the fiends that plague thee thus—
> 'Why look'st thou so?'—with my cross bow
> I shot the Albatross. (75–80)

The cross bow is a figure for many crosses, sacred and profane. One crossing it suggests is the intercourse of voices in this passage: the Mariner resumes speaking ("—with my cross bow/I shot the Albatross") without beginning a new sentence, letting his confession emerge, like Athena from Zeus's head, directly from the guest's question. Because the guest's interruption triggers the Mariner's confession, the crime enters the poem when two speakers sabotage each other. The speakers at cross purposes are the Mariner and the guest, but the poets crossed as well. It was even Wordsworth's idea that the Mariner should kill the Albatross; the poem owes its crime to the poets' intimate traffic.

Coleridge had described the "Sympathy of good & intelligent men" as a "Sea-breeze" that drives on his "Bark." In the "Ancient Mariner," active male forces impel the ship against its will, much as the Mariner restrains the passive listener: "'Still as a Slave before his Lord, / 'The Ocean hath no blast" (419–20). The sadistic wind controls the ship with the force of the narrator's imperatives ("Listen, Stranger!") mesmerizing the reader and the guest:

> The wedding-guest he beat his breast,
>   Yet he cannot chuse but hear:
> And thus spake on that ancyent Man,
>   The bright-eyed Marinere.
>
> Listen, Stranger! Storm and Wind,
>   A Wind and Tempest strong!
> For days and weeks it play'd us freaks—
>   Like chaff we drove along.
>
> Listen, Stranger! Mist and snow. . . . (41–49)

In the absence of breeze, the ship is "mov'd onward from beneath" by a masculine guide, a divine "He" (381):

> Under the keel nine fathom deep
>   From the land of mist and snow
> The spirit slid: and it was He
>   That made the Ship to go. (382–85)

Earlier, a She, "Mary-queen," had "sent the gentle sleep from heaven/ That slid into my soul" (287–88). The spirit slides beneath the passive soul of the Ship, as the Mariner slides his words into the wedding-guest's ready mind. In the 1798 edition, the sliding spirit moment was preceded by several stanzas about the listener's bodily passivity—stanzas that Coleridge cut in 1800:

> Listen, O listen, thou Wedding-guest!
>   'Marinere! thou hast thy will:
> 'For that, which comes out of thine eye, doth make
>   'My body and soul to be still.' (362–65)

This emanation of ego that "comes out" of the mariner's "eye" or "I" to ravage the guest's body is an unspeakable bit of *come*, fluid of reproduction.

The *Lyrical Ballads* thus begins with a narrator equally sadistic and inseminating. His power to hurt and to heal sets forth a moral on which the poets' collaborative enterprise depends: passive submission to a partner's authority bears fruit. But the apprenticeship that one must serve to another's authority entails, at first, silence. Collaborating with another male body (albeit a dead one), the Mariner grows to fear the sound of his own voice:

> The body of my brother's son
>   Stood by me knee to knee:
> The body and I pull'd at one rope,
>   But he said nought to me—
> And I quak'd to think of my own voice
>   How frightful it would be! (333–38)

The men are collaborators: together, they "pull'd at one rope." They are physically close: they stand "knee to knee." And yet they are silent: the brother's son has no voice, and the Mariner fears the sound of his own. In another passage, however, nearness to men's bodies, dead or living, revitalizes the Mariner. A seraph-man, standing upon a corpse, fills the flat body with a powerful "no voice"—as if the very experience of depletion, of being dominated, helps Coleridge find a music of silence:

> Each corse lay flat, lifeless and flat,
>   And by the Holy rood
> A man all light, a seraph-man,
>   On every corse there stood. (515–18)
>
> ....
>
> This seraph-band, each wav'd his hand,
>   No voice did they impart—
> No voice; but O! the silence sank,
>   Like music on my heart. (523–26)

Beholding a dead sailor's submission to a male seraph, the Mariner experiences a liberating paradox. Silence becomes music to the poet mystically resigned enough to flower under another man's sadistic and seraphic tutelage.

There is a connection between the various scenes of domination—Mariner over guest, wind over ship, seraph-man over corpse—and the poem's occasional references to cannibalism. The Mariner, remembering a moment of extremity on the high seas, tells the guest, "I bit my arm and suck'd the blood" (152). He bit his own arm, and he grips the guest's: storytelling might escalate into sucking and biting. There are firm historical connections between the Mariner's cannibalism and his oddly sexual relation to the guest: in naval lore, cannibalism serves as code for a range of unspeakable, often homoerotic, practices. (Certainly, in dire thirst, the Mariner would drink a fellow sailor's urine before sucking his own blood.[27]) Cannibalism masks affections—wishes to incorporate—so violent that they undermine the social contract; Wordsworth will mourn that contract's passing, and with it, the decline of generosity, and the separation of places from their former meanings. But he does not entirely disapprove of the kind of devouring that the Mariner recounts. The Mariner tells the guest that fathers act against nature, eating their young: "'And the owlet whoops to the wolf below / 'That eats the she-wolf's young" (569–70). Wordsworth repeats this image in "The Thorn," where it is the mother, not the father, who destroys the child, and in "The Mad Mother," where the mother begs the infant to consume her: "Suck, little babe, oh suck again!" (31). For Wordsworth, the urge to suck and to devour is maternal and, when not murderous, healing; it opposes social disintegration. Coleridge's tableaux of cannibalism, on the other hand, reinforce the Ancient Mariner's oral domination over the guest, and the poet's own legendary loquacity.

Doomed to repeat his tale, the Mariner must speak within the prison of Coleridge's stanza, which, with chiming inner rhymes ("Out of the sea came he"), hesitates to complete (82). Is the Mariner's tale quick or slow, and does its tempo have any bearing on his relation to the sexual punishment of storytelling? In a note to "The Thorn" in the 1800 edition, Wordsworth wrote: "It was necessary that the Poem, to be natural, should in reality move slowly; yet I hoped that, by the aid of the metre, to those who should at all enter into the spirit of the Poem, it would appear to move quickly."[28] The "Ancient Mariner" is hardly natural, but it, like "The Thorn," feigns speed while remaining stationary. The Mariner certainly enjoys being punished into speech; the poem's never-forward-moving stanza places Coleridge in the guest's posture of stillness. Writing verse that pretends to be quick but is actually slow (or, in Wordsworth's case, poems that pretend to be simple rural utterance but are in truth merciless), the poets escape the rule of appearances, the law ensuring that only one man must write a poem, and that when one man speaks the other man must be silent. The Mariner's stanza—mercurial, deceptive—shows Coleridge enjoying stillness under the mask of speed, and free choice (activity) under the mask of inexorable punishment (passivity).

Repetitions mimic the Mariner's immobility, and help him relive the unspeakable duration of his journey: "Alone, alone, all all alone/ Alone on the wide wide sea" (224–25). Wordsworth, in the note to "The Thorn," commented on such repetitions. He claimed that speakers repeat themselves because they are unsatisfied:

> now every man must know that an attempt is rarely made to communi-
> cate impassioned feelings without something of an accompanying con-
> sciousness of the inadequateness of our own powers, or the deficiencies

of language. During such efforts there will be a craving in the mind, and as long as it is unsatisfied the Speaker will cling to the same words, or words of the same character. There are also various other reasons why repetition and apparent tautology are frequently beauties of the highest kind. Among the chief of these reasons is the interest which the mind attaches to words, not only as symbols of the passion, but as *things*, active and efficient. . . . [T]he mind luxuriates in the repetition of words which appear successfully to communicate its feelings.[29]

Crippled by his own or language's deficiencies, the poet mistakes the word for the feeling, and clings to the word as if it were the missing thing. Like the Mariner or the wind, words have "active and efficient" powers. Relying on repetitions ("Water water, every where/Ne any drop to drink") to describe a state of lack and deprivation, Coleridge asks language to fill in the missing part, the absent comrade (117-18). But the repetitive structure of the Mariner's punishment, and of the stanza, keeps Coleridge in a state of perennial and passive "craving."

The blank verse poems in the *Lyrical Ballads*—in particular, Wordsworth's "Tintern Abbey"—describe returns to origins, but the fluctuating, overflowing blank verse, with its restless enjambments and its disdain for borders, escapes the compelled tautologies associated with the curse poems. When Wordsworth uses rhymed stanzas with tetrameter or trimeter lines, his poems bring to mind the punishment that the stanzas of the "Ancient Mariner" embody. By deferring the mature demands of the meditative poems that will fill the 1800 volume, and lingering in the deliberately idiotic byway of the curse poem, Wordsworth obsessively recapitulates Coleridge's "Ancient Mariner," and reaffirms its place as primogenitor. Reduced to an abstraction, a writing bond between two men is an instance of sameness; a tie between men marks itself by saying the same thing twice. The "mad mother" repeats: "Suck, little babe, oh suck again! . . . Oh love me, love me, little boy!" (31, 41). Wordsworth's expressions of affection for Coleridge were never that ecstatic or explicit; but in the mediating figure of the repeating mother, Wordsworth writes out his fraternal bond with the Friend, and satisfies that "craving in the mind."

Distressed Mothers and Idiotic Men

In the *Prelude*, summarizing their joint labor on the *Lyrical Ballads*, Wordsworth depicts the "Ancient Mariner" and "The Idiot Boy" as pendants:

> Thou in bewitching words, with happy heart,
> Didst chaunt the vision of that Ancient Man,
> The bright-eyed Mariner
>
> ....
>
> And I, associate with such labour, steeped
> In soft forgetfulness the livelong hours,
> Murmuring of him who, joyous hap, was found,
> After the perils of his moonlight ride,
> Near the loud waterfall. . . . (XIV, 398–406)

"Steeped / In soft forgetfulness," murmuring his "Idiot Boy" poem, Wordsworth finds a narcotic, amnesiac pleasure like opium-fond Coleridge's: as Wordsworth paints the scene, the long-ago paradise of 1798—"That summer, under whose indulgent skies, / Upon smooth Quantock's airy ridge we roved / Unchecked" (395–97)—borrowed some of its drowsiness from the idiot's own unformed mind, and from the conviction that by writing "The Idiot Boy," Wordsworth was echoing his friend's "Ancient Mariner." By claiming to be "associate" with Coleridge's maternal "labour," Wordsworth asserts himself as either the sire or the midwife of the "Ancient Mariner."

Even disregarding Wordsworth's rapturous account of 1798, internal similarities link the "Idiot Boy" and "Ancient Mariner," and show how carefully Wordsworth measured the shadow his friend's poem cast on the volume. Within the *Lyrical Ballads*, the "Ancient Mariner" and the "Idiot Boy" are the only two poems with their own title pages. Furthermore, Johnny the Idiot Boy is, like the Mariner, a "traveller bold" (458). On the proper performance of a Sisyphean dream-expedition rests the survival of his mother's friend, the hysteric Susan Gale:

> And he must post without delay
> Across the bridge that's in the dale,
> And by the church, and o'er the down,
> To bring a doctor from the town,
> Or she will die, old Susan Gale. (52–56)

The mission on which Betty Foy sends her son is covertly a banishment: like Cain or the Ancient Mariner, Johnny must wander the earth.

Wordsworth accused the Mariner of not acting, but being "continually acted upon." Similarly, Johnny is acted upon by his pony, who, "Feeding at will along the lane, / Or bringing faggots from the wood," has a greater *will* than its idiot rider (45–46). Johnny is also acted upon by his mother, who repeats her orders with the Mariner's willful obsessiveness:

> And Betty o'er and o'er has told
> The boy who is her best delight
> Both what to follow, what to shun,
> What do, and what to leave undone,
> How turn to left, and how to right. (62–66)

The pony can feed "at will," but *will* (sexual self-determination?) is part of a moral universe Johnny cannot rule. Wordsworth removes from his idiot hero any responsibility for choosing which geographic, ethical, and sexual direction he wishes to turn. Johnny finds his will only in narrating; in stories, he can, like the Mariner, beguile and mesmerize. Betty listens as raptly to her son's babblings as Dorothy Wordsworth listened to William's verses: "And Johnny makes the noise he loves, / And Betty listens, glad to hear it" (110–11); "Betty a drunken pleasure quaffs, / To hear again her idiot boy" (390–91).

The pony feeds "at will": as the guest could not resist the Mariner's (sexual) will, so the willful pony and the docile idiot boy experience a bliss so unspeakable that it is difficult to describe literally or to take seriously. The narrator teases the reader with the perverse sexual implications of Johnny's relation to his faggot-gathering horse: "Oh reader! now that I might tell/What Johnny and his horse are doing!" (322–23). Betty Foy is silly with desire, but Wordsworth's simpleton tone protects him from ribaldry. Betty, like her author, knows not, and so is not responsible for her improprieties: she "pats her pony, where or when/She knows not" (402–3). Wordsworth and Betty Foy are both made uneasy by intimacies that could be construed as sexual:

> She kisses o'er and o'er again,
> Him whom she loves, her idiot boy,
> She's happy here, she's happy there,
> She is uneasy everywhere;
> Her limbs are all alive with joy. (397–401)

She repeats her kisses "o'er and o'er again"; Wordsworth's own repetitions permit him to avoid saying exactly *where* Betty is "happy."

Wordsworth himself imposed Coleridge's mark on "The Idiot Boy" by including the poem in the joint volume. If interpreted within the book's frame, the rhetorical gestures of "The Idiot Boy" comment on male twinship. Through repetition, Wordsworth implies that doubling is a meaningless excess. For example, when Betty is surrounded by what she loves, but cannot touch it, she stutters, in the manner of the Ancient Mariner, over the same word: her cry, " 'Twas Johnny, Johnny, every where" (221), directly echoes the Mariner's "Water water every where." If "Johnny, Johnny" only expresses the impossibility of finding Johnny, then it is squandered language: it makes us understand her longing, but has no power as command. Collaborating, Wordsworth and Coleridge might be making an expenditure as futile as Betty Foy's verbal doubling: two men might be as useless for the purposes of poetic generation as they are for sexual reproduction. But Wordsworth gives us a second, more sanguine way to judge collaboration. He follows the dismal "Johnny, Johnny" moment with Betty's vision of her son drowning, like Narcissus, in his reflection:

> And now the thought torments her sore,
> Johnny perhaps his horse foresook,
> To hunt the moon that's in the brook,
> And never will be heard of more. (223–26)

The line "To hunt the moon that's in the brook," with its arrowy, figurative verb, "hunt," suggests that men speaking together might seize poetic prey. Hunting the moon, Johnny moves forward into a drowning element of difference: he appears to be engaged on a narcissistic homoerotic quest—the futile task of kissing his reflection in the water—but he is, according to his mother's fantasy, in search of something *not* himself: the moon.

In many of his ballads, Wordsworth indirectly asks: are two of the same thing—whether two words, two penises, or two writers—a redundance, or might doublings be generative? He may have felt cursed and burdened by the overhanging nearness of Coleridge's "Ancient Mariner," but he was also empowered by its urgent repetitions, which had enough will and momentum to drive the entire *Lyrical Ballads*. In 1800, Wordsworth appended his defense of repetition to "The Thorn," the volume's central image of maternal suffering; if the trope of repetition, within the *Lyrical Ballads*, invokes the Ancient Mariner's compulsion to narrate, then "The Thorn" is at once a poem about maternity, and a continuation of the Mariner's— or Coleridge's—troubled vector of voice. The first repeating narrator in "The Thorn" is Martha Ray, keening over the grave of the infant she killed: " 'Oh misery! oh misery! / 'Oh woe is me! oh misery!' "

(76–77). The second repeater is the nameless townsperson who bad-
gers the narrator: "'O wherefore? wherefore? tell me why / 'Does she
repeat that doleful cry?'" (87–88). The third repeater is the mariner
who narrates the poem, "a Captain of a small trading vessel," who
has, according to Wordsworth's note, become "credulous and talk-
ative from indolence." Wordsworth wished "to shew the manner in
which such men cleave to the same ideas."[30] Biblically, the word
"cleave" means to penetrate sexually: "Therefore shall a man leave
his father and his mother, and shall cleave unto his wife, and they
shall be one flesh" (Genesis 2:24). To cleave also means to split
asunder. Whether husband or axe, the poet who cleaves to the same
words phallically ravishes language. Language must be impregnated
to be fruitful; Wordsworth wished "to take care that words, which
in their minds are *impregnated with passion*, should likewise convey
passion to Readers."[31] There is a connection between the poem's
method—repeating words that are "impregnated with passion"—
and the poem's disastrously impregnated heroine, Martha Ray, who
bore a child out of wedlock, and murdered it. If both women and
words are liable to careless impregnation, what, in 1798, are words
worth? Restoring value to language by repeating it, Wordsworth
confirms that his language has been impregnated with passion, and
that it is of higher price—"More dear," as he will say in "Tintern
Abbey" (160)—because of Coleridge's influx.

The link between female reproduction and male doubleness is most
striking when the narrator describes seeing the baby's face in the
pond:

> The shadow of a babe you trace,
> A baby and a baby's face,
> And that it looks at you;
> Whene'er you look on it, 'tis plain
> The baby looks at you again. (227–31)

Confronting a mother's power to give birth to a child (and then to
murder it) induces linguistic repetition, like a hysterical tic: the male
narrator cannot forget the mother's gaze repeating and sending back
his own forceless stare, and he describes the mirroring in a sentence
that, like the Mariner, turns on itself as if to suck its own blood:
"Whene'er you look on it, 'tis plain / The baby looks at you again."
The poem's repetitions sprout from this moment of witnessing the
baby and Martha Ray, who, like the Medusa's head, petrifies Wordsworth's—and his narrator's—powers of speech: "I did not speak—
I saw her face, / Her face it was enough for me" (199–200). The

poem's motion halts with this repeated "Her face, / Her face." (Wordsworth later revised the punctuation to emphasize the speaker's paralysis: "I saw her face; / Her face!") But this instant of cleaving gives the poem its self-consuming momentum. Facing the woman's power to generate, the narrator and the poet must exceed it through compensatory strategies of repetition and collaboration.

In other, less substantial poems within the *Lyrical Ballads*, Wordsworth gives us more distressed mothers; each of these figures is, like Martha Ray, an echo of the Ancient Mariner, and so these poems of women read as skewed gestures of retribution or reconciliation aimed at Coleridge. The Mariner wore an albatross around his neck as emblem of his crime; these mothers, too, have committed a crime— sex out of wedlock—and they bear a child as punishment. The mother in "The Female Vagrant," like Coleridge's wanderer, is a guilty, cursed figure, forced "farthest from earthly port to roam," and to "shun the spot where man might come" (170–71). "The Mad Mother," too, is a mariner, for with her child "she came far from over the main" (4). The father of her child (like the idiot boy's father, who lives during the week as a "woodman in a distant vale" [39]), is "gone and far away" (80), and she seeks him "in the wood" (98). The child, an albatross hanging around her neck, may embody her sin, but its sucking alleviates her wretchedness:

> Thy lips I feel them, baby! they
> Draw from my heart the pain away.
> Oh! press me with thy little hand;
> It loosens something at my chest. . . . (33–36)

She bears a "something"—an unspecific, unspeakable burden—at her chest; similarly, the heroine of "The Female Vagrant" suffers a "perpetual weight which on her spirit lay" (270). Coleridge bore and then discarded the weight of poetic vocation, a bloody albatross, and handed it to Wordsworth, who trembled at this unnaturally sexual gift.

Wordsworth's decision to place these "mother" lyrics in a volume that opened with the "Ancyent Marinere" permits us to read backward from *mère* to Marinere: but what can we make of this alignment? These mother poems erase Wordsworth's debt to Coleridge by parodically unmanning the Mariner, the volume's suffering originator. But the poems also compromise Wordsworth, who cries to his companion, through the screen of the mother, "Suck, little babe, oh suck again!" The mothers in Wordsworth's poems cling to their infants as the poet hopes words will cleave to their meanings—with a revolutionary and erotic closeness. Read in the context of the *Lyrical Ballads*, these mad mother poems seem to participate in a worship of 1798—even if "The Female Vagrant" was written before that date. She remembers a moment of musical intercourse like Coleridge's and Wordsworth's collaboration, or William's and Dorothy's home life:

> 'Mid the green mountains many and many a song
> We two had sung, like little birds in May
>
> ....
>
> And I in truth did love him like a brother. . . . (66–71)

The mother, cut off from shared singing, is, like Coleridge in Nether Stowey, the lost half of a former whole.

We may associate this sense of abandonment, isolation, and truncation with Coleridge, but Wordsworth, too, rues the lost hour of sexual closeness to a mother tongue, and blames vagrant mothers for his own disaffection from language.[32] The steadfast "Mad Mother" resembles Nature in "Tintern Abbey": the mad mother says "I will always be thy guide" (53), which Wordsworth echoes in "Tintern Abbey" by invoking Nature as "the nurse, / The guide . . . and soul / Of all my moral being" (110–12). The mad mother regrets her altered looks: "Thy father cares not for my breast . . . and if its hue / Be changed, that was so fair to view, / 'Tis fair enough for thee, my dove!" (61–65). Similarly, in "Tintern Abbey," Wordsworth regrets both a changed Nature and his own altered self: he is "changed, no doubt, from what I was," and so he imagines that the visible world is also diminished (67). The heroine of "A Complaint of a Forsaken Indian Woman," who believes that "if I / For once could have thee close to me, / With happy heart I then would die" (65–67), sounds like Wordsworth crying, at the end of "Tintern Abbey," "Oh! yet a little while / May I behold in thee what I was once. . . . " (120–21). He enjoys the ferocity with which these mothers cleave to their children; in contrast, the mother in "The Thorn," who kills her child, represents a Nature or Imagination that Wordsworth fears will fail him.

Spectacles of maternal strength teach him that a "weight" on the spirit need not be Coleridge's albatross; the mad mother poems lighten the poet's burden by interpreting it as an infant whose sucking is a delight. "Tintern Abbey" promises that weight is transient, that "the heavy and the weary weight / Of all this unintelligible world" can be "lighten'd" in moments of vision

(40–43). Wordsworth moves through mad mothers, and toward "Tintern Abbey," as a way to imagine repetitions that generate (that "lead / From joy to joy"), and are not merely symptoms of a degenerate mind cleaving to dead and hollow words (125–26). Turning away from Coleridge's grip (the offer of unnatural intimacy that the "Ancient Mariner" seemed to extend), Wordsworth gives up the male oral cleaving of Mariner to guest, and asks for a potentially generative bond with Nature. The poems wonder, sometimes silently, sometimes aloud, whether such a bond is possible with another man. The next group of poems will demand that men turn to each other for succor, regardless of debilitating sexual implications, for these lyrics preach that the solitary man without a collaborator is, like Onan, merely a spiller of seed.

Degenerate Men

Wordsworth's men are degenerate because they resemble his friend's dread creation, the Ancient Mariner—a word hoarder, a Silas Marner who counts and recounts but hesitates to spend. The Mariner/Marner who must, as penance, become a mother, appears in Wordsworth's "Goody Blake and Harry Gill, A True Story," the tale of a woman who lacks, and a man who has more than enough, and how they trade places. It is indeed a true story: it is the story of the two collaborators. Like Wordsworth's voice, which threatened to incorporate both Dorothy's and Coleridge's, Harry Gill's "voice was like the voice of three" (20): he dominates by speaking. If the distinction between the powerful Mariner and the passive wedding guest was not entirely gendered (they were both men), "Goody Blake and Harry Gill" defines abundance and lack as respectively masculine and feminine. "Any man" can gloat over Goody's poor (genital) "hut": "And any man who pass'd her door/ Might see how poor a hut she had" (23–24). But Wordsworth's parable inverts this difference. Goody Blake, in need of sticks, leaves her fire, or bed, or fiery bed, to trespass on Harry Gill's property in a kind of sex-drenched quest: "She left her fire, or left her bed, / To seek the hedge of Harry Gill" (63–64). For that violation, he seeks "vengeance," and she, in turn, curses him; and so the fishy Harry Gill (a wet translation of the author Will) is burdened, like the Mariner, with perpetual repetition.

Harry's teeth make a chattering music that Wordsworth renders compulsively, using *repetitions* that are, in their chanting flatness, impossibly remote from *reproduction*:

> In March, December, and in July,
> 'Tis all the same with Harry Gill;
> The neighbors tell, and tell you truly,
> His teeth they chatter, chatter still.
> At night, at morning, and at noon,
> 'Tis all the same with Harry Gill;
> Beneath the sun, beneath the moon,
> His teeth they chatter, chatter still. (9–16)

Harry Gill's multiplicity (his many sticks and waistcoats) turns into meaningless repetition: each month is "all the same" to him. He is doomed to sameness because he used his difference from Goody Blake—a gender difference, and a disparity in property—to dominate her. Now, as retribution, he has "coats enough to smother nine" (8). If coats are poems (as Yeats would have it), then Wordsworth's strophic abundance—his full harvest of poems in *Lyrical Ballads*— becomes a signal of waste. Gill and Will have too many coats—"coats enough to s*mother* nine": the word "mother" hides in "smother," and suggests that through excess (too may coats, too many poems) and miserly counting, men strive to mimic a maternal state of plenty, an economic fullness that Wordsworth will call, in "Tintern Abbey," Nature's "Abundant recompence" (89). The power to reproduce is a female prerogative that Harry Gill miscontrues, reinterpreting multiplication as vengeance and compulsion. Rituals of enumeration in the "Ancient Mariner" and in Wordsworth's curse poems enact each male poet's futile wish to generate through doubleness. Homosexuality, though it does not reproduce, is hardly futile; but Wordsworth's curse poems approach that dire judgment when they present sameness as a punishment.

Encounters between men (or men and women) of unequal strength fill the *Lyrical Ballads*; these encounters are acts of self-retribution on Wordsworth's part, lovely rhymed reminders that a sin has been committed, that some inequity must be righted. Like "Goody Blake and Harry Gill," Wordsworth's "Simon Lee, the Old Huntsman" shows a man whose labors are repetitious and unproductive. Harry Gill's many coats could not keep him warm; similarly, Simon Lee repeats his efforts and, like the patriarch in "Michael," does not progress. Of Simon Lee, Wordsworth mourns:

> Few months of life has he in store
> As he to you will tell,
> For still, the more he works, the more
> Do his weak ancles swell. (65–68)

Solitary labor repeats itself within one line (*"the more* he works, *the more"*), and then, enjambed on the pivot word "more," spills into the next line, only to discover that this effort has been sterile and unprofitable—a useless swelling. The narrator's language is as fruitless as Simon Lee's labor, for the next lines depict the foolish raconteur's impotence to move on with the plot, his fear that this is "no tale":

> My gentle reader, I perceive
> How patiently you've waited,
> And I'm afraid that you expect
> Some tale will be related. (69–72)

I will leave "Simon Lee" for a moment, and digress to the somber and less lilting "Lines left upon a Seat in a Yew-Tree," for in that poem Wordsworth gives a generic instance of patience *not* bearing fruit—neither a tale nor any substantive issue germinating from a man's accretions. Words produce no issue for the man whose moral failings "Lines" obliquely sketches. The pleasure of staring at nature is a "morbid" process of *more and more*—of growth through repetition—which leads to nothing useful:

> And lifting up his head, he then would gaze
> On the *more* distant scene; how lovely 'tis
> Thou seest, and he would gaze till it became
> Far lovelier, and his heart could not sustain
> The beauty still *more* beauteous. (30–34, emphasis mine)

The man lifts up his "head": the eye's metaphorically sexual arousal leads "lovely" to grow "far lovelier," and "beauty" to grow "still more beauteous." Simon Lee's version of this visionary yet usurious phallic swelling is his vain endeavor to unearth an old tree's root:

> One summer-day I chanced to see
> This old man doing all he could
> About the root of an old tree,
> A stump of rotten wood.
> The mattock totter'd in his hand;
> So vain was his endeavour
> That at the root of the old tree
> He might have worked for ever. (81–88)

Like Michael or the Ancient Mariner, Simon Lee finds his repetitive endeavor never ending; but "Simon Lee" is a short poem, a parable with a clear finish, and so Wordsworth does not himself enact, through a wandering narrative line, the old man's perpetual, climaxless swelling.

Simon Lee is a "little man," and Coleridge once wrote of Wordsworth that "I feel myself a *little man by his* side."[33] Powerful Wordsworth takes Simon Lee's phallus in hand:

> 'You're overtasked, good Simon Lee,
> Give me your tool' to him I said;
> And at the word right gladly he
> Received my proffer'd aid.
> I struck, and with a single blow
> The tangled root I sever'd,
> At which the poor old man so long
> And vainly had endeavour'd. (89–96)

Wordsworth's "single blow" has the mythic abruptness of the instant the Mariner slays the Albatross, or the moment, equally magical, when "The Albatross fell off, and sank / Like lead into the sea" (282-83). These blows happen in spasms of violence so irrational as to seem exempt from time. The narrator, young and virile, usurps the old man's tool, only to use it to sever another symbolic phallus, the "tangled root." The tangled root represents Wordsworth's and Coleridge's vexed and cross-bred poetic past; by severing their bond at the root, Wordsworth acquires the patrimonial poetic "tool." Returning to Coleridge, however, leaves Wordsworth mourning at the knowledge of his own superior strength; but he mutes the certainty of his poetic power—his ability to sever the root, and to take over Coleridge's tool—by ending, with a whimper, on a feminine rhyme of "returning" and "mourning." The limping, failing trochees of "-turning" and "mourning" add to this poem's knowledge that farmers and writers may suffer losses of primal economies, reversals that invert their world and turn kind to unkind, natural to unnatural:

> —I've heard of hearts unkind, kind deeds
> With coldness still returning.
> Alas! the gratitude of men
> Has oftner left me mourning. (101–4)

The ascendancy of Wordsworth's imagination leaves him mourning because its growth, within this parable of their collaboration, has cost Coleridge's downfall.

In Wordsworth's chance encounters with faded men, he sympathizes with these simulacra of the Mariner, but finally chooses portraiture over passionate reconciliation. He will not touch these men; nor can he alter their lots. But he circles, curious, around them, and through his tetrameter lines, impersonates their simplicity. If the Mariner, wearing an albatross around his neck, suggested a brackish Pietà tableau, the outcast in "The Last of the Flock," too, is Mary to his last lamb. At the poem's start, Wordsworth witnesses a public display of unmanliness—as if he were to meet Coleridge on a public road:

> In distant countries have I been,
> And yet I have not often seen
> A healthy man, a man full grown,
> Weep in the public roads alone. (1–4)

This weeping man, who loved his lambs like children, has committed the sin of spontaneous germination or usury—making a profit through unnatural reproduction of an essence. His stock of lambs grew while he was still unwed:

> When I was young, a single man,
> And after youthful follies ran,
> Though little given to care and thought,
> Yet, so it was, a ewe I bought;
> And other sheep from her I raised,
> As healthy sheep as you might see,
> And then I married. . . . (21–27)

His stock grows—inexorable and charmed—*before* he marries and fathers: watching his flock rise, he hungers for a wild, unchecked, non-heterosexual increase like the "more and more"—barren swelling—of Simon Lee's pathetic (and pathic) labor.

In a letter of April 12, 1798, approximately the time he composed "The Last of the Flock," Wordsworth wrote, "You will be pleased to hear that I have gone on very rapidly adding to my stock of poetry."[34] The growth of the weeping man's "stock" resembles the magical burgeoning of Wordsworth's *oeuvre*:

> Year after year my stock it grew,
> And from this one, this single ewe,
> Full fifty comely sheep I raised. . . . (31–33)

A countinghouse pleasure suffuses the *Lyrical Ballads*, for the book's joys come from accretion ("Of sheep I number'd a full score, /And every year encreas'd my store" [29–30]). That these increases do not stem from intercourse or reciprocity dooms the man who gloats over plenty to suffer depletion. The man in "The Last of the Flock," for enjoying the spectacle of "more and more," must witness his flock's destruction. Whether or not Wordsworth wrote the poem with Coleridge in mind, this parable of excess and decay explores a sensation of burden that the reader of the entire *Lyrical Ballads* may associate with Coleridge's looming, sorrowful Mariner.

Wordsworth's poems of disempowered men preach that solitary labor is onanistic and destructive. But echoes from his poems to Coleridge's are instances of reciprocity that redeem the outcast and return him to society. Wordsworth's and Coleridge's intertextuality is comedic: it weds the men. These two passages, one from the "Ancient Mariner," the other from "The Last of the Flock," describe depletion, but by operating in unison, as a moment of camaraderie, their resemblance is a ritualized, if not a deliberate, coming together:

> Four times fifty living men,
> With never a sigh or groan,
> With heavy thump, a lifeless lump
> They dropp'd down one by one. ("Ancient Mariner," 208–11)

> And of my fifty, yesterday
> I had but only one,
> And here it lies upon my arm,
> Alas! and I have none;— ("The Last of the Flock," 95–98)

Numbers matter in the *Lyrical Ballads*. Three, for example: the Mariner "stoppeth one of three," and the book as a whole depicts the growth and vanishing of Dorothy's, William's, and Coleridge's community of three. Through enumeration (four times fifty ceremoniously unwinding to one), the poets describe their own relationship's unpiecing—a dream of collaboration dashed by the time that most of the volume's verse was written.

"The Last of the Flock" was written after the "Ancient Mariner," and with the *Lyrical Ballads* specifically in mind. The volume includes, however, remnants from the two poets' earlier work, fragmented poems about convicts and dungeon-dwellers which were written *before* collaboration was planned and cannot be considered literal products of their union. However, the placement of these stumbling, enigmatic poems within a book written in 1798's hour of fraternity casts them as half-achieved and premonitory emblems of situations that the later poems will more fully render. Even those poems that precede the fleeting moment of collaboration, and that seem only tangentially connected to the project's themes, become subject to the laws of poetic community once they are made citizens of a joint volume.

Read with hindsight, these fragmented early poems foreshadow Wordsworth's and Coleridge's collaboration; the enclosure of the *Lyrical Ballads* gives sanctuary to verses that seem meandering and unheightened when read apart from the volume's embrace. In "The Dungeon," Coleridge suggests that no prisoner could "endure/To be a jarring and a dissonant thing"—separate from fraternal harmony— once touched by nature (25–26); prison life deforms the soul, but "with other ministrations thou, O nature!/Healest thy wandering and distempered child" (20–21). A second prisoner, in Coleridge's "The Foster-Mother's Tale," escapes, and, like the Ancient Mariner,

> all alone, set sail by silent moonlight
> Up a great river, great as any sea,
> And ne'er was heard of more; but 'tis supposed
> He lived and died among the savage men. (78–81)

The prisoner leaves weddings and tales far behind him, fleeing to a land of "savage men" from which no stories leak. In these dungeon poems, male bonding salves the wound of imprisonment. In Wordsworth's "Old Man Travelling," a man visits his dying mariner son:

> 'Sir! I am going many miles to take
> 'A last leave of my son, a mariner,
> 'Who from a sea-fight has been brought to Falmouth,
> 'And there is dying in an hospital.' (17–20)

In Wordsworth's "The Convict," too, the prisoner finds repose in a man's attentions. This convict, like the Ancient Mariner, "wishes the past to undo," and is haunted by "his crime," a "weight" that "can no longer be borne" (22–24). The narrator is "come as a brother" to visit the prisoner, with no wish to compare poetic powers, sexual endowments, or economic lots:

> 'Poor victim! no idle intruder has stood
> 'With o'erweening complacence our state to compare,
> 'But one, whose first wish is the wish to be good,
> 'Is come as a brother thy sorrow to share.' (45–48)

The narrator suggests that he, as brother, could do Nature's work, helping the convict "blossom": "'My care, if the arm of the mighty were mine / 'Would plant thee where yet thou might'st blossom again'" (51–52). Ending with the word "again," this poem, which precedes "Tintern Abbey" in the *Lyrical Ballads*, leads directly to that poem's repeated *again*: "and again I hear / These waters. . . . Once again / Do I behold these steep and lofty cliffs . . . " (2–5). The convicts in these lopped-off poems, and the roaming child of nature in "Tintern Abbey," are as different as Coleridge's and Wordsworth's childhoods, a contrast that each poet stressed—gleeful Wordsworth bounding "like a roe," and poor Coleridge "pent 'mid cloisters dim" ("Tintern Abbey," 68; "Frost at Midnight," 52). The poems of disempowered men in the *Lyrical Ballads* right the balance between the two childhoods that the poets forged in retrospect: by depicting male weakness, Wordsworth does penance for his own strength. In the vocabulary of the "Ancient Mariner" and Wordsworth's curse poems, proud and self-sufficiently virile swelling is a sin; the male bonding enacted in poems of conversation and catechism saves words otherwise wasted on no ear.

Conversation and Catechism

This group of poems gives a body to Coleridge's and Wordsworth's collaboration by portraying conversation either as one man's willful domination over a passive partner, or, less frequently, as an erotic trade between equals. Two poems that directly infuse conversation with sexual meanings are Coleridge's "Lewti" and "The Nightingale." "Lewti, or the Circassian Love-Chaunt," was Coleridge's revision and enlargement of Wordsworth's early poem, "Beauty and Moonlight"; virtually a collaboration, "Lewti" was quickly removed from the volume after the first copies were printed, because the poem had been published already in the *Morning Post*. The two men wished the *Lyrical Ballads* to remain anonymous, and so they replaced "Lewti," whose signature had been exposed, with "The Nightingale," subtitled "A Conversational Poem," whose authorship, despite its narrator's lonely garrulity, remained safely unknown.

The speaker of "Lewti" is, like the Ancient Mariner, a rover by water who seeks to lift a punishing curse. The Mariner could not forget the slain Albatross, and the narrator of this slighter poem cannot forget his beloved Lewti: "At midnight by the stream I roved, / To forget the form I loved."[35] To bring on forgetfulness, he uses the familiar strategy of repetition, clinging obsessively to the refrain, "Image of Lewti! from my mind / Depart; for Lewti is not kind"

(13–14). The notion of "unkind"—not concerned with kind, with family, with generation—had worried Wordsworth in "Simon Lee," when "kind" turned into "unkind." Here, Coleridge's narrator succumbs to the appeal of the unkind, and longs for the sexual and poetic strength to thread Lewti's labyrinth:

> I know the place where LEWTI lies,
> When silent night has clos'd her eyes—
> It is a breezy jasmin-bow'r,
>   The Nightingale sings o'er her head;
> Had I the enviable pow'r
>   To creep unseen with noiseless tread,
> Then should I view her bosom white,
> Heaving lovely to my sight,
> As those two swans together heave
> On the gently swelling wave. (65–74)

Coleridge heaped sexual innuendo onto his friend's immature poem, and turned it into a vision of "two swans" heaving together. Only by impersonating and correcting his friend's verses could Coleridge attain this bower where the nightingale sings, and where swans heave in congress.

Coleridge was concerned with birds; they were apt, efficient emissaries to his friend. In a letter accompanying the manuscript of "The Nightingale," he sent Wordsworth a short lyric insinuating that birdsong and Coleridge's song were both impetuously erotic:

> In stale blank verse a subject stale
> I send *per post* my *Nightingale*;
> And like an honest bard, dear Wordsworth,
> You'll tell me what you think, my Bird's worth.
> My opinion's briefly this—
> His *bill* he opens not amiss;
> And when he has sung a stave or so,
> His breast, & some small space below,
> So throbs & swells, that you might swear
> No vulgar music's working there.
> So far, so good; but then, 'od rot him!
> There's something falls off at his bottom.[36]

The bird / bard throbs and swells, and a "something" (left ambiguous and hermaphroditic) falls off at his "bottom"—whether his buttocks, or the bottom of his vocal range. The bird may be entirely self-pleasuring, but Coleridge is not. He depends on Wordsworth, valued bard, to tell him what "his Bird's worth." Asking the worth of his poems, Coleridge subjugates himself to Wordsworth's economic eye. Talking prices with a fellow male poet, Coleridge asks, is my linguistic currency still sound?

In "The Nightingale" itself, Coleridge links the birds' erotic song with Wordsworth's sustaining presence. The birds' melodious conversation, which Coleridge enviously overhears and paraphrases, promises the democratic back-and-forth of a Socratic dialogue, a pastoral flirtation, and a consummated sexual act:

> They answer and provoke each other's songs—
> With skirmish and capricious passagings,
> And murmurs musical and swift jug jug
> And one low piping sound more sweet than all
> ....
>
> while many a glow-worm in the shade
> Lights up her love-torch. (58–69)

Coleridge displaces his desire for the coital "jug jug" of collaboration (which T. S. Eliot will lengthen into his own "jug jug jug jug jug jug") onto a "gentle maid," who "knows all their notes" (74)—as if the desire to linger in the nightingale's grove is more maidenly than manly. Coleridge describes surrendering to nature as a passive pleasure: "to the influxes / Of shapes and sounds and shifting elements /Surrendering his whole spirit . . . " (27–29). But Coleridge must return to care for his child, and cannot linger by the stream with his "Warbler," and with his "Friend" and "our Sister!" Paternal responsibilities interfere with the "jug jug" of Dorothy's and William's friendship, and the nightingale's "passagings." Coleridge's telltale delay when it comes time to head home reveals that obsessive repetitions and deferrals of closure keep him in a pleasure-bower with Dorothy and William:

> Farewell, O Warbler! till to-morrow eve,
> And you, my friends! farewell, a short farewell!
> We have been loitering long and pleasantly,
> And now for our dear homes.—That strain again!
> Full fain it would delay me! (87–91)

Delaying the return to his "dear babe," and to the fixtures—the curbs—of paternity, Coleridge repeats "farewell" three times. Repetition ("that strain again!") lets him loiter with Dorothy and William;

collaborating with the Wordsworths, a second family founded solely on affection and not biology, he could avoid his first family, embodied in the dreaded dear babe.

Coleridge ends "The Nightingale" by dismissing his words as merely a father's, and therefore of solely domestic interest: "Well!— / It is a father's tale" (105–6). By 1798, Wordsworth was also a father, though the illegitimate child he sired in France, and subsequently abandoned, stays concealed in the *Lyrical Ballads*. Wordsworth included a father's tale of his own: "Anecdote for Fathers, Shewing How the Art of Lying May Be Taught." Pedagogy so violent it approaches pederasty—the compulsive need to *teach* and thereby restrain a child-like passerby—haunted the Mariner: "The moment that his face I see / I know the man that must hear me; / To him my tale I teach" (621–3). In "Anecdote for Fathers," Wordsworth plays the Mariner's part by holding the boy's arm, like the wedding-guest's, in a catechismal grip:

> 'And tell me, had you rather be,'
> I said and held him by the arm,
> 'At Kilve's smooth shore by the green sea,
> 'Or here at Liswyn farm?'
>
> In careless mood he looked at me,
> While still I held him by the arm,
> And said, 'At Kilve I'd rather be
> 'Than here at Liswyn farm.' (29–36)

As the Mariner "stoppeth one of three," Wordsworth "three times" asks "Why, Edward, tell me why?," and each time, the firmness of the clasp intensifies: "I said and took him by the arm—" (26); "I said and held him by the arm" (30); "While still I held him by the arm" (34). Seeing the "glittering bright" vane of the weather-cock inspires the boy's answer (51); he is caught—seduced—by the vane's glittering, much as the wedding-guest was hypnotized into submission by the Mariner's "glittering eye." The boy responds with a piece of serious, deep-felt nonsense that rises from the fabular "Ancient Mariner": "'At Kilve there was no weather-cock, / 'And that's the reason why'" (55–56). The Ancient Mariner also reasoned by the presence or absence of weather-cock: he knew he was home when he saw how "moonlight steep'd in silentness / The steady weathercock" (505–6). The boy's response, however, is not thoroughly irrational; he asserts the phallic weathercock to undermine his abusive questioner. Indeed, the boy's answer unseats Wordsworth from his position as teacher: he admits that he "for better lore would seldom yearn, / Could I but teach the hundredth part / Of what from thee I learn" (58–60)—as distinctions between master and disciple, speaker and listener, collapse. "Anecdote for Fathers" is directed as a cautionary tale to other fathers, including Coleridge; Wordsworth warns them that no strict relation of dominance and submission between men can survive close colloquy's tendency to invert hierarchies.

Wordsworth's "We are Seven" continues the critique—through catechism—of the active / passive duality that thrilled the Mariner and gave his "Rime" the liberty to unfold. Even more than "Anecdote for Fathers," "We are Seven" points directly to the two men's collaboration, for Coleridge provided the poem's first stanza:

> A simple child, dear brother Jim,
> That lightly draws its breath,
> And feels its life in every limb,
> What should it know of death? (1–4)

By later removing the phrase "dear brother Jim," Wordsworth deleted the fraternal frame and obscured Coleridge's self-inscription; originally, the conversation between men—the narrator and his dear brother—encased the narrator's dialogue with the girl. To Wordsworth's obsessive questioning, the little maid obstinately repeats, "We are seven." More than any other Wordsworth creation in the *Lyrical Ballads*, she assumes the Mariner's prerogative, and demands to "have her will":

> 'Twas throwing words away; for still
> The little Maid would have her will,
> And said, 'Nay, we are seven!' (67–69)

"We are Seven" is certainly Wordsworth's answer to the "Ancient Mariner" (itself a poem in seven parts), for in the note to "We are Seven," he digresses to describe the origin of his friend's "Rime": Wordsworth confesses that he "furnished two or three lines at the beginning of the poem, in particular

> And listened like a three years' child;
> The Mariner had his will."[37]

Invoking the Mariner's will in a prologue to a poem celebrating a Maid's will, Wordsworth links the mesmeric powers of an innocent girl and a hoary man.

The Maid's exercise of will over Wordsworth—her disregard of the worth of his words—reflects his battle with Coleridge over the poetic identity to be purchased with words not thrown away, but carefully spent. Battling with her is a waste of words: "'Twas throwing words away." However, there are rewards in submitting to another's will. Through submission, the poet acquires a limpid voice, a sound of first, uncorrupted things. Here, Wordsworth's language seems purified by its position underneath the foot, as it were, of the Maid—who, like the seraph-man on board the Mariner's ship, fills with insubstantial voice the corpse it stands upon:

> 'The first that died was little Jane;
> 'In bed she moaning lay,
> 'Till God released her of her pain,
> 'And then she went away. (49–52)

"And then she went away" is an absurdly pure way to describe death. Wordsworth could not have attained that sublimity unless he let the Maid have her Will. The Mariner's childish emissaries, the little Maid and the boy Edward (in "Anecdote for Fathers"), teach Wordsworth that giving up his name (his Will) to the collaborator bears poetic fruit.

Wordsworth is prey to being inverted—whether by Coleridge's covering presence in the volume as a whole, or, as in the pendant poems, "Expostulation and Reply" and "The Tables Turned," by dialogue's tendency to turn tables. In these poems, two men scold each other: Matthew accuses William of idleness, and William accuses Matthew of sterile studiousness. "Expostulation and Reply" opens with Matthew asking,

> 'Why William, on that old grey stone,
> 'Thus for the length of half a day,
> 'Why William, sit you thus alone,
> 'And dream your time away? (1–4)

William, solipsistic on a stone, might well be suffering from the wedding-guest's anomie: seized by the Mariner's will, "The wedding-guest sate on a stone, / He cannot chuse but hear" (21–22). In "The Tables Turned," Wordsworth assumes the power to command, and assaults his friend: "Up! up! my Friend! and quit your books, / Or surely you'll grow double" (3–4). Growing double seems a dangerous fate to Wordsworth, who found it difficult to collaborate with Coleridge—the double assaulted in this pair of bantering poems.

Passivity is hardly the same as homosexuality; and yet the male mystic assumes a distinctly antimasculine posture of receptivity. Within the *Lyrical Ballads*, giving up one's will signals a readiness to accept the thrusting imperatives of Nature and of the male spirit guide. Both "Expostulation and Reply" and "The Tables Turned" celebrate passivity, and describe the mind's susceptibility to nature as a lack of "will" resembling the wedding-guest's prone mood. As the guest "cannot chuse but hear," Wordsworth's eye "cannot chuse but see":

> 'The eye it cannot chuse but see,
> 'We cannot bid the ear be still;
> 'Our bodies feel, where'er they be,
> 'Against, or with our will.
>
> 'Nor less I deem that there are powers,
> 'Which of themselves our minds impress,
> 'That we can feed this mind of ours,
> 'In a wise passiveness. (17–24)

Powers sway eye, ear, and body, as the Mariner captivated the wedding-guest; "Against or with our will," William Wordsworth proclaims the joys of receptivity to a masculine force. Because "Will" is also his name, when he gives up his will he is renouncing his autograph and his poetic patrimony: for Wordsworth, Coleridge's "*will*ing suspension of disbelief" is a self-denying enterprise.[38] William gives up will in the last lines of "The Tables Turned":

> Enough of science and of art;
> Close up these barren leaves;
> Come forth, and bring with you a heart
> That watches and receives. (29–32)

The heart must receive impressions from nature. But because Wordsworth chose to publish this poem in a collaborative volume, receptivity might also mean taking in another male poet. If receiving is unmanly, a heterosexual poet might well wish to discard his Friend as muse, and embrace a feminine Nature instead. In retrospect, the 1798 *Lyrical Ballads* might have seemed to Wordsworth merely "barren leaves"—fruitless precisely because they were generated by two men. In "Tintern Abbey," by blurring the line between the male "Friend" and the female "Sister," Wordsworth retains the services of Coleridge while saying farewell to him.

Memorializing Coleridge

The remaining poems in the volume—each a memorial to a specific place or season—come down hard on the sin of self-sufficiency. "Lines composed a few miles above Tintern Abbey" is the consummate address to Coleridge; the other "Lines" poems ("Lines left upon a Seat in a Yew-tree," "Lines written at a small distance from my House," "Lines written in early spring," and "Lines written near Richmond") insist, in varying degrees of heat or calm, that men must turn to each other—not, as in the curse poems, because supernatural calamity will befall them if they remain independent, but because it is more natural to be fused than separate, more "kind" to be double than single.

"Lines left upon a Seat in a Yew-tree," a stern piece, gestures toward the speaker's double, the "you" hidden in the phallic You-tree. The poem and the Yew-tree occupy positions of command, for the subtitle describes the tree (and implicitly the poem) as "commanding a beautiful prospect." The tree commands a vista, and the narrator commands the reader and a probably male "Stranger." Addressing this "Stranger," the narrator recalls the lonely life of a man, now dead, who was "by genius nurs'd" (13). Wordsworth emphasizes the onanistic sterility of this man who, according to the poet's later note, "died a bachelor in middle age":[39] sitting among "barren rocks," he "a morbid pleasure nourished, tracing here / An emblem of his own unfruitful life" (25–29). Weavings of syntax and line enable Wordsworth warily to identify with the bachelor, and then to detach himself:

> —Who he was
> That piled these stones, and with the mossy sod
> First covered o'er, and taught this aged tree,
> Now wild, to bend its arms in circling shade,
> I well remember. (8–12)

Wordsworth separates himself from his subject's morbid bachelor pleasures by Miltonically deferring the pronoun "I" ("he" and "I" wrenched apart by five tangled lines), and by casting the poem not as a meditation but as an accosting address to a stranger: the poem begins, "Nay, Traveller! rest." Echoing the Ancient Mariner's insistent "Listen, Stranger!," Wordsworth cries out, "Stranger!":

> with rash disdain he turned away,
> And with the food of pride sustained his soul
> In solitude.—Stranger! these gloomy boughs
> Had charms for him. . . . (19–22)

The outburst "Stranger!" interrupts the gloomy meditation on the man who consumed himself, as a "Thou"—placed rudely at a line's beginning—interrupts the man's gazing:

> And lifting up his head, he then would gaze
> On the more distant scene; how lovely 'tis
> Thou seest, and he would gaze till it became
> Far lovelier. . . . (30–33)

Making room for the reader—"how lovely 'tis / Thou seest"— Wordsworth turns the poem toward conversation, and away from a monologue uncomfortably similar to solitary "morbid pleasure." Wordsworth could see more clearly in the presence of collaborators: he later recalled that he used to escort an Irish boy to this very spot "to witness the pleasure I expected the boy would receive from the prospect of the islands below and the intermingling water."[40] Words- worth's pleasure grows by "intermingling" with the boy's; the poem cautions the reader against being a "man, whose eye / Is ever on himself" (51–52)—and implores the reader—"Stranger! henceforth be warned" (46)—to keep "pure" by restraining from self-nursing, a metaphysical version of the sin later generations would call self-abuse.

Wordsworth turns to the ambient world as alternative to self- nursing, but even the blended notes of pastoral turn discordant when he remembers male enmities. "Lines written in early spring" is haunted by a refrain that sees men's specular relation to each other as viperous: "And much it griev'd my heart to think / What man has made of man" (7–8). Although "man" and "man" cohabit one line and one volume, they have made ambiguous, sorrowful work of each other. In contrast, "Lines written near Richmond" uses nature—the Thames—to link the speaker with unseen men, and seems, despite its stiffly obeisant footnote to Collins's "Ode on the death of Thomson," to live in a moral air free from poetic rivalry:

> Glide gently, thus for ever glide,
> O Thames! that other bards may see,
> As lovely visions by thy side
> As now, fair river! come to me! (17–20)

The more supple "Lines written at a small distance from my House" feigns to abandon poetry altogether, urging sister Dorothy to come outside and to "bring no book" (15):

No joyless forms shall regulate
Our living Calendar:
We from to-day, my friend, will date
The opening of the year.

Love, now an universal birth,
From heart to heart is stealing,
From earth to man, from man to earth,
—It is the hour of feeling. (17–24)

The "friend" here is ostensibly Dorothy, but Wordsworth called Coleridge "Friend" in the *Prelude* and elsewhere. Read as an address to Coleridge through a sisterly screen, these lines praise the *Lyrical Ballads* as a product of "love," of a "universal birth"—as well as a "stealing," a bleeding of influence from one heart to another. Wordsworth considers that his poetic life is born from communion with Coleridge, and imagines 1798 as the Year One of poetry: "We from to-day, my friend, will date / The opening of the year." Anticipating the aesthetic pronouncements of the 1800 preface, which turns away from prisoning décorum, Wordsworth writes, "No joyless forms shall regulate / Our living calendar." In this short lyric, as in the more extended "Tintern Abbey," Wordsworth celebrates the "hour of feeling," the poetic "birth," that briefly linked him to Coleridge.

"Tintern Abbey" is a postscript to the volume: placed at the end, composed after the rest of the poems, it has the panopticon's power to peer into the hearts of the other lyrics, but remain unseen. It shrives the Mariner, and reconciles Wordsworth with the "Friend" whose poem of errancy opened the book. "Tintern Abbey" begins with a reunion of two wanderers, Wordsworth and the river Wye: he returns to the Wye "after many wanderings, many years / Of absence" (157–58), and addresses it as "Thou wanderer through the woods" (57). In this opening sequence, déjà vu overtakes Wordsworth not only because the landscape is uncannily resonant, but because he has populated it with guilty echoes of Coleridge's Mariner. In addition to the "Wanderer," Wordsworth imagines "vagrant dwellers in the houseless woods," and, more importantly, a hermit (21). (A hermit helped rescue and absolve the Ancient Mariner.) The freely meandering first verse paragraph is sobered by beholding, at its end, this hermit who seems Wordsworth's double, so powerfully does his unspeaking presence shape, in retrospect, the lines that came before. Wordsworth sees

wreathes of smoke
Sent up, in silence, from among the trees,
With some uncertain notice, as might seem,

> Of vagrant dwellers in the houseless woods,
> Or of some hermit's cave, where by his fire
> The hermit sits alone. (18–23)

Unwilling to enter the hermit's consciousness too closely, Wordsworth renders him as a patch of Spenserian scrim, and makes his very existence in the poem conditional, a mere hunch: "With some uncertain notice, as might seem. . . . " But the tentativeness of the phrase, "or of some hermit's cave," belies the hermit's strong position at the next line's beginning: "The hermit sits alone." Remembering that a mute double also inhabits these woods tames the boyish music of Wordsworth's repeated, leaping "once again do I behold," and the heedlessly enjambed movement of the opening lines; the hermit reminds Wordsworth that the uncanny business he must transact on the banks of the Wye will not end until he has faced the Friend.

In the next verse paragraph, the "purer mind" must face its debt not merely to "these forms of beauty" (25) ("I have owed to them, / In hours of weariness, sensations sweet" [27–28]) but to the Friend: Wordsworth records a memorial to "little, nameless, unremembered acts/Of kindness and of love" (35–36). This line—the slowest, most reluctant, in the entire bounding poem—matches another chastening reminder of his debt to other men:

> For I have learned
> To look on nature, not as in the hour
> Of thoughtless youth, but hearing oftentimes
> The still, sad music of humanity. . . . (89–92)

The realization that nature is infused with human deeds subdues the swift thrill of power Wordsworth felt while writing this poem. (Its composition was so inspired that "not a line of it was altered," he later claimed.[41]) He could not celebrate his return to the Wye without ending solemnly on the note of the hermit's solitude, nor could he recall those "sensations sweet" owed to nature, without remembering what he owed to Coleridge. These acts are "nameless" because Wordsworth does not name Coleridge, and because male friendship—even poetic fraternity—retains an unspeakable aspect. These acts are "unremembered" because Wordsworth's poems in the *Lyrical Ballads* have forgotten their debt to the Friend.

Fleeing from dependence, denying his need for a second presence to master and complete him, Wordsworth has been "more like a man/ Flying from something that he dreads, than one/Who sought the thing he loved" (71-73). Wordsworth's flight from the dread Something recalls the Mariner's paranoid flight from his own shadow:

> Like one, that on a lonely road
> Doth walk in fear and dread
> ....
> Because he knows, a frightful fiend
> Doth close behind him tread. (451–56)

No longer fleeing nature, Wordsworth now turns to him or her as to a human lover:

> Therefore am I still
> A lover of the meadows and the woods,
> And mountains; and of all that we behold
> From this green earth; of all the mighty world
> Of eye and ear, both what they half-create,
> And what perceive. . . . (103–8)

The odd verb, "half-create," could be a synonym for "collaborate." To the line, "both what they half-create," Wordsworth appends a footnote confessing a poetic debt: "This line has a close resemblance to an admirable line of Young, the exact impression of which I cannot recollect." Young's line, unrecollected, becomes another "little, nameless, unremembered" act "of kindness and of love" from a second male poet.

Wordsworth's confidence that nature remains loyal depends on a moment of gentle theft not only from Young, but, more prominently, from Coleridge's "Frost at Midnight," which cries:

> Great universal Teacher! he shall mould
> Thy spirit, and by giving make it ask.
> Therefore all seasons shall be sweet to thee. . . . (63–65)

Wordsworth's own "Therefore am I still / A lover" is a moment of false transition, like Coleridge's "Therefore all seasons": to say "therefore," and assume that a transition has been made, evades logic but attains rapture. The line "Therefore am I still / A lover" weds Wordsworth and Coleridge in the borrowed "therefore," and in its manifest meaning: Wordsworth is still the lover of ambient presences, including ghosts of past friends.

As this paean to the "mighty world / Of eye and ear" continues,

Wordsworth's description of nature begins to sound like praise of the Friend. The poet is

> well pleased to recognise
> In nature and the language of the sense
> The anchor of my purest thoughts, the nurse,
> The guide, the guardian of my heart, and soul
> Of all my moral being. (108–12)

"Nature" is an "anchor": Coleridge used the word "anchor" to describe his attachment to Southey, whom he prized as "the Sheet Anchor of mine!"[42] Describing a friend as anchor is appropriate in a volume so dominated by a nautical poem (the "Ancient Mariner") that sailors bought the *Lyrical Ballads* under the impression that it was a naval song-book.[43] Nature is a feminine "nurse," but, as guardian and anchor, also resembles the male Friend. Wordsworth turns to a Friend whose gender is at first unspecified:

> For thou art with me, here, upon the banks
> Of this fair river; thou, my dearest Friend,
> My dear, dear, Friend, and in thy voice I catch
> The language of my former heart, and read
> My former pleasures in the shooting lights
> Of thy wild eyes. (115–20)

Clinging to this unnamed Friend, Wordsworth cleaves to words, repeating "dearest," "dear, dear" in the manner of the mad mother or the narrator of "The Thorn." The Friend's "voice" gives Wordsworth back his original "language"; because this Friend is a writer, it is appropriate that Wordsworth "reads" his lost pleasures in the Friend's eyes. But these pleasures are "former": the Friend is at once present ("Thou art with me here") and departed. These former joys are satisfactions of male bonding that Wordsworth has renounced.

Indeed, the Friend's maleness departs when the adjective "wild" appears, for "wild" is a word attached to women in the *Lyrical Ballads*: "The Mad Mother," in fact, was retitled "Her Eyes Are Wild" in later editions. But if the word "wild" marks the gender of the Friend as female, the repeated long "I" sound—"thy wild eyes"— delays the verse and postpones the movement toward certainty; and the deferral of the word "sister" for two more lines enables Words-worth to maintain ambiguity. Gender remains unfixed for a moment: is the Friend Coleridge or Dorothy? After deciding that the Friend is Dorothy—

> Oh! yet a little while
> May I behold in thee what I was once,
> My dear, dear Sister! (120–22)

—Wordsworth again uses a floating "Therefore," sign of homage to Coleridge's "Frost at Midnight." Wordsworth writes:

> all which we behold
> Is full of blessings. Therefore let the moon
> Shine on thee in thy solitary walk. . . . (134–36)

Coleridge, in "Frost at Midnight," had described "silent icicles, / Quietly shining to the quiet Moon" (73-74). Wordsworth employs Coleridge's devices ("therefore" and moonlight) to depict a scene from Dorothy's future; borrowing from Coleridge to speak to Dorothy, Wordsworth makes the return to Tintern Abbey and the attainment of ripe language into triangular occasions.

The poem ends with the assertion that having once been fused with the Friend, Wordsworth finds nature "more dear." All of Wordsworth's future faith depends on one moment—"on the banks of this delightful stream / We stood together" (151–52). In the "Ancient Mariner," men also stand together:

> I woke, and we were sailing on
> As in a gentle weather:
> 'Twas night, calm night, the moon was high;
> The dead men stood together. (435-38)

Sharing a phrase, Wordsworth and Coleridge stand together as poets; like the "dead men" in the "Ancient Mariner," the two writers, by the end of 1798, have murdered the muse in each other. Through the screen of the Sister, Wordsworth extends to his Friend the consolation that whatever "solitude, or fear, or pain, or grief,/Should be thy portion" (144-45)—words resonant with Coleridge's future—the memory of standing together sustains them. When they are separated, Wordsworth will no longer be close enough to catch from Coleridge's eyes any inspiration:

> Nor, perchance,
> If I should be, where I no more can hear
> Thy voice, nor catch from thy wild eyes these gleams
> Of past existence, wilt thou then forget
> That on the banks of this delightful stream
> We stood together. . . . (147–52)

His very past unfolds to him only through the medium of his Friend's wild eyes and voice: "in thy voice I catch / The language of my former heart" (117–18). The "gleams / Of past existence" that Wordsworth mourns are intimations of immortality a child inherits, and embers of a year of language shared with Coleridge. The Friend's wild eyes, which give Wordsworth a voice, are arresting as the Mariner's eye:

> He holds him with his glittering eye—
> The wedding guest stood still
> And listens like a three year's child;
> The Marinere hath his will.

The Ancyent Marinere retains his will, for the Friend's mesmeric eye holds Wordsworth even in "Tintern Abbey," when "language of my former heart" is born out of the Friend's glittering eye.

The word "eye" is, of course, a pun for "I": by subjecting himself to the instructing, confining powers of Coleridge's eye, Wordsworth acquires the freedom to write autobiographically and independently. Despite the rewards of allying himself with Coleridge's "I," however, Wordsworth senses fatal links between the mad mother's wild eyes, the Ancient Mariner's glittering eye, and the rapacity of Coleridge's grip. In "Tintern Abbey," Wordsworth obscures his tie to Coleridge by addressing Dorothy: Wordsworth is not the only male writer in history to snap the bond between erotic entanglements and literary partnerships, to deny that he has used another man as muse. Poetry joins and divides Wordsworth and Coleridge; the dream of double writing dissolves as soon as Wordsworth's mature poetry begins. The first reference to the "Ancient Mariner" is November 1797, in a letter of Dorothy's. Wordsworth wrote "Tintern Abbey" in July 1798, in a flushed few days, eight or nine months after the "Ancient Mariner" was begun—enough time for a child's gestation. Once "Tintern Abbey" was completed, Wordsworth could move on from the nine-month sentence Coleridge's willful eye had imposed.

Coleridge's eye subdued Wordsworth, who saw no profit in being mesmerized; the *Lyrical Ballads* unfolds his resistance to the experience of being inseminated by a man. Wordsworth condemned sexual spending as wasteful: "The world is too much with us; late and soon/Getting and spending, we lay waste our powers. . . . " ("The World is Too Much With Us," 1–2.) T. S. Eliot, on the other hand, celebrated waste, and found submission poetically fruitful; he cooperated with Pound in enacting the dynamic of active Mariner and passive wedding-guest. Sexuality speaks louder in *The Waste Land* than in Wordsworth's and Coleridge's verse; because Pound and Eliot fall after Freud in time, I will return now to the vocabulary of my first chapter, and discuss *The Waste Land* as the collaboration of hysteric and analyst.

4
The Waste Land:
T. S. Eliot's and Ezra Pound's
Collaboration on Hysteria

Although the word "hysteria" has been muddied by years of misogynistic use, contemporary feminists have (if I may turn Pound's phrase) made it new. Hysteria now implies a linguistic condition—muteness alternating with disorderly, imaginative speech—and a covert antagonism to patriarchy. Hysteria is etymologically a woman's affliction, but it has also affected men, paralyzing them, sheltering them from exigencies of the bed and the battlefield, opening them up to passivity as a sexual and social position. When I write of "hysteria" I mean to invoke not the specific experiences of women, but a set of male emotions and responses. The problem of hysteria helped Eliot and Pound articulate their own relationship, as it had helped Freud and Breuer nearly thirty years before.

The Waste Land is a portrait of hysteria over which two men brooded—a repetition, in verse, of Freud's and Breuer's 1895 experiment. It is problematic to call *The Waste Land* collaborative, because standard notions of authorship deem it Eliot's. Its manuscript, however, reveals that Ezra Pound determined its final shape, transforming a "sprawling, chaotic poem"[1] into something hard and powerfully disjunctive, and that this supposedly impersonal icon of New Criticism has profound connections with Eliot's own emotional disturbances. Despite its sibylline discontinuities, *The Waste Land* was used to shore up that monolith, the male modernist. Joyce wrote that it "ended the idea of poetry for ladies," and Pound commented that "Eliot's *Waste Land* is I think the justification of the 'movement,' of our modern experiment, since 1900."[2] Critics have patiently sought a male protagonist in the poem, and identified this quest figure with the male reader. In 1934, I. A. Richards described the obstacles this quester faces: "Even the most careful and responsive reader must reread and do hard work before the poem forms itself clearly and unambiguously in his mind. . . . And it is easy to fail in this undertak-

112

ing."[3] Delmore Schwartz, in 1945, hailed Eliot's protagonist—and Eliot himself—as an "international hero," and D. C. Fowler, in 1953, touted the poem's protagonist as "both hero and king."[4] These heroic readers, whom John Crowe Ransom, in 1966, called "those sturdy people who studied *The Waste Land*," formed a brotherhood of critics who "were as tough-minded as they were competent, and when they succeeded they were elated like professional sportsmen over their triumphs."[5]

This sportsman-reader of Eliot's kingly poem has, until recently, obscured the affinities between the style of high male modernism and the discourse of the female hysteric. Hysteria's ruptures, discontinuities, and absences are similar to the "pre-Oedipal semiotic babble"[6] which Julia Kristeva finds in experimental literature: "for at least a century, the literary avant-garde . . . has been introducing ruptures, blank spaces, and holes into language." If "the moment of rupture and negativity" is feminine, then fissures in a text (even if its author is male) unseat literary convention *and* patriarchal rule.[7] Eliot's poem—semiotic, negative, riddled with absences—is "feminine" not because women always sound like *The Waste Land*, but because, in 1922, its style might have seemed more recognizably a hysterical woman's than a male poet's.

Hysteria is a disturbance in language, and the very word "hysteria" marks it as a woman's affliction. In *Studies on Hysteria*, where the patients are all women, female speech is both illness and cure: talking is the sickness cured by talking. Anna O. suffered

a deep-going functional disorganization of her speech. It first became noticeable that she was at a loss to find words. . . . Later she lost her command of grammar and syntax; she no longer conjugated verbs, and eventually she used only infinitives, for the most part incorrectly formed from weak past participles; and she omitted both the definite and indefinite article. In the process of time she became almost completely deprived of words. She put them together laboriously out of four or five languages and became almost unintelligible. . . . At times when she was at her very best and most free, she talked French and Italian.[8]

Discontinuities like Anna O.'s, however, offer openings for analytic entrances; the hysteric's riddles cry out for a collaborator's interpretation. Freud refers to a patient as "*our* oracle"[9]—a puzzle to be solved in complicity with male readers and colleagues. By interpreting this enigma, Freud and friends become midwives helping draw sense out of hysteria's "narrow cleft":

The whole spatially-extended mass of psychogenic material is in this way drawn through a narrow cleft and thus arrives in consciousness cut up, as it were, into pieces or strips. It is the psychotherapist's business to put these together once more into the organization which he presumes to have existed.[10]

Freud's analogy is clear: the analyst plays midwife to the laboring hysteric. The hysteric undergoing analysis may resemble a woman giving birth, but Freud (as I observed earlier) slips into the masculine pronoun when discussing the patient as intellectual partner; Freud tried to make the hysteric "himself into a collaborator," and to "induce him to regard himself with the objective interest of an investigator."[11] The very process of cure, then, makes over the dissembling woman into a cooperative male colleague.

Breuer's and Freud's collaboration on hysteria illuminates Eliot's and Pound's partnership because the manuscript of *The Waste Land*, even more than the "finished" poem, resembles hysterical discourse— a private theater of fantasy like Anna O.'s, a female language which Pound, acting the analyst's part, remade in a man's image. The two poets can unite because they see the discontinuous poem as a woman in need of cure. The poem's ailing body stands in for Eliot's body, and for the body of his "mad" wife, Vivien: the poem is a hysteric with whom the two men form a triangle. Containing hysteria within the bounds of verse may have repaired Eliot's wounded masculinity, and yet he wrote a maimed poem in the first place as a way of obtaining Pound's powerful services. *The Waste Land* asked for Pound's curative arrival; Eliot's act of giving his "chaotic" poem as a gift to another man exists as a gesture intrinsic to the poem, and prior to the two men's sexually resonant moment of exchange.

A Poem Is Born

In the years preceding *The Waste Land*, Eliot was preoccupied with nerves—his own and his wife's; together, they suffered from vague emotional and somatic disorders.[12] His deepening nervous crisis led to therapeutic retreats—Margate and Lausanne—and to the writing of *The Waste Land*: Eliot's mental breakdown was one circumstance provoking the poem. Hysteria is a legitimate term for his condition; male hysteria—sanctioned as shell shock during World War I—certainly existed,[13] and Eliot knew of the disease in at least its female form. In "Sweeney Erect," he writes of an epileptic on a bed who "curves backward, clutching at her sides" in an *arc-en-cercle*; Eliot wryly observes, "hysteria/Might easily be misunderstood."[14]

He most explicitly confronts the sickness, however, in his prose-poem "Hysteria." Seeing the disturbance in a woman, Eliot finds it in himself, for the male "I" is hardly separate from the female hysteric he watches: "As she laughed I was aware of becoming involved in her laughter and being part of it."[15] Lost "in the dark caverns of her throat," he has entered her very organ of speaking, a vagina dentata with "unseen muscles" and a row of teeth like "accidental stars." To separate himself from the hysteric, Eliot invokes an "elderly waiter"—a paternal spirit guide who seems part of the hysteric's conspiracy: hands "trembling," the waiter speaks in a stutter reminiscent of one of Freud's hysterics, Frau Emmy von N., whose speech "was from time to time subject to spastic interruptions amounting to a stammer."[16] The old man repeats, "If the lady and gentleman wish to take their tea in the garden, if the lady and gentleman wish to take their tea in the garden ... " Eliot must confront hysteria without the waiter's help: "I decided that if the shaking of her breasts could be stopped, some of the fragments of the afternoon might be collected, and I concentrated my attention with careful subtlety to this end." Eliot proposes an extreme solution to his identification with female hysteria: the woman must be "stopped"—tranquilized, terminated. Fragments can cohere, and he can begin to write, only after he stops the sympathetic vibrations that the hysteric's shaking breasts set off in his language.

Although Eliot had this long poem on his mind as early as 1919,[17] he found himself, like Anna O., almost completely deprived of words. Feeling that he had "dried up completely," he wrote poems in French to outwit his paralysis.[18] Anna O. knew that trick, called "hysterical conversion"; she spoke English when she had suddenly lost the ability to speak her native German. Conrad Aiken related that although every evening Eliot "went home to his flat hoping that he could start writing again . . . night after night the hope proved illusory: the sharpened pencil lay unused by the untouched sheet of paper."[19] In 1918, Eliot's doctor ordered him not to write any prose for six months; at Margate, the work he did on *The Waste Land* was against medical advice. Eliot remembers being told by his doctor to "go away *at once* . . . not exert my mind at all, and follow his strict rules for every hour of the day."[20] Enforced abstention from fatiguing brain-work was standard practice in treating female nervous patients: Eliot, like Alice James, Virginia Woolf, or Charlotte Perkins Gilman, was diagnosed as mentally exhausted. He suffered from a paralysis similar to the literal immobility that afflicted Freud's patients: in 1918, Eliot wrote that "the experiences I have been through have been paralys-ing,"[21] and in 1921, he complained of "an aboulie and emotional

derangement which has been a lifelong affliction."[22] Freud's hysteric
Emmy von N. suffered from abulia, a state of impaired will, and so
did Coleridge's wedding-guest. In a woman, barrenness, paralysis,
and abulia were labeled hysteria. By displaying these symptoms in the
years he was contemplating and composing *The Waste Land*, Eliot
invoked the aid of what any middle-class or aristocratic hysteric, after
1895, could expect: a male analyst.

Conrad Aiken believed, in fact, that a male analytic "intrusion" cata-
lyzed the composition of *The Waste Land*. A friend of Aiken asked a
psychiatrist about Eliot's writing block, and the doctor pronounced
that Eliot "thinks he's God." Aiken wrote: "When I told Eliot . . . he
was literally speechless with rage. The *intrusion*, quite simply, was one
that was intolerable."[23] Eliot may have protested, but this strong man's
"intrusion" fertilized his imagination and freed him to write *The Waste
Land*. At Lausanne, under the care of Dr. Vittoz, Eliot enjoyed further
intrusions: the doctor performed a laying-on-of-hands similar to the
pressure technique Freud describes in *Studies on Hysteria*.[24] Freud
would press his hand to a patient's forehead and command her to recall
repressed material; under the alienist's hand, one patient fell into a
trance and saw "curious signs looking rather like Sanskrit."[25] Eliot,
too, saw curious Sanskrit signs—*Datta, Dayadhvam, Damyata*, and
Shantih; while under Vittoz's care, Eliot wrote the body of "What the
Thunder Said," lines he considered the best in the poem.[26] He was able
to compose them because of his illness, not in spite of it; in his essay on
Pascal, he wrote that "it is a commonplace that some forms of illness
are extremely favorable, not only to religious illumination, but to artistic and literary composition."[27] Illness opened Eliot to a state of grace,
fecund as Anna O.'s transcendental *condition seconde*, her auto-hyp-
notic *absence*, which, according to Breuer and Freud, "may well be
likened to a dream in view of its wealth of imaginative products and
hallucinations, its large gaps of memory and the lack of inhibition and
control in its associations."[28] Eliot believed that sickness could inspire:
in *The Use of Poetry and the Use of Criticism*, he approvingly quoted
Housman's comment, "I have seldom written poetry unless I was rather
out of health," and added that "ill-health, debility or anaemia, may
. . . produce an efflux of poetry in a way approaching the condition of
automatic writing." For Eliot, poetic composition was a cathartic birth.
Though he did not labor as literally as Anna O., he reached to childbirth
for a description of a poem's "long incubation," the suspense of not
knowing "until the shell breaks what kind of egg we have been sitting
on."[29] Eliot felt that the male poet, as if pregnant, "is oppressed by a
burden which he must bring to birth in order to obtain relief."[30]

Hysteria, in Eliot's prose-poem, was a feminine sickness that a man could catch. T. S. and Vivien Eliot spent their marriage sharing this pathology; in 1919, for example, while Vivien complained of migraine, swollen face, tiredness, and depression, Eliot was depressed, bedridden, and exhausted.[31] Vivien's mother feared that her daughter had inherited "moral insanity," including an "irregular and over-frequent menstrual cycle"; on the other hand, a doctor told the poet, "Mr. Eliot, you have the thinnest blood I've ever tested."[32] Thin-blooded Eliot linked Vivien's "over-frequent" bleeding to his own less frequent poetry: when Aiken praised Eliot's 1925 *Poems*, he responded with a page ripped from *The Midwives' Gazette*, on which he had underlined a description of vaginal discharge: "*blood, mucous, and shreds of mucous . . . purulent offensive discharge.*"[33] Vivien's bleeding, Eliot's interest in vaginal discharge, and his description of poetry as a cathartic birth, suggest that female procreation and male poetry were linked in his imagination; he might have felt that his wife, with her "over-frequent bleeding," embodied the hysteria (the wandering uterus) that *The Waste Land* both suffers and portrays.

Eliot's alliance with Vivien was more than symbolic: she was part of his work. He invited her to Margate, where she wrote letters for him; as he worked on *The Waste Land*, "her approval was the prime consideration."[34] In treatment at Lausanne, his aim was to get well enough to "place less strain upon Vivien who has had to do so much *thinking* for me."[35] She found *The Waste Land*'s publication painful, since the poem was so tied to her. "As to Tom's *mind*, I am his mind," she wrote.[36] Confined under mysterious circumstances to an asylum in 1938, she died, still confined, in 1947. Eliot turned his hysteria into a poem that quickly and deliberately became an institution; Vivien suffered a more concrete institutionalization. It is a telling coincidence that Pound and Vivien, accomplices to Eliot's hysterical poem, each spent long years locked in asylums—Vivien at Northumberland House, Pound at St. Elizabeths.

The most conspicuous midwife of *The Waste Land* was Ezra Pound, who had a decisive effect on Eliot's life and work. In 1915, Pound stimulated him to begin writing after a three year lapse, and encouraged him to settle in England and marry Vivien.[37] In personal and poetic matters, Eliot depended on his friend's blunt mediation and superior strength. Two days after the Eliots married, Pound wrote to the groom's father in America: "Your son asks me to write this letter, I think he expects me to send you some sort of apologia for the literary life in particular."[38] The father had not been told of the marriage; Pound writes to defend his friend's commitment to poetry, not to praise the bride. By omitting any reference to Vivien or the wedding, Pound poses as suitor for the eligible son's hand, and agrees to share Eliot's literary life in sickness and in health.

Pound, in fact, was the only friend in whom Eliot confided his marital problems.[39] These confidences eased the difficult exchange of poetic powers. Eliot learned from the example of Wordsworth and Coleridge how a shared woman helps male poets intertwine:

> This reciprocal influence [of Wordsworth and Coleridge] would hardly have been possible to such a degree without another influence which held the two men together, and affected both of them more deeply than either know, the influence of a great woman. No woman has ever played so important a part in the lives of two poets at once—I mean their poetic lives—as did Dorothy Wordsworth.[40]

By qualifying "the lives of two poets" with an aside ("I mean their poetic lives"), Eliot blurs the line between life and poetry: if two men share a great woman they might also share a poetic corpus equivalent to her body. Writing to Pound in 1915, Eliot enclosed two poems about formidable women: "Portrait of a Lady," and "Suppressed Complex," about a woman in bed—either asleep or hysterically paralyzed.[41] Discussing "Portrait," Eliot calls the poem a Lady. Were all of Eliot's poems symbolic Ladies? Asking Pound to burn "Suppressed Complex" after reading it, Eliot begs his friend to destroy, by fiery sympathetic magic, the woman that the poem embodies. Eliot sends his friend portraits of problematic women because he knows that Pound has mysterious and virile powers of judgment, a will to incinerate the weaker man's affinity with hysteria.

Given Pound's power over hysteria, it is not surprising that Vivien should turn to him for advice, and as a go-between in her troubled relations with her husband. In letters, she thanks Pound for his medical attentions, and begs him to strong-arm Eliot into rescuing her from The Stanboroughs, a hydrotherapy institution.[42] She also confesses her powers as medium, her ability to fall into trances: Vivien, like many of the women in *The Waste Land*, had a sibyl's gifts. When Eliot went to Lausanne to be treated by Vittoz, he left his wife in Pound's care—along with, the evidence suggests, the manuscript of *The Waste Land*.[43] Eliot disburdened himself of two hysterics—poem and wife; he saw Pound as the man who could make both right.

Sending Aiken the clipping from *The Midwives' Gazette*, Eliot linked female fluids and male poetry, but the connection did not necessarily please him. Desire to extricate male verse from vaginal discharge may have inspired his paranoid dislike of women writers.

In a letter of 1915, he comments disparagingly on how women have taken over literature; in 1917, he describes a literary gathering marred by too many women, and suggests that the men meet separately. Contemporary life, he complains, has grown too feminine. In another letter of 1917, he mocks Edith Sitwell (finding the word "shit" in her name), and remarks on the scarcity of gifted women.[44] But a more vituperative misogyny is unleashed in John Quinn's letters to Ezra Pound. Quinn, a lawyer and agent, helped mastermind the practical and financial aspects of Eliot's literary career; in recognition of those efforts, he gave Quinn the original manuscript of *The Waste Land*. Though no *miglior fabbro*, Quinn was, like Pound, granted custody of a poem that its author was loath to hold by himself. Pound, Eliot, and Quinn were close friends. In Quinn's letters to Pound, misogyny is so continuous and unrestrained that it might have served as common ground for the three men. Quinn, like Eliot, was intrigued and disgusted by waste, and imagined it was intimately connected to words and to women. In this letter to Pound, Quinn excoriates the two women who edited *The Little Review*:

> These people seem to sweat urine and probably urinate sweat. . . .
>
> I don't mind the aberrations of a woman who has some openness and elasticity of mind . . . in whose execrations there may occasionally be cream; but, by God! I don't like the thought of women who seem to exude as well as bathe in piss, if not drink it, or each other's. . . .
>
> Without being personal, I think of female literary excrement; washy urinacious menstruations; with the mental stink but without the physical hardihood of the natural skunk . . . a feeling of stale urine exuded in the place of the cream of the jest.
>
> Putrid ignorance, imbecile brazenness, banal pretense—that make the sight of a squatting bitch dachshund pouring a sheet of urine into a ditch a poetic, if not a pitiful sight.[45]

These are the sentiments about literary women that distinguish the man whom Eliot gave, in gratitude, his manuscript of *The Waste Land*. Did Eliot and Pound share these passions, or merely tolerate them in Quinn? Describing female literary activity as excrement, and obsessively focusing on a woman's urine, Quinn forms a bond with Pound. The conviction that a woman's urine, excrement, or blood are substances connected to her literary products underlies the omitted Fresca passages from Eliot's "The Fire Sermon": Quinn's execrations tap the same prejudices as Eliot's description of the typist's "dirty camisoles and stays," and of Fresca (blessed with a "good old hearty female stench") producing a "needful stool" while reading *Clarissa*. Eliot, who made "waste" the center of his poem, shares Quinn's concerns; *The Waste Land*, as its title announces, is about excrement—the anal land over which, Quinn hopes, women hold sovereignty.

The two poets indulged together in a bawdiness like their friend Quinn's. Eliot wrote poems filled with penises and sphincters—parts of an epic, "King Bolo and His Great Black Queen"—and incorporated the verses into letters to Pound, who wrote his own counterparts.[46] In a letter to Eliot suggesting revisions to *The Waste Land*, Pound includes comic verses describing himself as midwife, and Eliot as mother, of *The Waste Land*. Unfortunately, D. D. Paige expurgated the poem in his *Selected Letters of Ezra Pound*.[47] I will quote the entire poem; the lines that Paige omitted I enclose in brackets.

SAGE HOMME

These are the Poems of Eliot
By the Uranian Muse begot;
A Man their Mother was,
A Muse their Sire.

How did the printed Infancies result
From Nuptials thus doubly difficult?

If you must needs enquire
Know diligent reader
That on each Occasion
Ezra performed the caesarean Operation.

                                                              E.P.

/ / / / / / / / / / / / / / / / / /

Cauls and grave clothes he brings,
Fortune's outrageous stings,
About which odour clings,
            Of putrifaction,
Bleichstein's dank rotting clothes
Affect the dainty nose,
He speaks of common woes
            Deploring action.

He writes of A.B.Cs.
And flaxseed poultices,
Observing fate's hard decrees
            Sans satisfaction;
Breeding of animals,
Humans and canibals,
But above all else of smells
            Without attraction

Vates cum fistula

                                                              E.P.

[E.P. hopeless and unhelped
Enthroned in The marmorean skies
His verse omits realities,
Angelic hands with mother of pearl
Retouch the strapping servant girl,

The barman is to blinded him
Silenus bubling at the brim, (or burbling)
The glasses turn to chalices
Is his fumbling analysis
And holy hosts of hellenists
Have numbed and honied his cervic cysts,
Despite his hebrew eulogists.

Balls and balls and balls again
Can not touch his fellow men.
His foaming and abundant cream
Has coated his world. The coat of a dream;
Or say that the upjut of his sperm
Has rendered his senses pachyderm.

Grudge not the oyster his stiff saliva
Envy not the diligent diver. et in aeternitate][48]

The first verses revealed that Pound was the midwife of *The Waste Land*, and that Eliot was the mother, but left ambiguous how he had been impregnated. Insemination depends on sperm that the expurgated verses supply: "His foaming and abundant cream / Has coated his world." Receptive Eliot takes in Pound's sperm, for E.P., the "blinded him" who, merely masturbatory, cannot "touch his fellow men," is the source of the upjutting "cream." Pound, Eliot's male muse, is the sire of *The Waste Land*.

Pound's talk of semen here is not an isolated instance. Six months earlier, June 1921, in a postscript to his translation of Rémy de Gourmont's *The Natural Philosophy of Love*, Pound expatiates on the relation between creativity and semen, and describes semen as a shaping force vast and omnipotent as Coleridge's "esemplastic power." Pound writes: "the brain itself is, in origin and development, only a sort of great clot of genital fluid held in suspense or reserve," and "creative thought is an act like fecundation, like the male cast of the human seed." Pound believes that men have a privileged power to "exteriorize" forms—to mold works of art: men are masters of "the new upjut, the new bathing of the cerebral tissues in . . . *la mousse* of the life sap." Pound's belief that "the mind is an up-spurt of sperm" influenced his assessment of a literary man's prospects in 1920s London; he compares the phallus "charging, head-on" into "female chaos," to the frustration of "driving any new idea into the great passive vulva of London."[49] Trying to create a revolution in poetry was a phallic act.

Pound disparaged London's "passive vulva," but enjoyed Eliot's receptivity to suggestion. Pound, casting himself as the source of "foaming and abundant cream," implies that Eliot played the passive part, and that the poem was sired in a scene of intercourse between the two men. That imagined moment of upjut clarifies the nature of Eliot's "Uranian muse": the phrase not only refers to Milton's muse, but to the Uranian poets, homosexual verse-writers of the late 19th and early 20th centuries—a group that included John Addington Symonds. Rendered "hopeless and unhelped" by the spectacle of Eliot's magnificent (and now manly) *Waste Land*, Pound is "wracked by the seven jealousies," and condemns his own verse as effeminate; he confesses to Eliot, "I go into nacre and objets d'art."[50] Pound's reference to "foaming and abundant cream" strives to be merely bawdy; so does Quinn's "feeling of stale urine exuded in the place of the cream of the jest." But dirty jokes supported more unsettling complicities. Eliot took Pound's comic verses seriously enough to suggest that they be published in italics at the beginning of *The Waste Land*—a gesture which would have publicly established the poem as collaborative. The substance of Pound's dirty joke is that he has impregnated Eliot. Fantasies of maternity buttress male modernism: Pound dates this letter *24 Saturnus, An 1*, signifying that 1922, the year *Ulysses* was published, is the Year One of modernism, and that Joyce's epic gave birth to a new world. The Latin date *An 1*, spelled out, reads *An Unus*. Pound's playful reference to an(un)us as modernism's birthsite brings the poem's scene of gestation even closer to anal intercourse. In the same letter, Pound calls Eliot a "bitch," and refers, in the comic verse, to "his cervic cysts," which have been "honied by hellenists." In Pound's world, men have cervixes (with cysts) that have been lubricated by hellenists—men who, like Symonds, turned to Greece. Pound makes a further suggestive reference: a male oyster's "stiff saliva." Pound, who goes "into nacre," might have seen himself as having, like the oyster, a hermaphroditic opening that gestates pearly art, a hole that leaks an androgynous "saliva." Pound further conflates anality and birth by yoking "breeding of animals" to the excremental "smells/Without attraction" and the "odour" of "putrifaction" [sic]. In a 1921 letter to Eliot, Pound writes that "Yeats has given birth to a son."[51] Pound wished to believe that Joyce, Eliot, and Yeats, the mothers of modernism, had each given birth in 1921/1922.

Pound took cervic cysts even further: the scene of anal penetration that gestated Eliot's poem-child acquired vividness with the phrase, *"Vates cum fistula." Vates cum fistula* means poet with reed-pipe; it also means poet (or seer) with an ulcer in his bowels. The OED cites: "Fosteryng continually this fretting Fistula within the Bowels of the Christian commonweale." Earlier in the "obstetric" letter of December 1921, Pound wrote, "Some day I shall lose my temper, blaspheme Flaubert, lie like a shit-arse and say 'Art shd. embellish the umbelicus.'"[52] "Shit-arse," more than jest, reinforces the sense that the male poet has given birth, and that his "umbelicus" is in his arse, site of his cervic cysts. The poet *cum fistula* is a bard with anal cysts, signs of venereal disease. When Eliot sent Aiken the clipping from *The Midwives' Gazette* describing "blood" and "purulent offensive discharge," Aiken was in the hospital suffering from an anal fistula. Eliot, toying with the resonances of male anal bleeding, wrote to the ailing Aiken, "Have you tried Kotex for it? . . . KOTEX. Used with success by Blue-eyed Claude the Cabin Boy." In a farcical poem attached to this letter, Eliot described the Cabin Boy as a "clever little nipper/who filled his ass with broken glass/and circumcised the skipper."[53] Claude bleeds from his "ass" because he was penetrated by a bottle that broke internally. Offering Kotex to Aiken, Eliot connects female menstruation to a male anal bleeding that seems, in the Claude the Cabin Boy verse, a consequence of sexual play. Like Freud and Fliess, Eliot and his friends were conscious of the male anus as a tender and charged site where metaphors of reproduction and creativity intersect. The male modernist anus, a barren, intrinsically unprocreative zone, achieves a weird flowering—lilacs out of the dead land—when men collaborate; Pound penetrates Eliot's waste land, and fills the hollow man with child.

According to Freud and Breuer, "hysterics suffer mainly from reminiscences";[54] *The Waste Land* suffers from reminiscences of Jean Verdenal, a medical student with literary interests whom Eliot befriended in Paris before the war, and who died in 1915, one month before Eliot's hasty marriage to Vivien.[55] There is a link between the poem's homosexual conception (Pound's sperm, Eliot's "arse") and the poem's mourning for a dead man. The "nuptials" of Eliot and Pound act out the poem's secret love for Verdenal, but Pound's revisions bury that subtext, for he urges the omission of "The Death of Saint Narcissus," "Song for the Opherion," "Exequy," and "Dirge"—poems "elucidative" of Eliot's mourning for the dead friend.[56]

After Eliot revised the poem, Pound made final suggestions. Paige published Pound's letter, but omitted a telling passage:

Aristophanes probably depressing, and the native negro phoque melo-
dies of Dixee more calculated to lift the ball-encumbered phallus of man
to the proper 8.30, 9.30 or even ten thirty level now counted as the
crowning and alarse too often katachrestical summit of human
achievement.
I enclose further tracings of an inscription discovered recently in the
buildings (?) outworks of the city hall jo-house at Charleston S.C.
May your erection never grow less. I had intended to speak to you
seriously on the subject, but you seemed so mountany gay while here
in the midst of Paris that the matter slipped my foreskin.[57]

What evidence did Pound witness of Eliot being "mountany gay"? In
the phrase, "the matter slipped my foreskin," Pound substitutes the
word "foreskin" for "mind," implying that the poet's mind is in
his penis, and that the foreskin, missing or intact, is a place where
remembering and forgetting occurs. (Eliot, too, noted foreskins: in
his "Claude the Cabin Boy" verse, he mentioned the skipper's circum-
cision.) Given Pound's yoking of sperm and creativity, the "erection"
for which he congratulates Eliot is anatomical and literary: with
Pound's help on *The Waste Land*, Eliot regains sexual potency and
poetic power.

Eliot admitted that he "placed before [Pound] in Paris the manuscript of a scrawling, chaotic poem";[58] in his hesitation to claim those
discontinuities as signs of power, he resembles Prufrock—unerect,
indecisive, unable to come to the point. Pound treats the manuscript
of *The Waste Land* as if it were an effeminate Prufrock he wishes to
rouse: he cures the poem of its hysteria by suggesting that representations of the feminine be cut, and by urging Eliot to make his language
less qualified. Pound, who wrote to Eliot, "May your erection never
grow less," approved of neither the poem's nor the man's sexual
neurasthenia. Within a sequence of opposites, pairs that glide into
each other and, in my hands, often blur (straight / gay, man / woman,
active / passive, willful / indecisive), Pound urges his friend to inhabit
the primary term; however, by metaphorically impregnating Eliot,
Pound places him in a passive position that they must have considered
unmanly. Pound's gestures are paradoxical; he denounces instances
of linguistic effeminacy, and yet the very act of intruding commentary
is homosexually charged. In the "erection" letter to Eliot, Pound
writes, "I merely queeried the dialect of 'thence'; dare say it is
o.k."[59] The act of queerying—critiquing, editing, collaborating—has
suspicious overtones of queerness, inferences which Pound highlights
and denies. In discussing Pound's ambiguous "queeries," I will put
aside questions of literary quality. Focusing only on whether or not
Pound's suggestions were justified blinds us to other motives for his

excisions. I would like to offer a different reading of Pound's Caesarian performance.

Because Pound sought to establish Eliot's primacy in literary history with *The Waste Land*, he disapproved of beginning the poem with an epigraph from Joseph Conrad, a living writer. In the "obstetric" letter, Pound wrote to Eliot: "I doubt if Conrad is weighty enough to stand the citation." I suspect that Pound objected not merely to Conrad's lack of eminence, but to the epigraph's content: a passage from *Heart of Darkness* ("The horror! the horror!"), it records a man crying out in fear of the dark (and feminine) continent. Beginning the poem with a cry of emasculated terror would not help keep Eliot erect. However, in this letter to Eliot, Pound criticizes another portion of the poem by echoing the very language of horror he disliked in the epigraph: "It also, to your horror probably, reads aloud very well. Mouthing out his OOOOOOze." Pound uses words that reflect *The Waste Land*'s fear of things that gape: he mentions "the body of the poem," and describes his Sage Homme verses as a "bloody impertinence" which should be placed "somewhere where they would be decently hidden and swamped by the bulk of accompanying matter." Pound describes the poem's body in a language of mouths, horror, blood, and swamps—a vocabulary calculated to affect Eliot, who thought of his verse as a woman's "purulent offensive discharge."

Pound separated *The Waste Land* from dread female discharge by criticizing Eliot's portraits of women. Pound questioned the lines— " 'You gave me hyacinths first a year ago;/'They called me the hyacinth girl' "—with the marginal annotation, "Marianne," which, according to critic Barbara Everett, refers to the heroine of the Pierre Marivaux novel *La Vie de Marianne*, a work whose "Frenchness" attracted Eliot.[60] Did Pound object to these lines because "hyacinth" signified homosexuality, and because Eliot—impersonating a hyacinth girl—was indulging in French tendencies? (Pound remembers the note as a possible reference to Tennyson's Mariana: perhaps he disapproved of Eliot's identification with this pining hysteric, an emblem of the kind of Victorian poetry that modernists condemned as effete.) Pound tersely indicts these lines as mere "photography":

"My nerves are bad tonight. Yes, bad. Stay with me.
"Speak to me. Why do you never speak. Speak.
"What are you thinking of? What thinking? ~~Think~~ What?
"I never know what you are thinking. Think." (11)

Pound wrote "photo" beside the line, "Are you alive, or not? Is there nothing in your head?" (13). Pound faulted these passages for their photographic style—cheaply realistic, insufficiently wrought by artistic muscle—and for their subject: these snapshots portray Eliot as neurasthenic, silent, unable to satisfy his wife, and portray Vivien as hysterically adamant. Nothing fills the husband's head: he is the gaping "horror" of the cancelled epigraph. Vivien, the camera's subject, commented that these lines were "WONDERFUL," and added a further photographic line which Eliot kept: "What you get married for if you dont want to have children" (15). Lil may refuse to have children, but the "nothing" husband was guilty of a truly hysterical reluctance—the refusal to speak.

The portrait of a lady that Pound most wholeheartedly blotted out was a swathe of Pope-like couplets concerning Fresca. In the typescript, Pound dismissed the whole passage with the comment, "rhyme drags it out to diffuseness" (39), but only crossed out the four lines which portrayed her as poet:

> From such chaotic misch-masch potpourri
> What are we to expect but poetry?
> When restless nights distract her brain from sleep
> She may as well write poetry, as count sheep. (41)

Eliot had described his poem as "chaotic"; Pound called it a "masterpiece."[61] Pound, as male collaborator and editor, divides Eliot's discourse from Fresca's, and ensures that readers do not confuse the chaotic *Waste Land* with Fresca's chaotic potpourri, Eliot's masterpiece with Fresca's hysteric fits, Eliot's Uranian muse with Fresca's forays into gay and lesbian writers: "Fresca was baptised in a soapy sea / Of Symonds—Walter Pater—Vernon Lee" (41). Pound's revisions intend to save Eliot from seeming like soapy Symonds. By crossing out Fresca, Pound suggests that Eliot begin "The Fire Sermon" with the narrator, an "I," "Musing upon the king my brother's wreck / And on the king my father's death before him." Pound lets this depiction of a dead king and wrecked brother remain: male royalty, even when dismembered, seemed preferable to a woman reading lesbian literature in the bathtub.

Pound particularly objected to syntactic inversion—which suggests, in turn, sexual inversion. The word "inversion" mattered to Pound. He wrote, in a letter to Eliot, "I should leave it as it is, and NOT invert,"[62] and commented in the manuscript, "Inversions not warranted by any real exigence of metre" (45). For Pound, inverted word order, a dated poetic affectation, implied the aesthete's "nacre" and "objets d'art." Pound wrote "1880" and "Why this Blot on Scutchen *between* 1922 & Lil'" beside

And if it rains, the closed carriage at four.
And we shall play a game of chess:
The ivory men make company between us
Pressing lidless eyes and waiting for a knock upon the door. (13)

These lines clashed with the nearby jazzy "O O O O that Shakespeher-ian Rag" and "HURRY UP PLEASE IT'S TIME." But Pound disliked the passage for reasons other than its dated tonality; he found fault with the scene of sexual inaction between husband and wife, and accused Eliot of a sexual and stylistic listlessness. Modernism defined itself in opposition to that "1880" of literary and sexual ennui.

Removing traces of inversion from the poem, Pound also quibbled with Eliot's diminutives, writing "'one' wee red mouse" (from a Rudyard Kipling poem) in the margin of "From which one tender Cupidon peeped out" (11). Pound, disliking hesitation, defined linguistic effeminacy as the art of qualifying statements excessively. He put a box of disparagement around the word "little": "Carrying / Away the little light dead people" (13). In the passage,

> Above the antique mantel was displayed
> In pigment, but so lively, you had thought
> A window gave upon the sylvan scene,

he objected to the "had": "had is the weakest point" (11). Pound deplored the limpness of "little" in the line, "Spread out in little fiery points of will," and objected to the phrase "of will" because it was a "dogmatic deduction but wobbly as well" (11). Eliot's wobbliness was made flesh in Prufrock, echoes of which Pound sought to cut: writing "Pruf[rock]" and "Pr[ufrock] or Por[trait of a Lady]" in the margins, he objected to "Time to regain the door" and to "And if I said 'I love you' should we breathe / Hear music, go a-hunting, as before?" (107). Instead of the inverted "should we breathe," he suggested the straightforward "we should breathe." Inversion was, like Prufrock's disorder, a pathology Pound could cure.

Accusing Eliot of Prufrock's indecision, Pound wrote, beside the line "Across her brain one half-formed thought may pass": "make up yr. mind you Tiresias if you know know damn well or else you dont" (47). Pound, impatient with Eliot for limping verbs like "may," conflates ambiguous words and ambiguous men. Eliot took the accusation seriously, and responded by declaring in a footnote that Tiresias is "the most important personage in the poem," the character where "the two sexes meet." Indeed, Tiresias is the poem's quintessential male hysteric—one of Freud's "double flowers" containing male and female parts. It was once fashionable to say that *The Waste Land* portrays a crisis in Western civilization. That interpretation still holds: through Tiresias, Eliot describes (from the inside) an epoch we might call The Age of Inversion, when heterosexuality was in the process of being undermined and traduced by its eerie opposite.

Consistent with his dislike of wavering, Pound encourages Eliot to act, whatever the sexual act in question may be. Where the "I" makes a date with the apparently homosexual Mr. Eugenides, Eliot had vacillated: Mr. Eugenides

> asked me, in demotic French,
> To luncheon at the Cannon Street Hotel,
> And perhaps a weekend at the Metropole. (31)

Beside the "perhaps," Pound wrote: "damn per'apsez." This phrase appears in a letter that Coleridge wrote to Robert Southey in September 1794, describing their Pantisocratic scheme. Coleridge exclaimed, "Perhaps you have not heard from Bath—perhaps—damn perhapses—My God! my God!"[63] Pound, echoing Coleridge's "damn per'apsez," suggests that his modernist partnership with Eliot follows the path of their Romantic predecessors. Pound's reiterated "perhaps" has a second resonance. In a 1922 volume of short stories about unmarried and implicitly homosexual men and women, George Moore used "perhaps" to signify indecision about gender and sexual preference: "neither man nor woman, just a perhapser," sighs one of Moore's celibates.[64] Pound thought that Eliot relied on "perhaps" because he was reprehensibly unsure about sex: "perhaps" is the symptom of Eliot's inabilty to act, erotically or linguistically. Pound cures this hysterical paralysis by cutting the "perhaps." In the margin of the line, "Perhaps his inclinations touch the stage," Pound wrote "Perhaps be *damn*ed" (45). Pound seizes on that "perhaps"—the code for Eliot's ambiguous "inclinations"—as a hysterical tic. Pound objects to a third "perhaps," writing "Georgian" beside the line, "Perhaps it does not come to very much" (99). Consistent with the sexual sense of "come," the "it" that does not come to very much is an erotic temptation beyond the narrator's reach: "The golden foot I may not kiss or clutch / Glowed in the shadow of the bed" (99). This "I" is a Prufrock, afraid of desire and of direct statement; the golden foot he may not kiss or clutch is a poetic foot. Eliot's fear that "perhaps it does not come to very much" is a fear that the poem, *The Waste Land*, does not come to very much. Crossing out that doubt, Pound asserts the poem's power.

When Eliot confessed hysterical speechlessness—"I could not /

Speak"—Pound underlined the phrase (7). Did he dislike that confession, or did he underscore it because he recognized its importance? By emphasizing these words, Pound points out that Eliot *has* spoken: the very act of confessing "I could not speak" means silence is over. By articulating hysteria, Eliot conquers it: because Eliot gave his manuscript to Pound, every instance of hysteria in *The Waste Land*— whether described, or enacted as linguistic symptom—invites Pound's attention and affection. I will examine the poem's hysterical plots and fits as moments where Eliot opens his body up to Pound.

The Poem's Hysterical Body

The Waste Land was originally titled "He Do the Police in Different Voices." Eliot may have tried to impersonate the police, arm of male law, but he ended up doing woman. The poem lost a title but remained inhabited by the voice of sexual difference—a sequence of women's voices hysterical because of their multitude and their character. The original title implied states of speech which Freud glorified as "oracular": the hysteric utters cryptic and premonitory fragments, like "I want to die," spoken by the epigraph's Sibyl. Indeed, the poem's opening lines, which express a fear of April's regeneration, resume the epigraph's death-wish, and so seem the lament of a sibyl whose agony is capacious enough to include the poem's diverse narrators. The metamorphosing narrator—now the Sibyl, now Marie, now Tiresias—is herself or himself a hysteric, moving, like Charcot's Geneviève, through the stylized phases of a fit.

The opening lines are resigned to a fated and terrifying process of generation. "Breeding," "mixing," "stirring," "covering," "feeding"—each enjambed line finishes with a reproductive word that does not resolve, but throws unsatisfied weight back into the next line's initial stress:

> April is the cruellest month, breeding
> Lilacs out of the dead land, mixing
> Memory and desire, stirring
> Dull roots with spring rain.

The hysteric is terrified by waste's unnatural ability to breed: the site of excrement (the anus) makes the speaker remember and desire, and even generates new life. However, the verse dreads its own strategies of propulsion: the poem gains life by submitting itself to Pound in a constructed scene of anal intercourse, but it denies the place where male collaborative births occur.

The poem avoids this specter of male-male breeding by deflecting its hysteria and its vatic powers onto women. The figures of commanding wisdom in the poem, though maligned by the hypnotically detached narrator, are sibyls and hysterics. After the epigraph's Sibyl, the next oracle is Madame Sosostris, "known to be the wisest woman in Europe"—a cross-dressed Ezra Pound, whom Eliot certainly thought the most prescient *man* in Europe. Like frigid Marie, who goes "south in the winter," Madame Sosostris suffers from the hysteric's chronic neuralgia: she has a "bad cold." Though ill, she reads Eliot's cards; Pound, too, read his friend's cards—the leaves of *The Waste Land*'s manuscript, which, as late as 1969, he called "the lost leaves."[65] (Pound reading Eliot's leaves disguises a more intimate haruspication: reading his friend's entrails.) Madame Sosostris is both an oracle and a fake; similarly, hysterical women stunned audiences and relatives with fits, but were accused, as well, of malingering. By distrusting Madame Sosostris (she "had a bad cold"), Eliot accuses the Tarot symbolism—the thread of his entire poem—of fraudulence. The poem maintains an ironic and paralyzed distance from the events and personae it unfolds: Eliot throws his voice equally into the throat of the oracular hysteric, believed and believing, and into the mind of the modern analyst / reader who recognizes the allusions and knows the hysteric's tale to be a sequence of simulations.

The other female hysteric in "The Burial of the Dead" is Marie, the poem's first "I" (if we do not include the epigraph's "I want to die"). The voice that spoke "April is the cruellest month" may have seemed equally Eliot's and the Sibyl's, but the androgynous dirge on memory and desire modulates into Marie's distinctly female recollection:

> And when we were children, staying at the archduke's,
> My cousin's, he took me out on a sled,
> And I was frightened. He said, Marie,
> Marie, hold on tight. And down we went.
> In the mountains, there you feel free.
> I read, much of the night, and go south in the winter.

This affectless reminiscence, spare and banal, hauntingly omitting, reads like a childhood trauma in *Studies on Hysteria*, a memory drained of meaning and emotion. Marie only remembers holding on tight, going down, and feeling free. "Hold on tight" and "down we went" are ingenuous screens for sexual acts that Marie's hysteria protects her from precisely recalling. Instead of going down, now she reads: the women in *The Waste Land* are serious readers—Madame Sosostris studying her cards, Fresca savoring Vernon Lee. Marie reads "much of the night" because she is not having sex and because she is insomniac. She goes south, in search of warmth and a cure, much as Eliot fled to Lausanne. Eliot grants Marie the poem's first dramatic monologue: by beginning androgynously but then shifting into a specifically female voice, he locates the poem within the blanched mind of a woman whose hysteria has taken away memory and desire.

Marie's male counterpart in "The Burial of the Dead" is the speaker who remembers the scene in the hyacinth garden; he remembers desire but not its anatomical configurations. Marie's screen memory was parched and pleasureless because of its failure to remember the past and because of its present desperation, while the hyacinth garden speaker's memory is glamorously burnished by the failure to specify and to act ("I could not/Speak, and my eyes failed, I was neither / Living nor dead, and I knew nothing"). Anna O. suffered loss of speech, as well as "a high degree of restriction of the field of vision: in a bunch of flowers which gave her much pleasure she could only see one flower at a time."[66] Eliot's vision here is restricted not to one flower, but to one head of hair—the hyacinth girl's wet locks, which bring on hysterical muteness and blindness. Freud claimed that the Medusa's head represents the vagina dentata.[67] The diffused narrator of *The Waste Land* is twice haunted by Medusas: a cut line exclaims, "Around that head the scorpions hissed!" (117), and a woman (whom Pound did not excise) "drew her long black hair out tight / And fiddled whisper music on those strings." The hysteria-inducing music of the Medusa's hair is an image of Eliot's own hissing poetry.

Indeed, the powerful women in *The Waste Land* are emanations of Eliot's verbal incandescence. One particularly glowing woman— whom the poem both admires and undermines, without announcing a point of view which consciously does either—appears on a "burnished throne" at the beginning of "A Game of Chess":

> The Chair she sat in, like a burnished throne,
> Glowed on the marble, where the glass
> Held up by standards wrought with fruited vines
> From which a golden Cupidon peeped out
> (Another hid his eyes behind his wing)
> Doubled the flames of sevenbranched candelabra
> Reflecting light upon the table as
> The glitter of her jewels rose to meet it,
> From satin cases poured in rich profusion. . . .

Despite the iambic pentameter's intrinsic verve and height, the meter is subtly nervous, always about to miss a beat and turn modern:

"Reflecting light upon the table as / The glitter of her jewels rose to meet it." The tone may be archly Elizabethan or neoclassical, but it veils a wish to malign modern women: the narrator hates the woman for her supremacy and hopes to steal the "chair" she sits in. *Chair* is French for meat or flesh: the chair she sits in is a fleshliness, a corpulence, that is *like* a burnished throne but is a seat far less lofty—her buttocks, or that conflation of toilet and excrement that Eliot called Fresca's "needful stool" (39). She holds court over an array of vials which "troubled, confused / And drowned the sense in odours." If this passage is narrated by a man, his identity is buried in the passage's deflecting ironies; the smell of a woman drowns his sense, as, in "Prufrock," the "we" were drowned by human and genderless voices, and as female smells broke up Prufrock's logic ("Is it perfume from a dress / That makes me so digress?"). In "A Game of Chess," men go blind from women's odors: a parenthetical Cupidon hides his eyes—"(Another hid his eyes behind his wing)"—as if anticipating the woman's fragrant vials. This Cupidon makes himself blind as Eliot in the hyacinth garden ("my eyes failed"), or "Tom, boiled to the eyes, blind," in the omitted opening, or blind Tiresias (5). Hysterically blinded by the woman's flesh, Eliot's huge terraced sentence passively refuses a firmer orientation of part to part. A weird evenness of texture takes over, and it grows difficult to find the sentence's main verb: "doubled," "glowed," or "poured"? The refusal to subordinate the different fragments of waste that make the poem both jeweled and excremental is—in a poet who appreciated hierarchy—a species of hysteria, a willful blindness to his own meanings.

The male "I" admits "I could not / Speak"; Philomel is too far gone in her hysteria for even those four words. Raped and tongueless, she converts her speech into unintelligible bird-song, replaying her trauma in hysterical code that is powerless as protest:

> Above the antique mantel was displayed
> As though a window gave upon the sylvan scene
> The change of Philomel, by the barbarous king
> So rudely forced; yet there the nightingale
> Filled all the desert with inviolable voice
> And still she cried, and still the world pursues,
> 'Jug Jug' to dirty ears.

Eliot avoids limning the barbarous king's rape: "So rudely forced" sounds like a minor breach of décorum, not a tragic violence. But the appearance of the raped woman breaks up the stillness of the set piece, and hurls the poem into the modern world. Philomel, rendered on an antique mantel, metamorphoses into an acidic and contemporary portrait of Vivien, complaining, " 'My nerves are bad to-night. Yes, bad. Stay with me. / 'Speak to me. Why do you never speak? Speak." The wife confesses bad nerves, but the husband is truly the hysteric, speechless as the man in the hyacinth garden so enraptured by the woman's hair that he could neither speak nor see. The husband can only remember "Those are pearls that were his eyes." The line depicts hysterical blindness, and describes the trauma that sparked the symptom: he cannot speak because he remembers his drowned friend, eyes turned to pearl. Pearl's preciousness links this elegaic image to the sexual treasures of the regal woman's jewel box—her "glitter of jewels" which "from satin cases poured in rich profusion." Pearls, too, come from the oyster to which Pound made glancing reference ("his stiff saliva") in the Sage Homme verse. Eliot's Game of Chess involves a choice between pearls of the dead man and jewels of the throned woman. The hysteric husband, with "nothing" in his head, cannot choose and cannot remember, and so Vivien acts the part of the interrogating analyst: " 'Do / 'You know nothing? Do you see nothing? Do you remember / 'Nothing?'" Under the pressure of her questions he breaks into a song—"O O O O that Shakespeherian Rag": this rag is "Full Fathom Five," an elegy for drowned men—Ferdinand, Phlebas the Phoenician and, obliquely, Verdenal. Memories of beloved dead men induce the poem's forgetful and hysterical weaving from plot to plot and voice to voice. Tom is "boiled to the eyes, blind" so that he can remain blind to a memory of some erotic significance—a glimpse of the "handsome and tall" drowned man.

The speaker mourns a drowned man but speaks in the voice of a woman about to drown herself: Eliot impersonates the Victorian's favorite image of the madwoman, Ophelia—who is, with Marie and the Sibyl, one of the poem's primary hysterics. Ophelia's drowning seems to represent narrative itself sinking into hysteria, for the story of Lil and Albert disintegrates, interrupted by the importunate syncopation of the bartender closing shop: "HURRY UP PLEASE ITS TIME." Self-interruption is hysterical; a verbal tic, "HURRY UP" punctuates and disturbs the story. Ophelia is given the privilege of closing "A Game of Chess," as Marie had the honor of opening "The Burial of the Dead." By intoning, "Good night, ladies, good night, sweet ladies, good night, good night," Ophelia performs a poetic closure that eluded Eliot. Using a madwoman's voice to end "A Game of Chess," which contained a "photographic" portrait of his own marriage to Vivien, he conflates Ophelia and Vivien, and shows female hysteria to be a suitable mask for a Shakespeherian (Willful) man. In this ending, Eliot addresses his

lady readers in the voice of a woman; previously, in the conclusion
of "The Burial of the Dead," he used a male voice to propitiate his
gentleman readers—"You! hypocrite lecteur!—mon semblable,—
mon frère!" The text may be disjunct and allusive, but it ends, in both
sections, with a direct, accosting cry to a reader/double, first man then
woman, whose "hypocrite" schismatic nature is the poet's own. Of
course, the final goodnight—"Good night, ladies"—inaugurates neither sex nor sleep. Marie, we have learned, reads much of the night: no
nights in the waste land are good.

In the original "Fire Sermon," Eliot satirized what Fresca reads;
however, like Madame Sosostris's cards, Fresca's reading matter lies
close to the poem's heart. Eliot first meant her to attempt "a page of
Gibbon," whose chronicle of imperial decline overlaps with "broken
Coriolanus" and his "falling towers," the poem's emblems of toppled
patriarchy (23). Later, Eliot replaced her Gibbon with the "Daily
Mirror": in Dickens's *Our Mutual Friend*, Sloppy (who does the
police in different voices) is a "beautiful reader of a newspaper,"[68]
and so Fresca's newspaper reading is a thread leading back to the
poem's original male subject. She also reads "the pathetic tale of
Richardson," *Clarissa*—pathetic because she was, like Philomel,
raped (23). Rape has broken Fresca's speech, making it useless as
Philomel's bird-song, or the silence of Eliot in the hyacinth garden:
like the poem's other hysterics, Fresca has "much to say— / But
cannot say it—that is just my way" (23). Eliot values ineffability as
a sign of powerful feeling, and yet through satire he distances himself
from this image of the poet as a depressed woman who "scribbles
verses of such a gloomy tone / That cautious critics say, her style is
quite her own" (27). He must separate his verse from hers because,
to paraphrase Breuer and Freud, hysteria and poetry spring from the
same source:

> The Scandinavians bemused her wits,
> The Russians thrilled her to hysteric fits.
> From such chaotic misch-masch potpourri
> What are we to expect but poetry?
> When restless nights distract her brain from sleep
> She may as well write poetry, as count sheep. (27)

Marie reads and Fresca writes: nighthawks, Eliot's hysterical women
fasten on the written word. By doubling up with Pound, Eliot separates his *Waste Land* from Fresca's feminine "potpourri"—a sweet-
smelling collage that derives, etymologically, from "rotten pot."

Eliot's misogynistic portrait of Fresca, however, is a manuscript page he turned over. On Fresca's back side, he began writing the first draft of "The Fire Sermon" as it finally stands: "The rivers tent is broken and the last fingers of leaf / Clutch and sink into the wet bank" (25). With languid stresses separated by lax unstressed syllables, these lines lyrically depict the state of being *broken*, and do not translate fear of homosexual rape into a scatological satire of a woman. Much is broken in *The Waste Land*: the river's tent, fingernails ("The broken fingernails of dirty hands"), and Coriolanus. The name "Coriolanus" itself suggests broken places. A "broken (Coriol)anus" was the fate of Claude the Cabin Boy (with broken glass up his "ass"), and of the *vates cum fistula* in Pound's comic verse. Despite New Critical smokescreens about Fisher Kings and symbolic wounds, castration is not the unmanning that the poem fears. It dreads the anal penetration that has already occurred: the cracked earth in "those hooded hordes swarming / Over endless plains, stumbling in cracked earth." Eliot may have longed for Pound's editorial insemination, but the poem's hysterics experience it as rape. Like the raped and tongueless Philomel, the poem has translated its experience of being penetrated (by Pound) into a hysterical method of speaking.

In the figure of Tiresias, Eliot announces his affinity with the violated hysteric. The typist "awaited the expected guest," and Eliot can participate in the typist's erotic expectancy by invoking a Tiresias who has "foresuffered all/Enacted on this same divan or bed." Wise Tiresias, unafraid of sexual passivity, is not so much a token of an epic past, as a figure from a radical present—an Urning. Tiresias, however, is the only man in the poem to acknowledge passivity. More often, the poem enacts its fractured masculinity in sketches of sexually violated women—Philomel, the typist, the Rhine Maidens—who each respond in hysterical code to rape. "Twit twit twit / Jug jug jug jug jug jug" (like the "Drip drop drip drop drop drop drop" of Eliot's water-dripping song, which he considered the sign of his cure) comes from a condition like Anna O.'s "deep-going functional disorganization" of speech in "moments of extreme anxiety." Several characters in *The Waste Land* share Anna O.'s feeling of "profound darkness in her head, of not being able to think, of becoming blind and deaf, of having two selves."[69] The poem's author has two selves, Eliot and Pound; Tiresias, too, is a double figure, half-woman, half-man. The husband in "A Game of Chess" recapitulates Anna O.'s sensation of not being able to think, for he knows, sees, and speaks nothing. All the characters in *The Waste Land* seem emanations of one hysterical voice trying to describe a past violation; as Eliot commented in the notes, Tiresias unites the poem's various characters, for "all the women are one woman, and the two sexes meet in Tiresias."

The connection between the female hysteric's plaint and Eliot's own lament glimmers in the song of the Thames-daughters, in "The Fire Sermon." Here, the Rhine Maidens wail (in hysterical code) that their river has been violated, its gold stolen: "Weialala leia." The anality of gold means the Rhine Maidens are, in part, screens for the ghostly male protagonist's suffering. This song of the Rhine Maidens shifts directly into Eliot's confession, though he does not claim it for himself. In semaphore, he confesses breakdown at Margate:

> 'On Margate Sands.
> I can connect
> Nothing with nothing.
> The broken fingernails of dirty hands.

In a draft, Eliot included a grammatical subject to clarify whose hands were dirty, and to specify the aggressor's gender: "He had/I still feel the pressure of dirty hand" (53). From this remembered violation, Eliot moves directly into his echo of St. Augustine's "caldron of unholy loves":

> la la
>
> To Carthage then I came
> Burning burning burning burning
> O Lord Thou pluckest me out
> O Lord Thou pluckest
>
> burning

Repression plucks away, word by word, his language.

Losing his language, Eliot (or the hysteric "double flower" whose oscillation between speech and silence the poem traces) resembles Anna O., who, deprived of words, "put them together laboriously out of four or five languages and became almost unintelligible."[70] Each of the poem's five sections follows the same trajectory of depletion: memories of desire return intensely enough to break Eliot's language down by each section's end. In the conclusion of "The Fire Sermon," the hysteria of "Burning burning burning burning" arises from the sexual scenes that came earlier: the intercourse of typist and young man, the rape of Philomel, the theft of the Rhine gold, the trysts of the nymphs and their City Directors, and the narrator's weekend with Mr. Eugenides. In "What the Thunder Said," the hysteria of the final pastiche of tongues is also a response to preceding sexual scenes. First, rain has come—a "damp gust." Second, Eliot remembers a moment of sexual surrender: "My friend, blood shaking my heart / The awful daring of a moment's surrender / Which an age of prudence can never retract." This moment of surrender, unspeakably awful, is given brief body in the phrase "seals broken by the lean solicitor," and the sexual image of a key turning in the prison door: "I have heard the key / Turn in the door once and turn once only." There is only one chance for escape from a dry life: fortune occurs in the turning of a key, the breaking of a seal (or hymen). In this context, the suggestive broken (Coriol)anus occurs. Third, Eliot remembers a romantic scene on the water, a moment when "your heart would have responded / Gaily, when invited, beating obedient / To controlling hands." Hands, once dirty, are now pleasantly controlling: Eliot does not mind obedience here, and even considers it gay—"your heart would have responded / Gaily." But these sudden turns of keys in locks are followed by the conclusion's extreme retreat from desire into hysteria:

> London bridge is falling down falling down falling down
>
> *Poi s'ascose nel foco che gli affina*
> *Quando fiam uti ceu chelidon*—O swallow swallow
> *Le Prince d'Aquitaine à la tour abolie*
> These fragments I have shored against my ruins
> Why then Ile fit you. Hieronymo's mad againe.
> Datta. Dayadhvam. Damyata.
>   Shantih shantih shantih

Eliot's disorderly endings translate sexual desire into mystical language. In "The Fire Sermon," the "burning" of lust alternates with impassioned prayer, "O Lord Thou pluckest"; in "What the Thunder Said," the rape of Philomel encoded in "O swallow swallow," and the sexual impotence figured in *"Le Prince d'Aquitaine à la tour abolie"* (aboulie?) or "London bridge is falling down," give way to the mysticism of "Shantih." (If "swallow" is a verb, the phrase "O swallow swallow" turns into a sexual command.) The poem's closures modulate from profane to sacred rapture; similarly, the hysteric's *attitudes passionnelles* alternate between sexual and spiritual ecstasies. "Burning burning burning burning" is a linguistic *attitude passionnelle*, like a tableau staged by Charcot's Geneviève, who "would fall and tumble on the floor as if making love, then in a minute strike the crucifixion pose or be in ecstasy like a saint."[71]

As hysterical discourse, *The Waste Land* remains as passive as Coleridge's wedding-guest: the poem invites a reader to master it. Unwilling to explain itself, requiring a reader-as-collaborator ("mon semblable,—mon frère!") to unravel its disguises, it remains passive toward a "frère" whose attentions it solicits by this technique of direct presentation without transitions. Modernist ideograms refuse to soften the image's blow with commentary, and place the reader in the active though reluctant role of elucidator. Between two men, passivity and activity have sexual valences that the poem bodies forth in its thematics of violation, and the hysterical discontinuities, aphasias, and amnesias that follow from the repressed moment of surrender. Eliot's abulia creates antitheses of itself in the "flushed and decided" young man carbuncular, or the sailor (in excised portions from "Death by Water") who aims his "concentrated will against the tempest and the tide" (63). Despite these representations of sexual will, the poem's heart is in its passivity toward interpretation, the moments of collage, potpourri, and fragmentation which place enormous faith in the reader as analyst. In this sense, Eliot's manuscript reads like the premonition of Pound's arrival: the text implies a second man who might interpret its absences. Eliot's dismissal of his work as merely chaotic, and his passivity toward revision, correspond to the poem's own willingness to stay broken. Eliot could "connect nothing with nothing"; it remained for Pound to redefine disjunction, to convert female hysteria, through male collaboration, back into a powerful discourse. Indeed, Pound's revisions changed *The Waste Land* from a series of *poems* into a unity which he trumpeted as "the longest *poem* in the English langwidge," nineteen pages "without a break."[72] With its feigned seamlessness, the poem avoids the bodily breaks that Claude the Cabin Boy, Philomel, and Coriolanus must suffer. Though Pound himself penetrates the poem by editing it, Eliot owed him the illusion of unbroken textual hymen, and the accompanying sense of power.

By giving his text to Pound, Eliot set up the paradigm for the relationship that readers and critics have established with *The Waste Land*: man to man. The footnotes embody the implied male reader: they invite him to enter and understand the poem. They demonstrate that the poem has absences which an external body must fill. The footnotes give value to the poem's hysteria, and transform it from meaningless chaos into allusiveness. Readers armed with the notes have approached *The Waste Land* not as if it were a fragment of hysterical discourse, but an artifact converted, by Pound's mediation, into something masculine. Conrad Aiken, on the poem's publication, wrote that it succeeds "by virtue of its incoherence, not of its plan";[73] if a woman had written a proudly incoherent text, how would its absences have been judged? *The Waste Land* has always been a scene of implicit collaboration between the male poet and his male reader, in which Eliot's hysterical discourse—by the act of collusive interpretation, by the reader's analytic listening—suffers a sea-change into masculinity.

Eliot used hysterical discourse to invoke the corrective affections of another man. Together, they performed an ambiguous act: they engaged in a symbolic scene of homosexual intercourse while freeing themselves from imputations of inverted style. Collaboration was particularly popular in the fin de siècle among men who wrote together to define their distance from homosexuality: sometimes this distance was not more than a few inches, though they made it seem like miles. In the next section, by reading doubly authored works of the 1880s, 1890s, and early 1900s (texts contemporaneous with *Studies on Hysteria* and *Sexual Inversion*), I hope to reveal the roots of Pound's and Eliot's Uranian experiment. By 1922, when *The Waste Land* emerged, its double authorship concealed, male collaboration had already earned a reputation for perversity.

Part III

The Hour of Double Talk

5
Manuscript Affairs:
Collaborative Romances of
the Fin de Siècle

In 1902, Henry James fell so in love with H. G. Wells's *Two Men* that he proposed they write a novel together about Mars. James begged to be his friend's "faithful finisher" (to add chiaroscuro to his friend's two-dimensional creations), but Wells, wary of the implications of "finishing," refused the offer.[1] Though he never collaborated, James brooded on the process in "Collaboration," an 1893 short story that can be read as documentary, a knowing vignette about the preponderance of double writing among British literary men, many of them James's friends and admirers, at the turn of the century—a troubled time when the Author split in two, and when sexuality divided into a straight original and its inverted mirror image.[2]

James, though hardly an avowed homosexual (few of these double writers were), cannily described the sexual implications that had gathered by 1893 around the word "collaboration." The act of double writing, he implies, emerges from enervated artistry and depleted power. Appropriately, the narrator of "Collaboration" has given up painting, and runs a fashionable salon instead, where the story's protagonists, a French poet and a German composer, agree to transcend national enmities by collaborating on an opera. Vague charges of immorality hover around the pair; it is unclear whether their collaboration is immoral because of xenophobic prejudices, or because the act of collaboration suggests homosexual ties. Furthermore, the French poet is engaged to marry a girl whose father was slain by a German soldier; the poet offends his fiancée by collaborating with a compatriot of her father's murderer. The collaborators know that the public will think them "immoral and horrible" for working together (129); the fiancée's mother accuses the poet of dragging the family into "abysses of shame and suffering," and charges that his "perversity was monstrous" (138–39). At the end, the poet gives up

143

marriage and escapes to the Riviera to consummate the "unnatural alliance" and "unholy union" with his collaborator (142).

When the narrator exclaims, "Herman Heidenmauer and Félix Vendemer are, at the hour I write, immersed in their monstrous collaboration" (141), James indicates that double writing is the activity of the hour, and that it masks a deeper monstrosity of which he, uncomfortable with Oscar Wilde's flamboyance, hesitated to take the full measure.[3] In James's story, artistic and sexual motives are inseparable: the poet and composer work together to consummate a sexual union and to create a masterpiece. The ambitions of fin de siècle collaborators concealed impoverished aesthetic means; when the narrator, wanly optimistic, ends the story by exclaiming, "Don't say art isn't mighty!" (144), James implies that art's virile days are past.

James's story summarizes what this chapter will document in detail: a historical moment when collaboration gave rein to desires considered monstrous if enacted anywhere but on the page. Resemblances between the several collaborators in this section, and their very number, suggest that double writing was a sustained and widespread effort in the fin de siècle (loosely defined to mean the period between the fall of Wilde and the birth of modernism), and that these collaborators understood the act's symbolic properties. The importance of the sexual struggle that these fin de siècle fictions embody, and not their literary value, explains this chapter's length.[4]

If one writer dominated this collaborative renaissance, it was Robert Louis Stevenson, whose primary writing partner was his stepson, Lloyd Osborne, and who pioneered a genre, called the "romance," which introduced homosexual desire under the guise of boyish escapism. The other important romancers of the 1880s and 1890s were Andrew Lang and H. Rider Haggard, whose novel, *The World's Desire*, is the era's exemplary collaborative text, emerging from a fear of female authority—both literary and political—and a desire to confirm male bonds. After discussing the work of Stevenson, Osborne, Lang, and Haggard, I will survey a range of other collaborators whose number and variety indicate the perimeters of fin de siècle double writing. I will then enter the 20th century to discuss Joseph Conrad's and Ford Madox Ford's *Romance*, which brings the tradition I trace in this chapter to modernism's threshold. Not all fin de siècle collaborators were men. I close the book by discussing two prominent female partnerships, Michael Field (Katharine Bradley and Edith Cooper), and Edith Somerville and Martin Ross (Violet Martin), who fall in a history of lesbian collaboration that this study does not include.

Stevenson's Queer Yarns

Though Robert Louis Stevenson was a unifying figure of his age, beloved by men of every political and aesthetic stripe, homosexual writers paid him special court. At 17, Marc-André Raffalovich, author of *Uranisme et unisexualité* and sometime collaborator of the poet John Gray, sent Stevenson an essay in homage;[5] Symonds dedicated poetry to him and classed him among the "tribe" of Walt Whitman.[6] Andrew Lang, summarizing the devotion that Stevenson inspired, claimed that he "possessed, more than any man I ever met, the power of making other men fall in love with him."[7] Male contemporaries particularly praised Stevenson's works for omitting women. Andrew Lang felt that Stevenson did himself "most justice in novels without a heroine,"[8] and Henry James, who applauded his friend for giving to the world the "romance of boyhood," observed that Stevenson's "books are for the most part books without women, and it is not women who fall most in love with them. But Mr. Stevenson does not need, we may say, a petticoat to inflame him." Continuing the conceit of dress and undress, James hypothesized a nude authorial body that Stevenson shyly withheld from his readers: Stevenson "would never, if I may be allowed the expression, pose for the nude."[9] James sounds disappointed. Women perceived this affectionate network between Stevenson and his readers to be covertly misogynistic: the feminist critic Alice Brown tartly observed that "quite evidently he is a boy who has no mind to play with girls. They are somewhat in the way. He is absorbingly satisfied with games made up of guns and boats, and in such matters girls . . . unsex them quite."[10] Stevenson needed the company of playmates, and preferred them not to be girls.

Stevenson's first collaborator was poet W. E. Henley; they wrote several plays together, including *Deacon Brodie, or, The Double Life*, predecessor of that more incisive tale of doubleness, *The Strange Case of Dr. Jekyll and Mr. Hyde* (1885).[11] Sessions with Henley, however, were so stimulating to consumptive Stevenson that they were "prohibited by the doctor as being too exciting."[12] In contrast, Stevenson's collaboration with his stepson, Lloyd Osborne, could circumvent all medical and legal prohibitions; the seeming innocence of a stepfather's devotion masked a darker purpose. Their partnership began as a game: their first collaborative efforts were accounts of the battles they fought with toy soldiers.[13] When Lloyd showed signs of a literary vocation, Stevenson joined him in writing three novels, *The Wrong Box* (1889), *The Wrecker* (1892), and *The Ebb-Tide* (1894). Because Stevenson's implicit subject was, as James observed, the "romance of boyhood," collaborating with a real boy brought Stevenson closer to

146 / The Hour of Double Talk

his material. He understood the sexual implications of his relationship with Lloyd, or so he implies in a letter to Henley. Describing his love for Lloyd as a craving and a problem, Stevenson worries that it resembles homosexuality: "Perhaps as we approach the foul time of life, young folk become necessary? 'Tis a problem. We know what form this craving wears in certain cases. . . . Thus perhaps my present (and crescent) infatuation for the youth Lloyd."[14] The stepson's expressions of love were braver: remembering the day that his mother and Stevenson became engaged, Lloyd recalls that "at last my hand crept into Luly's [Stevenson's], and in that mutual pressure a rapturous sense of tenderness and contentment came flooding over me. It was thus we returned, still silent, still hand in hand, still giving each other little squeezes."[15] Little squeezes led directly to literary collaboration.

Even before they actually collaborated, Lloyd helped generate his stepfather's work. In the preface to *Treasure Island*, Lloyd remembers being called to Stevenson's bedroom to hear the opening chapter of the novel: "I was called up mysteriously to his bedroom (he always spent his mornings writing in bed), and the first thing I saw was my beloved map lying on the coverlet." Lloyd congratulates himself on the seminal role that his own handpainted map played in the conception of a great romance: "Thus one of greatest . . . of all romances came to be written, and that I should have had a share in its inception has always been to me a source of inexpressible pleasure. Had it not been for me, and my childish box of paints, there would have been no such book as *Treasure Island*."[16] The "inception" scene of *Treasure Island* happens on Stevenson's bed, and Lloyd imagines his map to be an integral partner. Once Lloyd outgrew his box of paints, he could play a man's part in his stepfather's career by responding as critic. Embracing Stevenson in the dark, Lloyd told him that his book, *The Weir of Hermiston*, was perhaps the greatest novel in the English language. Lloyd recalls:

> Never had I known him to be so moved; never had I been so moved myself; and in the all-pervading darkness we were for once free to be ourselves, unashamed. Thus we sat, with our arms about each other, talking far into the night. Even after thirty years I should not care to divulge anything so sacred as those confidences . . . no words can convey the tenderness of its expression—the softened voice, the eyes suffusing in the starlight, the lingering clasp of the hand.[17]

Lloyd blazons this scene as a sign of his intimacy with the great writer, but refrains from confessing sexual motives. Stevenson and Osborne used double writing as a sanctioned venue for handclasping, a way to make homoerotic tenderness seem a virile matter of "guns and boats." The last of their collaborative works, *The Ebb-Tide*, compels attention as evidence that collaboration, in the fin de siècle, had erotic uses.

Stevenson's tuberculosis drove him, with his family, to Samoa, and *The Ebb-Tide* begins, appropriately, with a shocked tribute to the spread of disease from England to the Pacific: "Throughout the island world of the Pacific, scattered men of many European races and from almost every grade of society carry active and disseminate disease."[18] These men are exiled to islands because of a disease linked to semen and sex by the words "disseminate" and "active," and because of disgrace in England, where each man had "made a long apprenticeship in going downward; and each, at some stage of the descent, had been shamed into the adoption of an *alias*" (5). The word "shame," understood in the 1890s to mean homosexuality,[19] has particular relevance to "going downward," for men who go down are guilty of moral decline and of fellatio. As in *Dr. Jekyll and Mr. Hyde*, which mentions illicit "down-going men," the social trajectory of downfall implies a reputation ruined by homosexuality.[20]

The Ebb-Tide repeats words like "shame" and "queer," whose significances were rapidly changing in the fin de siècle. "Queer," at the time of *The Ebb-Tide*, nearly meant "homosexual," for the notorious Marquess of Queensbury, the year before he prosecuted Oscar Wilde, accused a group of prominent men of being "Snob Queers."[21] The uncertainty of the word's meaning helps it designate incomplete knowledge: "queer" signifies an illogical stab of doubt, the sensation of wavering between two interpretations—a hesitation that marks the literary genre of the fantastic.[22] Stevenson's *Dr. Jekyll and Mr. Hyde* defines queerness as the horror that comes from not being able to explain away an uncanny doubleness. According to the butler, there was "something queer" about Hyde, "something that gave a man a turn—I don't know rightly how to say it, sir, beyond this: that you felt in your marrow—kind of cold and thin" (68). Hyde makes the witness feel queer: he enters the man's "marrow" (his bowels) and executes a cold thin turn. In *The Ebb-Tide*, Stevenson and son enjoy the freedoms of the word "queer," using it with manic randomness. The ship that the crew take over is "a queer kind of outfit from a Christian port" (52); a sailor confesses that he is a "queer kind of a first officer" (82); two men agree that "this is a queer place and company for us to meet in" (150); and another remarks, "It was a queer case" (199). Stevenson's and Osborne's previous novel, *The Wrecker*, calls its story-within-a-story a "queer yarn"; an illustration, with the caption "'Yes, it's a queer yarn,' said his friend," shows two men conversing on a dark porch (a young swell smoking a cigar, the older man discoursing from a cane chair), as if yarns were most queer when shared by two men.[23]

As "queer" connoted sexual ambiguity, "cruise" suggested erotic freedom to Stevenson, who complained to Henley of the pleasures that marriage had taken away: "What in the name of fate is to become of an R. L. S. who can no longer (1) spree, (2) walk, (3) cruise, (4) drink, (5) or smoke?"[24] In *The Ebb-Tide*, he connects cruising to unspecified lusts, remarking on the crew's "prolonged, sordid, sodden sensuality as they sailed, they knew not whither, on their last cruise" (102). Because sailors lived far from marriage in all-male communities, maritime objects carried homoerotic associations. In *The Ebb-Tide*, an aroused man exclaims that there is "nothing so affecting as ships! . . . The ruins of an empire would leave me frigid, when a bit of an old rail that an old shellback leaned on in the middle watch would bring me up all standing" (167–68). Because Stevenson and Osborne considered collaboration to be a boyish game, they could describe these sexual responses without embarrassment.

This ingenuous novel disregards its own double entendres; sexual meanings pour forth with no emancipatory intent. Nonetheless, a certain blustery pleasure blows from the book's inadvertencies. We learn that the Captain was "one whose hand you could take without a blush" (12), and Stevenson and son hardly flinch when they record the Captain's confession of affection for a male friend:

> "I tell you Herrick, I love you," the man broke out. "I did n't take to you at first, you were so Anglified and tony, but I love you now; it's a man that loves you stands here and wrestles with you" (57).

The stalwart Attwater also loves Herrick, and tells him, "You are attractive, very attractive" (175). Appropriately, the word used to describe their conversation's climax is "orgasm": "For how long he walked silent by his companion, Herrick had no guess. The clouds rolled suddenly away; the orgasm was over" (182). Male size fills them with joy: the Captain was "flushed, but not so much with wine as admiration; and his eyes drank in the huge proportions of the other with delight" (199). In several scenes, men contemplate shooting each other, and the two authors suggestively describe the gun's hunger for the body. Attwater is a fine shot because, he says, "I believe my balls will go true" (183). On this island, "a fragrance of strange meats was in the air" (183), and so the men, like cannibals, ardently plan the angles from which they will shoot each other. One man feels "the butt of his revolver" and thinks, "It should be done now, as he went in. From behind?" (212–13). Another man wishes to send in the shot from behind, and addresses his intended victim: "Your back view from my present position is remarkably fine" (226). The sexual heat expended in this collaborative romance, however, does not end blindness and lead to knowledge; these double entendres reaffirm ignorance. Stevenson and Osborne collaborate to ensure that homosexual references are lost within the doubletalk of a dishonest genre—the romance—that courts the boy reader with a tale of adventure while hiding its pederastic intent.

The many sexually suggestive scenes between men in *The Ebb-Tide* are tied to biography by a single slip: the authors named a character Dr. Symonds. Both Stevenson and Osborne were friends of John Addington Symonds, who was no doctor, though he collaborated with one. J. A. Symonds had died the year before the novel was published, and a character in *The Ebb-Tide* eulogizes him by saying: "Pity Symonds is n't here! He is full of yarns. That was his part, to collect them" (197). Stevenson might have known that Symonds was collecting yarns—case studies—for *Sexual Inversion*, and might even have provided him with a history, for Stevenson longed to speak out, and was disappointed that *The Ebb-Tide* did not involve fuller disclosure. Complaining of the "veil of words" that hung over it, Stevenson said, "I like more and more naked writing; and yet sometimes one has a longing for full colour and there comes the veil again."[25] Reviewers, however, saw through the veil and detected sexual misconduct. The decadent poet Richard Le Gallienne, himself fond of collaborating, questioned the novel's scene of love-making between men: "would a rough seaman like Davis say 'I love you' to another man? Wouldn't he express affection for a comrade in some blunter idiom[?]."[26] Another critic complained that "there is not so much as the shadow of a woman cast upon the story," and indicted the novel for portraying "the fag ends of certain useless and degraded lives."[27] Although in the 1890s the word "fag," like "queer," had not yet attained its present homosexual meaning, Stevenson urged the word toward that destination. In *Dr. Jekyll and Mr. Hyde*, he describes the *doppelgängers* as "incongruous faggots" who were "bound together" (82). He means bundles of wood; but Jekyll's and Hyde's relationship bears a sexual charge as well. The story of their bondage to each other shows that male doubleness—the divided self and the double writer—had acquired, by 1885, associations of homosexuality.

Dr. Jekyll and Mr. Hyde, like many of Stevenson's works, was written in bed; any appraisal of his works or his bed must measure the impact of Mrs. Stevenson, the former Fanny Osborne. She was herself a writer, though he had bragged, several years before their wedding, that "certainly, if I could help it, I would never marry a wife who wrote."[28] Resentful of her powers, he described her to Henley as a literate vagina dentata who deprived him of his gay self: "I got my little finger into a steam press called the Vandergrifter [Fanny Van de Grift Stevenson] . . . and my whole body and soul had to go through it. I came out as limp as a lady's novel . . . I am what she has made of me, the embers of the once gay R.L.S."[29] He may have disparaged the lady's novel as a limp thing, but he entered the steam press of his wife's mind enough to collaborate with her on *More New Arabian Nights: The Dynamiter* (1885), and to involve her intimately, that same year, in composing *Dr. Jekyll and Mr. Hyde.* Forbidden by the doctor to talk, Stevenson resorted to hand-signals, which Fanny translated back into speech; because he was too ill for much company, she stood guard outside his room with a watch, ready to warn the visitor when the fifteen minute interview must end.[30] Stevenson resented his wife's control over his bed, his voice, and his novel: she had woken him from the dream in which the germ of *Jekyll and Hyde* came to him, and she had so trenchantly criticized the tale in an early draft that he burned and then rewrote it.[31] Stevenson, in his essay on dreams, denied the help of "unseen collaborators," and claimed, with hysterical adamantness, that "the meaning of the tale is therefore mine. . . . Mine, too, is the setting, mine the characters. . . . Will it be thought ungenerous, after I have been so liberally ladling out praise to my unseen collaborators, if I here toss them over, bound hand and foot . . . ?"[32] Eager to drown any rumor of assistance, whether from the "brownies" of unconscious prompting or from his wife, Stevenson urgently claimed *Jekyll and Hyde* as his work entirely—though he would not feel such anxiety about the three novels he happily confessed were composed with Lloyd.

Jekyll and Hyde, over which such a custody battle raged, is a parable of male twinship; given Stevenson's fondness for collaborating, Jekyll's split self seems a figure for the schismatic activity of double writing. Nor should it come as a surprise that their duality has homosexual meanings. One of the novel's characters, reluctant to probe too deeply into the strange friendship of Jekyll and Hyde, and not yet aware that they are two halves of one man, ventures this truism: "the more it looks like Queer Street, the less I ask" (33). It looks like Queer Street because the doctor's nervous friends think that Hyde had a liaison with Jekyll and is now blackmailing him; Jekyll's colleagues call Hyde's place "Blackmail House" (33). Jekyll's and Hyde's intimacy must have seemed queer to the first readers of the novel, who could not yet know that Jekyll and Hyde were the same person, and who might have assumed—confronting Jekyll's "strange preference" for Hyde, an unexplained "intimacy"—that the two men were lovers (38, 52).

Andrew Lang implied that *Dr. Jekyll and Mr. Hyde* was a parable of male sexual crisis as well as of literary collaboration when he compared it to the romance he wrote with H. Rider Haggard, *The World's Desire* (1890). Lang claimed to have turned Jekyll / Hyde into a woman: "Haggard and I have written a novel which borders on the slightly improbable . . . especially when the hero, having gone to bed with Mrs. Jekyll, wakes up with Mrs. Hyde."[33] Toying with the Jekyll / Hyde and Mr. / Mrs. polarities, Lang conceives of his collaboration with Haggard as a response to Stevenson's story of the double life. *The World's Desire* deserves a more sustained glance than I gave to *The Ebb-Tide*, for Lang's and Haggard's venture, no mere *jeu d'esprit*, emerged from a coherent if pernicious political agenda: Lang and Haggard, reactionary married men, were shaken enough by currents of sexual change to tamper with the division between He and She, in the hope of restoring a beleaguered masculinity to its former height.

Lang and Haggard: He or She?

Andrew Lang, now best known for his fairy tale books, was in 1890 an influential man of letters; Rider Haggard was the author of sensational adventure novels, most notably the best-selling *She* and *King Solomon's Mines*. When the friends at last wrote a novel together, they chose a subject dear to Lang's Hellenist heart. *The World's Desire*, picking up the *Odyssey* where Homer left off, shows a widowed Odysseus voyaging to find his heart's desire, Helen of Troy. Two men writing together about Greece—a homosexual utopia that Symonds celebrated in his "Greek Ethics" essay—is an act calculated to reassert the masculinity of British fiction and to steal fire back from women writers, whose success Haggard decried, fondly remembering the time that Andrew Lang threw a novel by Mrs. Humphry Ward out a train window.[34]

Lang learned to love books at the same time as he learned to love the company of other men, in a public school whose literary and fraternal institutions he warmly recalls: "We had a common roof, common dinners, wore scarlet gowns, possessed football and cricket clubs, and started, of course, a weekly magazine. It was only a manuscript affair."[35] Remembering his first manuscript affair, Lang suggests that adult literary institutions are modeled after adolescent crushes. Indeed, the subjects he found in youth remained with him in age, and his tastes in literature, like his tastes in love, never swerved. Remembering his early passion for chap-books about Robert Bruce, William Wallace, and Rob Roy, Lang writes, "I can still see Bruce in full armour, and Wallace in a kilt, discoursing across a burn, and Rob Roy slipping from the soldier's horse into the stream."[36] Fond of books about boys, Lang is also fond of boys. Lang sees no difference between boys and books:

> People talk, in novels, about the delights of a first love. One may venture to doubt whether everybody exactly knows which was his, or her, first love, of men or women, but about our first loves in books there can be no mistake. They were, and remain, the dearest of all; after boyhood the bloom is off the literary rye. . . . One's literary equipment seems to have been then almost as complete as it ever will be, one's tastes definitely formed. . . . My own first essays were composed at school—for other boys.[37]

To a man who thought literary life merely an extension of schoolboy camaraderie, collaboration was a pleasing sport in which women were unwelcome.

On the dedication pages of their separate works, Lang and Haggard carried on a public correspondence, using the boy-reader as a medium for their intercourse. Dedicating to Haggard a collection of essays, *In the Wrong Paradise*, Lang invoked the boy: "Dear Rider Haggard,— I have asked you to let me put your name here, that I might have the opportunity of saying how much pleasure I owe to your romances. They make one a boy again while one is reading them."[38] Haggard dedicated *King Solomon's Mines* to "all the big and little boys who read it,"[39] and specified a boy-reader in the sequel, *Allan Quatermain*, dedicated to his son "Jock" (whose real name was Arthur) and to those boys, including Lang, who became his sons by reading it. Haggard hoped that, by reading this novel, his son and "many other boys whom I shall never know" might attain "the state and dignity of English gentleman."[40] Haggard envisioned Arthurian and heroic possibilities unfolding for the boy who took the father's adventure novels to heart as guides to masculine conduct. However, Lang's and Haggard's privileged boy-reader—often a grown man—was a boy only in the ancient Greek sense: the Greeks called any male lover a "boy," regardless of age.[41]

Indeed, the boy-reader was a figure of erotic interest, for Haggard and Lang considered these textbooks in masculinity to be specimens of "romance"—a genre that Stevenson favored, and that critic George Saintsbury, among others, invested with reactionary and anti-feminist values. Saintsbury advocated a "return to pure romance," a revolt against "the more complicated kind of novel" with its "minute manners-painting and refined character analysis."[42] These complicated and realistic novels were either by women—such as George Eliot— or they focused on women's lives and on marriage; in contrast, Haggard's romances, like Stevenson's, slighted women altogether. The term "romance," then, has nothing to do with the heterosexual romance of Victorian fiction; Stevenson's and Haggard's romances made room for pederasty by excluding marriage.

The world of "pure romance" offered men a refuge not only from women's fiction, but from an England that they imagined Queen Victoria had feminized. In 1887, the year of her Jubilee, Lang wrote poems hailing Haggard and Stevenson as saviors who brought the castrated romance novel back to life:

> King Romance was wounded deep,
>   All his knights were dead and gone. . . .
> Then you came from south and north. . . .
> Blazoned his achievements forth,
>   King Romance is come indeed![43]

Fellowship with Stevenson and Haggard gives Lang the confidence to assert that British letters might be ruled again by male monarchs virile enough to "come." Though they longed for the symbolic overthrow of the Queen, these romance writers were hardly anarchists: dreaming of flight, they remained in power at home. At the Savile Club, where Lang and Haggard often ate together while working on *The World's Desire*, Henley would insist that Haggard tell a Zulu tale at each meeting.[44] The structure that upheld their communal spinning of romances was British patriarchy.

Lang's and Haggard's imperialist celebration of King Romance, however, diverged from Wilde's homoerotic aestheticism: Wilde was not even admitted to the Savile Club, even if James, Haggard, and Henley supported his candidacy.[45] Though the Savile clique tried to distance itself from what Henley called, during the Wilde trials, the "pleasant sight" of "Oscar at bay,"[46] Lang and Haggard made discreet overtures to each other in letters. It was perhaps these gestures that compelled Lang's widow to destroy her late husband's correspondence with such "heart-rending completeness" that, according to his biographer, "she used to complain that her wrists ached for weeks and weeks after tearing up Andrew's papers."[47] In the remaining correspondence, any statements of mutual affection are restrained. Lang wrote to his collaborator: "You have been more to me of what the dead friends of my youth were, than any other man, and I take the chance to say it, though not given to speaking of such matters." Haggard responded in kind: "My dear Lang, that friendship to which you make such touching allusion always has been, is, and will be returned by myself. I will say no more."[48] A golden O sealed their unspeakable bond: before he died, Lang asked his wife to give Haggard a ring once belonging to the Egyptian Queen Taia, and henceforth, as photographs show, Haggard always wore it.[49]

The two men prepared for *The World's Desire* with an extended courtship of implicit collaborations. Lang helped Haggard plan and revise *She, Allan's Wife, Beatrice, Eric Brighteyes,* and *Nada the Lily,* and added poems to *Cleopatra,* about which Haggard wrote, "Perhaps Lang and I shall collaborate in the final copy."[50] Lang begged to see proofs of his friend's novels, claiming that "two pairs of eyes are better than one," and, on another occasion, that "two pairs of peepers are better than one."[51] Like collaboration, composing parodies was a way to peep into another man's private property. By spoofing their friends' works, writers like Lang and Haggard could engage in inversions that they would not otherwise dare. For example, Haggard dedicated *She* to Lang, and Lang responded with two sonnets—dedicating one of them, called "Twosh," to "Hyder Ragged": Lang's biographer calls the poem "an amusing emanation of the 'gay mind.' "[52] (Haggard pasted "Twosh" inside his own copy of *King Solomon's Wives,* a pseudonymous Hyder Ragged's parody of the genuine Haggard's *King Solomon's Mines.*[53]) The transformation of Rider Haggard into Hyder Ragged inverts the author's initials and seems to turn patronymic and patriarchy upside down. The journal *Punch* played along with the inversion game, publishing a cartoon that called *The World's Desire* a "Romance by Rider Laggard and Andrew Hang."[54]

Lang performed his most radical inversion when he collaborated with the obscure W. H. Pollock on *He* (1887), a parody of Haggard's *She.*[55] In a notebook, Haggard had described She as a "mental vampire in the shape of a woman sucking the life out of a man who worships her."[56] The purpose of *He* was to unsex *She;* Lang and Pollock, however, do more than repudiate strong women. They question gender itself by uniformly reversing the sexes of all the characters in *She,* turning She into He, Holly into Polly, and Leo into Leonora. The collaborators even make a man of Queen Victoria; dedicating the work to Haggard's fictional hero, Allan Quatermain, they unsex Victoria by saying that "His Majesty is a Merry Monarch." They replace She's matriarchal kingdom of Kôr with the world of masculine literary clubs: *He* takes place not in She's Africa but on Grub Street, in the male sanctuaries of the Academy and the Athenaeum. The sexual undertones of Lang's and Haggard's literary Clubland are wildest in the scene where a crocodile and a "catawampuss" swallow each other. A bystander cries, "Ah . . . he's going for him!" as the two monstrous male animals seize each other by the tail. "The interview was hurried and tumultuous," Lang and Pollock drily comment, and then exclaim, *"They had swallowed each other!"* (47–48). Lang and Pollock, collaborating on *He* to mock and pay homage to their friend Haggard, hope to swallow the object of their mockery, and to incorporate each other.

One goal of Lang's carnivorous partnership with Haggard was the exclusion of women. Though married, Haggard was, according to his nephew, "not very good with the sex as a whole."[57] The women in his fiction were not well rendered, and Lang deplored their presence. He wrote to Haggard: "I hope *Beatrice* will come off. But I prefer your males. Don't let her flirt."[58] Claiming that women were incapable of understanding male romance novels, Lang commented, "Unluckily I think the dam[n] reviewers never were boys—most of them the Editor's nieces."[59] Disparaging their abilities, he nonetheless profited from their labors: his wife, Leonora Blanche Alleyne, wrote most of Lang's acclaimed fairy tale books, although he and not she took the credit. He describes their collaboration pithily: "Eve worked, Adam superintended."[60] It is not surprising that this enslaved Eve should have destroyed her husband's letters, in retribution, after his death.

Despite the erasure of his wife from the fairy tale books, Lang and other male writers of his generation lived in the shadow of female literary precursors; one reason men collaborated was to deny the emergence of women's voices since the 1840s. In the Rabelais Club's volume of *Recreations*, privately printed for circulation among its male members, Walter Besant's poem, "Of He and She," wonders whether men (and male literary efforts) are merely offshoots of female originators:

> In lonely slumber lay the earliest He,
> While from his rib was framed a lesser She.
> Lo! now the miracle reversed we see:
> From She unconscious springs a lesser He.
> Of He and She doubts fall on me and thee.
> How if the old tale with the new agree?
> How if 'twas She that slumbered, and that He
> Was from the first a parody of She?[61]

The writers in Lang's and Haggard's circle indulged in parodic gender inversion, using jokes to disguise a fear that male authority had been fatally weakened.

Haggard had reason to brood over the relation of male to female authority: his mother, Ella Haggard, was a writer, and she died in 1889, the year before *The World's Desire* appeared. In 1890, Charles Longman published her long poem, *Life and Its Author*, prefaced by Rider's tribute, "In Memoriam": he claimed that her great disappointment in life was that owing to "endless cares and occupations, she was unable to devote herself to literature."[62] In a letter thanking Rider for the dedication to *Cleopatra*, she remarks that "circumstances, in my case, have always been steadfastly against me, a little disappointing I must confess, now in the evening of my life."[63] Her poem, *Life and Its Author*, tries to right the balance between Rider's authority and hers. Praising the universe's secret power, she seems to be describing her own fecundity:

> Germ of Eternity, conceived of Time;
> Though meanly reared, yet by thy birth sublime:
> Force launched in space by the Primeval Power . . .
> Faint reflex of the great Omniscient Mind.

Rider Haggard, though by his birth sublime, is but a "reflex" of his mother's "great Omniscient Mind." *The World's Desire*, emerging in the same year as Ella Haggard's poem, tries to wrest primacy from the woman writer's Mind. This particular woman's name, Ella, is the Spanish word for *She*. Revolting against Ella Haggard, the woman-writer-who-must-be-obeyed, Lang and Haggard join boyish forces on *The World's Desire*.

Although Haggard had initially suggested to Lang that they write about "the quest for the divine, which must, for the purposes of the story, be symbolized by a woman," he was finally more concerned that their novel be manly: he wanted to do "something grand and pure and simple, something to lift up!" He added: "Let's do a big thing for once and die happy."[64] Thirst for a big thing that might lift up, however, carried sexual meanings that compelled Lang to lose the novel's manuscript for three months and then find it again in a folio where he had placed it "to keep it clean."[65] Well aware of their project's unclean tone, he wrote to Haggard of the slip between fiction and flirtation, complaining "*I'm* no good at fictions [?or *flirtations*?]" [sic].[66] The purpose of their collaboration was to toy with flirtations they dared not pursue except in fiction, and to undermine gender polarities which, as British men, they felt bound to uphold. Many of their first ideas for a collaborative project involved switching genders: Lang mentions St. Germain as "a grand subject," a "male She of the last century," and notes "what a good character some male Elizabeth would have been."[67] Eager to turn She into He, they were, however, not happy with instabilities in maleness. When Haggard began a scene featuring a bearded character, and Lang, revising it, inadvertently described the man as clean-shaven, Lang saw the error and commented, "*You* gave Loi a white beard! I shaved it!"[68] The beard, a common motif in homosexual literatures of almost every culture, marks the mature man, and keeps him differentiated from his boy-lover.[69] Lang's and Haggard's failure to keep the detail of the beard consistent means they have not kept masculinity stable. Compensating for this vacillation, they made their novel belligerently woman-hating: Lang proudly called it "rather a misogynistic book on the whole."[70] Stevenson, their idol, recognized and celebrated its misogyny, and wrote a parodic poem which calls the novel "suspicious/An' queer," and disparages its heterosexual plot:

> In stunt and in strife
> To gang seeking a wife—
> At your time o' life
> It was wrang.[71]

According to Stevenson, Lang and Haggard were foolish to make their aged Odysseus seek a wife. Among Stevenson's characters, matrimony was never a motive.

Lang and Haggard collaborated not only to flirt, but to flee an emasculated modernity. They opened their novel with a poem that urges, "Come with us, ye whose hearts are set/On this, the Present to forget."[72] Other fantasy novels of the period expressed a similar longing to flee what maleness had come to mean. H. G. Wells, for example, complained in *The Time Machine* (1895) that "you cannot move at all in Time, you cannot get away from the present moment."[73] Wells hid his nostalgia in scientific décor, while Lang and Haggard retreated through collaboration into romance. Lang's embroidered, archaic style dominates the novel; his language mystifies and impedes the reader, and seems to evade a distinctly modern predicament. The Labouchère Amendment made men newly conscious of the sexual implications of close male friendship; Lang and Haggard longed to retreat to a time before homosexuality was "invented," for they recognized in the prologue that "all things were possible in a life whereof so little was understood."[74] Using archaism to obscure the contemporary motives for their collaboration, they begin with a tableau of a "silent isle" (both Ithaca and England) in which their impotent hero seeks regeneration. In this waste land, Odysseus finds a singing bow whose sound is "faint" at first, "a thin note," but it swells into a voice "clear, strong, angry, and triumphant" (11). The collaborators seek in their heroic subject, and in the act of double writing, a movement from effeminacy to virility. Indeed, male body hair marks the landscape through which Odysseus travels: he passes rocks "covered over with bush that grew sparsely, like the hair on the limbs of a man" (291). The landscape looks like a man, as in Browning's "Childe Roland to the Dark Tower Came," because the terrain Odysseus must experience and overcome is his own body.

Tennyson, too, found it tonic to write about Odysseus: he composed "Ulysses" to rouse himself from torpor after the death of Arthur Hallam. Lang's and Haggard's title, *The World's Desire*, alludes to the moment in Tennyson's *In Memoriam* when, addressing Hallam, the poet imagines a divinely gifted man who, "moving up from high to higher, / Becomes on Fortune's crowning slope / The pillar of a people's hope, / The centre of a world's desire" (LXIV, 13–16). Because *In Memoriam* is a preeminent poem of homosexual love, Lang's and Haggard's allusion to it suggests that a similar passion moves their novel. Lang even wrote his own thin *In Memoriam*—a handful of elegies for a male friend. Echoing Tennyson, Lang mourns, "I count the years passed over since the sun / That lights me looked on him"; "Once more I watch you, and to me / It is as if I touched his hand!"[75]

This discrete and derivative homoeroticism is far less radical than the vacillation between He and She that Lang and Haggard perhaps unwittingly perform in *The World's Desire*. Lang's and Haggard's opening poem describes the quicksilver alternation between the star and the snake, symbols of sexual difference:

> The fables of the North and South
> Shall mingle in a modern mouth.
> There lives no man but he hath seen
> The World's Desire, the fairy queen . . .
> Not one but he hath chanced to wake,
> Dreamed of the Star and found the Snake.

Lang and Haggard "mingle in a modern mouth": they collaborate, two mouths speaking as one. By calling this mingling "modern," they imply that collaboration, and the propensity to confuse star and snake, are contemporary urges. Lang and Haggard caution the male reader to be vigilant:

> Beauty has many shapes, now it is that of Helen, now that of Meriamun, each sees it as he desires it. But the Star is yet the Star, and the Snake is yet the Snake, and he who, bewildered of his lusts, swears by the

Snake when he should have sworn by the Star, shall have the Snake for guerdon. (246)

Odysseus wavers between Star and Snake because he cannot decide which woman he loves, holy Helen or wicked Meriamun; but the Star's and Snake's refusal to remain distinct brings on an even more bewildering erotic choice, a confusion over which sex to love—whether to swear allegiance to the "blood-red" menstrual star on Helen's breast or to the snaky phallus. Lang and Haggard encourage the male reader, "bewildered of his lusts," to stare down Protean mirages and hold fast to old fables of intrinsic sexual difference.

The novel's fiercest energies are spent in Meriamun's and Helen's rivalry over a man, not in the hero's quest for a woman. Meriamun loves Odysseus "with a love unspeakable," the standard euphemism for homosexuality (71); to describe her love, Lang and Haggard call on the less guarded language of Plato's *Symposium*. Because in a previous lifetime her love for Odysseus was taboo (it dared to waken "That which slept" and to warm "That which was a-cold"), she is divided from him, and must seek the lost half of her self across the mediating body of a rival: "From Two be ye made *Three*, and through all Time strive ye to be twain again" (72). Lang and Haggard must also seek each other across a rival's body: because their love is unspeakable, they must strive to unite across the body of the novel they write together.

Lang and Haggard fuse by depicting the fierce Meriamun, an embodiment of the independent New Woman they disliked: she demanded to be "the equal of Pharaoh," and to be "the Queen leading Pharaoh by the beard" (66, 73). Lang and Haggard may detest female autonomy, but they are titillated by Meriamun; she is so sexually open-ended that it is difficult to say whether she is a man in a woman's body or a woman in a man's. In one extraordinarily perverse scene, Meriamun reaches into a forbidden box to which she alone has the key; she is clearly masturbating, for she finds the key in her girdle, and must thrust her hand "deep into the chest" to draw forth "a casket of dark metal that the people deemed unholy, a casket made of 'Typhon's Bone'" (189). Only Meriamun knows where to touch herself: "She pressed a secret spring. It opened, and, feeling within, she found a smaller casket" (189). Although the lid, opening "like a living mouth," appalls her, she puts her hand into the box with renewed application (189). The consequence of Meriamun's masturbation is, however, a scene of labor: she gives birth to a snake. A similar image—a rod emerging from a woman's lap—appeared as the frontispiece of *Cleopatra*, the novel Haggard dedicated to his mother.

Meriamun is represented in this scene as a mother giving birth, as a woman coming, and as a woman dominated by a penis that seems to emerge so organically from her own being that she *is* the penis, and has no existence apart from it. She takes off her robe and laid a "gleaming toy," like a dildo (she calls it a "snake of stone") on her breast (190). Waiting for transformation, she is "shaken with throes like the pangs of childbirth" (190). Gradually, the implement on her breast grows erect; it "undid its shining folds and reared its head to hers," and finally slips to the floor, where it slowly rises and winds about her body, "wrapping her in its fiery folds till it reached her middle" (190-91). When the snake reaches her "middle" (her crotch), it suddenly changes ontological direction, and seems not to approach her from without but to emerge from within her body. As in a mirror, she stares at a snake and sees herself; Meriamun becomes the phallus that ravishes her. She sees it rear "its head on high," and sees that "lo! its face was the face of a fair woman—it was the face of Meriamun!" (191). Indeed, she and the snake have much to say to each other. After they kiss, they perform a conversational 69, the snake laying its ear against her lips and Meriamun laying her lips against its ear: "there in the darkness they whispered, while the witch-light glittered down the gray snake's shining folds, beamed in its eyes, and shone through the Queen's dark hair and on her snowy breast. At length the tale was told" (192). The scene is both gossip and sex: the snake and the woman-in-a-snake's-image tell each other stories and imitate a serpent devouring its own tail. As the crocodile and the catawampuss swallowed each other in *He*, Haggard and Lang achieve, on the body of a woman, an intercourse with each other. Meriamun's name itself suggests male marriage: Marry-a-man. If, playing Lang's inversion game, we reverse the first and last letters, her name becomes Neriamum: Nary-a-Mum.[76] Once Ella Haggard died, Lang and Haggard were free to celebrate, through double writing, the successful revolt of men liberated from the authority of She-who-must-be-obeyed.

James M. Barrie summarized the critical judgment on *The World's Desire* when he wrote that "collaboration in fiction, indeed, is a mistake, for the reason that two men cannot combine so as to be one."[77] Barrie, who celebrated an eternal and erotic boyhood in his *Peter Pan*, admits that two men might well wish to join bodies and voices, even if he insists that the feat is impossible. He assumes that those who are anatomically the same cannot unite, and that writing must be a solitary act, never shared. But *The World's Desire* was hardly an isolated instance of attempted fusion. It was part of a collective treasure hunt, among the debris of old sexual codes, for a lost virility of voice and a new justification for male authority. Before I turn to Conrad's and Ford's *Romance*, which shares Lang's and Haggard's concerns, I will outline a range of fin de siècle men, from aesthetes to knights, who gamboled with the bodily and metaphysical question of whether it was possible, in Barrie's words, for two men to combine so as to be one.

Men of Might

The fifth volume of *The English Catalogue of Books*, which lists all works published in Britain during the 1890s (except for private or limited editions), includes an enormous number of collaborative texts; however, because the catalogue often omits the author's full first name, gender remains unknown.[78] Subjects range from electricity to gynecology—D. C. and J. P. Jackson's *Alternating Currents and Alternating Current Machinery* (1896) to L. and T. Landau's *History and Techniques of Vaginal Radical Operation* (1897). One text that recalls both *Studies on Hysteria* and *Sexual Inversion* is Italian criminologists Cesare Lombroso's and Guglielmo Ferrero's *La donna delinquente, la prostituta e la donna normale*, published in English as *The Female Offender* (1895).[79] Many of the collaborative works are lost novels, though their titles alone—W. G. Moffat's and J. White's *What's the World Coming To? A Novel* (1893)—promise connections between double writing and the fin de siècle's apocalyptic fears. Other collaborations are hagiographic jingoism, such as *Men of Might: Studies in Great Characters* (1892), by Herbert F. W. Tatham and A. C. Benson. Benson edited Queen Victoria's letters and was brother to E. F. Benson, who traveled up the Nile with Lord Alfred Douglas;[80] both Bensons were homosexual. The Carlylean *Men of Might* made room for sexual ambiguity and foreignness by featuring Michelangelo as a man of "might": a maybe man, a perhapser.[81]

Among male collaborators of this era, none were more earnest or prolific than Sir Walter Besant and James Rice. Lang, Haggard, and Stevenson were friends of Besant, and certainly knew of the series of novels, including *The Seamy Side* and *Ready-Money Mortiboy*, that Besant and Rice churned out in the 1870s and early 1880s. Few writing teams were as professional and mechanical. In his memoirs, Besant boasts that "no other literary collaboration" has been "comparable, in this country, with ours for success."[82] Besant was clearheaded and unabashed in his conception of writing as a profession; he collaborated because it was more efficient to write with a partner. No trace of psychological need contaminated the purely financial origin of their bond; it came about because, as Besant and Rice assert, every man has "a thing to sell, whether it be the offspring of his brain, or something he has bought from others."[83] Buying and selling dominated their conception of writing, and yet capitalist competitiveness finally led Besant to denounce the lucrative practice of collaboration: an artist, he claims, "must necessarily stand alone," while double writing compromises virile self-sufficiency by demanding that "the two men must be rolled into one." Mingling finally grew distasteful: "There will come a time when both men fret under the condition; when each desires, but is not able, to enjoy the reputation of his own good work; and feels, with the jealousy natural to an artist, irritated by the loss of half of himself."[84] Besant insists that male writers need to keep themselves intact; collaboration only leads to dismemberment. In 1883, the year after Rice died, Besant helped found a writer's union, the Society of Authors, with the purpose of defining and defending literary property; Besant denied his long career as collaborator by establishing a system to codify and restrict the nature of authorship. The year before, Besant had sought to solve other ambiguities in his misogynist tract, *The Revolt of Man* (1882), an explicit program for a kind of final solution to the "woman question."

The collaborative practice that Besant and Rice honed to a commercial and manly art was taken up by 1890s aesthetes and decadents—most prominently, Baron Corvo (pseudonym of Frederick Rolfe), author of the homosexual novel, *The Desire and Pursuit of the Whole: A Romance of Modern Venice* (1934). Corvo had several collaborators; all his writing relationships had a sexual core. In 1896, inspired by the "wondrous beauty" of John Holden, his landlady's nephew, Corvo proposed collaboration: "You are the man I have been waiting for. We are flint and steel to each other. I need you and you need me."[85] Composing essays, triolets, and rondeaux, they pinned manuscript pages on their studio walls and worked in tandem, reserving Saturday nights for revision. Corvo also collaborated with his friend C. H. C. Pirie-Gordon. Devout Roman Catholics, they sunbathed nude while revising the rules for the Order of Sanctissima Sophia; under the pseudonyms Prospero and Caliban, they published two collaborative novels, *Hubert's Arthur* (1909) and *The Weird of the Wanderer* (1912), inspired by *The World's Desire*.[86] Corvo attempted to write a biography of Thomas à Beckett with the eldest brother of A. C. and E. F. Benson, Robert Hugh Benson, who eventually claimed the book for himself. Corvo found a more passionate mate in Sholto Douglas, with whom he produced "stuff" which was "as rich and as pregnant and as aromatic as a Christmas pudding."[87] They began by translating *The Songs of Meleager*, and then tried to work up two fantasias, *Thirty Naughty Emperors* and *Reviews of Unwritten*

Books. Corvo hoped that Douglas would be that "Divine-Amicus, Much Desired," both collaborator and ideal lover; Corvo wrote provocatively to him, "You wave your hot luxurious quill and jet sugared words: I with adulterate complexion heave hecatombs of sighs and submit."[88] Corvo submitted to Douglas's spermatic jet of language, but the partnership ended unproductively.

Other decadents collaborated, though none so consistently and theatrically as Corvo. Oscar Wilde invited Lord Alfred Douglas to translate *Salomé* (1894), and looked forward to seeing both of their names on one title page, but Douglas's translation proved inadequate.[89] John Gray, model for Wilde's Dorian Gray, collaborated with his lifelong companion Marc-André Raffalovich on a play, *The Blackmailers*, so raffiné it was never even printed. Before taking religious orders in terrified response to the Wilde debacle, Gray and Raffalovich collaborated on so-called "duologues": "A Northern Aspect" and "The Ambush of Young Days," published in 1895 with the caveat "Not for general circulation."[90] Decadent poet Richard Le Gallienne collaborated with Robinson K. Leather on a volume of vignettes, *The Student and the Body-Snatcher* (1890), inspired by Stevenson's story, "The Body-Snatcher"; Le Gallienne's and Leather's collection included the suggestive tale of David and Jonathan.[91] A more prolific collaborative team was aesthete poet Ernest Dowson and lawyer Arthur Moore, friends from Oxford; together they wrote four novels and published two, *A Comedy of Masks* (1893) and *Adrian Rome* (1898). These novels, like *Jekyll and Hyde*, are tales of the double life. Adrian Rome is an unsubtle variant of Dorian Gray: the writers transposed "Dorian" to "Adrian," and in his last name, "Rome," encoded the interest in Catholic ritual among fin de siècle homosexuals.[92] By collaborating, Dowson struggled to reconcile his Wildean sensibilities with a reactionary desire for literary manliness. Dowson's conflict between sexual styles is representative, and warrants a closer look.

In Dowson's first joint venture, he deliberately followed the path of Wilde by suggesting a volume of verse to poet Victor Plarr, to be called, "ROSES AND RUE by Two Authors." When Plarr suggested "Vineleaf and Vine" as an alternate title, Dowson responded with an invitation to entangle their voices—and bodies—as in a wreath:

> Violets, and leaves of Vine
> Into a fair frail wreath,
> We gather and entwine!
> A wreath for Love to wear . . . [93]

The aesthetes used vine-leaves as emblems of homosexual seduction: in a letter to Dowson, Wilde enticed him, "Come with vine-leaves in your hair."[94] Dowson may have enjoyed playing the hyacinth boy, but when he began to collaborate with Moore, he asked to be cured of artistic sterility:

> I can not conceive another story. I feel barren, sterile. . . . What a man you are! I assure you I am aghast when I think of your unconquerable energy! . . . Indeed it is as much as I can do at the present moment to hold a pen.[95]

Dowson took very literally the equation between pen and penis; he asked Moore to "castrate & emend Chap X as much as you can."[96] Although in a more maternal vein Dowson described their story as an "embryo," he hoped to procreate without women's help, and proposed keeping their pens chaste by avoiding depictions of heterosexuality, suggesting to Moore "a novel without any love-making in it at all," on which they could work "with no prostitution of our most chaste pens."[97] Dowson feared that portraying heterosexuality might compromise their commitment to pure art; collaboration was a way of keeping clean.

Purity, however, was not Dowson's strong suit; notorious for his relations with young girls, he sighed to Moore, "Quelle dommage that the world isnt composed entirely of little girls from 6–12" [sic].[98] He considered his affairs "experiments," grist for the collaborative mill, and urged Moore to "start up an 'experiment' of your own," so that they might "compare notes with mutual advantage and work our result when the disillusionment comes, into an agreeable étude—in collaboration."[99] They savored heterosexual experience as subject matter for collaboration, and yet their interest in the opposite sex was severely qualified: they traded photographs of child actresses, but hated adult women. They particularly admired Stevenson's novels for excluding women characters, and they dreamed of spending long evenings together when they could "ignore the existence of the [female] sex altogether & talk of kings, cabbages, & what you will."[100] For Dowson and Moore, male literary bonding offered an escape from the threat of female autonomy and power.

The dominant tone of fin de siècle collaboration, however, was playfulness. One of the least serious and most star-studded collaborative texts of the period was never even published. On December 28, 1899, virtually the turn of the century, a play by ten men, *The Ghost*, was performed at Stephen Crane's house: by then, the 19th century was almost a ghost, the new century an emergency requiring unified male response. Of this farce, only the program survives intact, but its roster of authors includes James, Gissing, Haggard, Conrad, Wells, and Crane. Not all of its writers had an equal share: Crane asked them "to write a mere word—any word 'it,' 'they,' 'you'—any word and thus identify themselves with the crime" [sic].[101] Crane, advocating a random use of personal pronouns, does not distinguish singular from plural, subject from object, masculine from feminine, and he considers ambiguity a crime; collaboration on *The Ghost* demanded a momentary disregard of private enterprise.

Collaborators share the blame of authorship; anonymous publication disperses blame entirely. In the 1890s, certain shades of shame automatically meant Oscar Wilde, who is believed, with little evidence, to have masterminded *Teleny, or the Reverse of the Medal, a Physiological Romance of Today*, a homosexual pornographic novel. Its manuscript circulated like a chain letter among several men: in 1889, a "Master" (perhaps Wilde) left it at a London bookshop, and asked the proprietor to pass it to a "friend." After this friend returned the manuscript, another man, and then another and another, called for it. By the time it reached the Master again, it had become a promiscuous jumble of different hands. When published in 1893, the advertisement praised it as "the most powerful and cleverly written erotic Romance which has appeared in the English language during recent years":[102] the genre of the Romance evidently encompassed Stevensonian yarns and Sadean pornography. The strange case of *Teleny* proves that men in 1889 who wished to compose homosexual scenes turned to collaboration as a useful means. Doubtless, they wrote *Teleny* to arouse themselves as well as their readers. One of its climaxes, an orgy scene, represents a group of men collectively and ecstatically writing the novel: "we understood that the last moment had come. It was like an electric shock amongst us all. 'They enjoy, they enjoy!' was the cry, uttered from every lip" (152). "They enjoy, they enjoy!" might well be the orgasmic battle cry of collaborators, invoking a paradise of plural pleasures in which no single author or type of desire predominates.

Group sex and group writing, available to this clique in 1889, would have been less conceivable after 1895, when Oscar Wilde was sentenced, and homophobic consciousness sharpened. Joseph Conrad and Ford Madox Ford, writers from a very different tradition than Wilde, began writing their own *Romance* in 1898; it shares important values with the more overtly homosexual "Physiological Romance of Today." Romance was the preferred mode of the fin de siècle collaborative renaissance; the roots of Conrad's and Ford's *Romance* go back to Stevenson/Osborne, Lang/Haggard, and the daisy chain of *Teleny*. Such a genealogy implicates Conrad's and Ford's austere modernist impulses in a sexual underground.

Conrad's and Ford's Criminal Romance

Although Conrad was 41 and Ford was 24 when they began in 1898 to write *Romance,* the most substantial of their three collaborative novels, neither writer was master. Ford later claimed that Conrad had sought him out because he was the most "boomed" writer in England at the time, while partisans of Conrad considered that Ford was an interloper "shamelessly laying eggs" in the other man's nest; and yet *Romance,* an apprentice novel on which they lavished six years, hatched both men's careers.[103] Pound turned Yeats into a modernist; Conrad and Ford did the trick for each other. They described the gestation of their collaborative novels in terms of childbearing, even if they claimed the results were more manly than maternal.

When Conrad and Ford began writing *Romance,* each of their wives had recently delivered a first child. Their second collaborative novel, *The Inheritors* (whose title suggests its concern with issue and generation), was written while Elsie Hueffer, Ford's wife, was pregnant. Women's biology affected the men's pronouncements on collaboration. In the preface to their third and last joint novel, *The Nature of a Crime* (1909), Conrad described the work as a mystery born and then forgotten: "the details of its birth . . . remain for me completely forgotten."[104] Ford continued the birth metaphor when describing the difficulties of urging his collaborator to write: Ford pushed him "towards writing as the drake manoeuveres the sitting duck back to the nest when she has abandoned her eggs."[105] They also turned to language of male reproductive sexuality: Conrad, commenting on their extravagant writing sessions, exclaimed, "This is collaboration if you like! Joking aside the expenditure of nervous fluid was immense."[106] Debt follows from excessive spending: Conrad owed Ford money, which remained unpaid as late as 1921, though they had quarreled in 1909 and parted ways.

Despite their investment in maternity, Conrad and Ford tried to keep their prose clear of women. They could remove women from their fiction because they never admitted women into their conversation—or so Ford claims, insisting that "in all our extreme intimacy, lasting for many years, neither of us ever told what is called a smoking-room story. We never even discussed the relations of the sexes."[107] The women who appeared in their collaborative novels were Ford's exclusive responsibility, and were so bothersome to Conrad that he once exclaimed, "*Damn* Ford's women."[108] Though he included women in their novels, Ford omitted Conrad's wife from his 200-odd page memoir, *Joseph Conrad: A Personal Remembrance;* she retaliated by denouncing Ford in a letter to the *Times Literary Supple-*

ment. Ford's literary technique of "impressionism" permitted him to sentimentalize the bygone days of the two men's friendship and to do away with all evidence that Conrad had a wife.

Pining for a past of pure form and beauty (much as Pater and the aesthetes yearned for a homosexual Renaissance), Conrad and Ford turned to Stevenson's name and works for succor. Though they consciously imitated that progenitor of the boy's book, Conrad professed surprise when W. E. Henley invoked the master in connection with their paltry plans for *Romance.* Conrad humbly exclaimed that Stevenson and Dumas were "big names and I assure You it had never occurred to me they could be pronounced in connection with my plan to work with Hueffer [Ford]."[109] Conrad, who assumed that Stevenson would never have stooped to collaborate, feared "sneers at collaboration—sneers at those two men who took six years to write 'this very ordinary tale' whereas R. L. S. single handed produced his masterpieces."[110] Conrad implies that only weak men collaborate, and forgets that Stevenson's labors were not all singlehanded. Like many writers of their time, Conrad and Ford demanded that prose be manly. Ford considered his collaborator a "he-man," and envied his few but virile contributions to *The Inheritors*: whenever words of Conrad's appear, they "crepitate from the emasculated prose like firecrackers amongst ladies' skirts."[111] Ford assumes that prose is most masculine when it can shock and harm women.

Despite their hostility to women, and their reactionary conviction that "the writing of novels is the only pursuit worth while for a proper man,"[112] they attempted a new kind of novel that might undermine masculinity by complicating it. Ford believed that narrative chronology, when shattered, would unmask the British man and reveal his secret neurasthenia. The problem with the British novel, according to Ford, was that "it went straight forward"; however, when getting to know an "English gentleman at your golf club," you only discover his character gradually, and never "go straight forward." The man who originally seems "beefy, full of health, the moral of the boy from an English Public School of the finest type," turns out to be "hopelessly neurasthenic." The only way to capture such a man in fiction is to "work backwards and forwards over his past," and to eschew chronological order.[113] Conrad and Ford avoided moving "straight forward"; indulging in temporal weaving, they could present a man who was *not* straight. Ford used the very word "queer" to describe his loathing for *The Inheritors*, "a queer, thin book which the writer has always regarded with an intense dislike." Only a "psychopathic expert," Ford claimed, could find the "obscure nervous first cause" that motivated his "hatred and dread."[114] Ford associated queerness with an illogical hatred, and straightness with a traditional fiction that was, however, unable to register finer points of degenerate character.

Conrad, too, used the word "queer" to demarcate a region of feeling he could not explain. In the veiled autobiography of *The Mirror of the Sea*, he described his "queer symptoms"—"inexplicable periods of powerlessness, sudden accesses of mysterious pain."[115] For this hysteria, the captain ordered a silent rest cure. Ford, who played the doctor's part within the collaboration, remedied Conrad's writing block by applying hypnotic pressure: according to Conrad, his partner exerted that "gentle but persistent pressure which extracted, from the depths of my then despondency, the stuff of the Personal Record."[116] Pulling unformed "stuff" from depths, an act of midwifery, places Ford in the analyst's position; and yet he, too, suffered hysteria, seeing a specialist who diagnosed nervous breakdown, prescribed sea voyage, and forbade work for six months.[117] Both Conrad and Ford suffered from a hysteria that collaboration could successfully treat.

Collaboration may have alleviated their hysteria, but it also inspired new anxieties. Writing with another man meant entering his prose's body: Wells, afraid that Ford would wreck Conrad's style, warned, "It's as delicate as clockwork and you'll only ruin it by sticking your fingers in it."[118] Wells, who narrowly avoided collaborating with James, describes double writing as a matter of fingers stuck where they do not belong. Conrad and Ford, however, enjoyed this sensation of transgression, and proudly labeled their work criminal. Conrad wrote, "You cannot really suppose that there is anything between us except our mutual regard and our partnership—in crime"; and Ford remembered Conrad shuffling the manuscript pages of *Romance* "distastefully as if they had been the evidence of a crime."[119] Their collaboration was criminal because its ambitions were so revolutionary: they meant to alter the techniques that fiction used to represent masculinity. Working with Conrad on *Romance* at night, Ford recalls whispering "in a conspiracy against the sleeping world."[120] *Romance* provides evidence of other, more tangible crimes that double writing displaced.

Romance is caught between an allegiance to the "boy's book" and to an enameled perfection that the collaborators associate with Flaubert. A primer in *le mot juste*, the novel also indicts literature as an effeminate pastime, and longs for the rough sea life. The boyish protagonist, John Kemp, flees England to rebel against the literary impotence of his father, a man "powerless and lost in his search for rhymes," who sits all day, "happy in an ineffectual way," "inscribing 'ideas' every now and then in a pocket-book."[121] Kemp wistfully remarks, "I think he was writing an epic poem" (5). Anti-imperialist as Conrad's and Ford's politics might have been, the novel mistily renders this boy's desire for a patriarchal strength his father's poems could not attain; the novel broods on the chimerical vision of an "England stable and undismayed, like a strong man who had kept his feet in the tottering of secular edifices shaken to their foundations" (120). Although Conrad and Ford depict empire as morally murky, the ardor in the novel arises from scenes of men exerting sexual power over each other, a charismatic influence that the novel cannot say is either good or evil. The novel's very artfulness makes it hard to tell the villains and the heroes apart; leaving the reader in the dark, the novel will not decide whether one man's sexual sway over another man is base or ecstatic.

Like Stevenson, Conrad and Ford declare this ambiguity through the word "queer." In *Romance*, everything is queer, from ships ("Queer-looking boats crawled between the shores") to the knowledge garnered from long voyage ("I was another man by that time, with much queer knowledge and other desires")(34). Leaving England, Kemp is transformed into the very pirates he fears; indeed, he enters the outlaw's life under the grip of a hypnotic Carlos who looked him "straight in the face with a still, penetrating glance of his big, romantic eyes," and "whispered seductively," "I like you, Jack Kemp" (37–38). Kemp, fascinated, noted that Carlos "was all eyes in the dusk, standing in a languid pose" (38). This seductive man, whose proposition, according to the recipient, rings "so sweetly and persuasively that the suggestiveness of it caused a thrill in me" (38), and whose hand-clasp "thrilled me like a woman's" (40), urges the narrator to enter a Romance; through this scene of homosexual seduction, Conrad and Ford describe the allure of a collaborative practice associated with Stevenson's genre. When Carlos leaves, he "leaned over and kissed me lightly on the cheek, then climbed away. I felt that the light of Romance was going out of my life" (40–41). The "Romance" that so sways Kemp and his authors is a homosexual love affair, a literary genre, and a nimbus of attractive degeneracy surrounding fantasies of English power.

The novel is so filled with near-naked men, in postures of threat and repose, that one searches, baffled, for the node in the narrator's voice from which these scenes emanate. Are Conrad and Ford indifferent to the flesh they depict? The scenes pass as realism and local color; they convey menace—for the naked ones are usually pirates who might easily murder the narrator or expose his identity. And yet the flesh exceeds its apparent purpose; Conrad and Ford interpret "romance" to mean a man's life among men and wish sexual implications to go undetected. Hairy pirates populate the book; the more bloodthirsty they are, the less clothed. A ruffian "paused, and undid his shirt, laying bare an incredibly hairy chest; then slowly kicked off his shoes. 'One stifles here,' he said. 'Ah! in the old days—'" (100). This pirate turns to Kemp "with an air of indescribable interest, as if he were gloating over an obscene idea" (100). Conventions of the Stevenson-forged "romance" novel permit Conrad and Ford to depict, as objects of desire, men whose menace prevents the scenes from lapsing into sex. A man who almost murders Kemp on board a ship turns lovely a few pages later: "To this day I remember the beauty of that rugged, grizzled, hairy seaman's eyelashes. They were long and thick, shadowing the eyes softly like the lashes of a young girl" (245). The pirate's life, like the career of the fin de siècle homosexual, is circumscribed by threat of blackmail and entrapment; secret signs help him recognize possible sexual partners. Kemp spies a man who might be enemy or friend: "From a wine-shop . . . issued suddenly a brawny ruffian in rags, wiping his thick beard with the back of a hairy paw" (360). In one inchoate instant, Kemp sees nakedness and the telltale earring: "I noticed the glitter of a gold earring in the lobe of his huge ear. His cloak was frayed at the bottom into a perfect fringe and, as he flung it about, he showed a good deal of naked skin under it" (360). But how is Kemp or the reader to sort this information? If Kemp succumbs to the erotic invitation, he risks discovery: he dares not say yes to a "young smooth-faced mulatto" who wore "new straw slippers with blue silk rosettes over his naked feet," and who "lounged cross-legged at the door." Beckoning the narrator, "he held a big cigar tilted up between his teeth, and ogled me, like a woman, out of the corners of his languishing eyes" (359). Because Kemp is a wanted man traveling incognito, acquiescence to this straw-slippered flirt might mean arrest and death.

Kemp's susceptibility to discovery and unveiling makes any attack "romantic"; the sensation of being ambushed taps the energies of Stevenson's adventure fiction and of homosexual pornography.

> Something hairily coarse ran harshly down my face; I grew blind; my mouth, my eyes, my nostrils were filled with dust. . . . I had no time to resist. I kicked my legs convulsively. . . . Someone grunted under my weight. . . . My surprise, rage, and horror had been so great that, after the first stifled cry, I had made no sound. I heard the footsteps of several men going away. (74–75)

In another scene, Kemp feels six men fling "their arms round me from behind"; with a sudden "exaggerated clearness of vision," he can see "each brown dirty paw reach out to clutch some part of me." Night falls as they fight, and afterwards the narrator finds himself "lying gasping on my back on the deck of the schooner; four or five men were holding me down" (94). The authors may have dedicated *Romance* to their wives, but the novel centers on male bodies fighting each other in a distant past that Conrad and Ford, at the novel's end, call "Romance": "And, looking back, we see Romance—that subtle thing that is mirage—that is life" (428). Like "queer," "romance" is a word meant to obscure.

Heterosexual love does occur in *Romance*, and yet the narrator confesses that he came to it rather late: before he met Seraphina, daughter of the patriarch Don Riego, he "had never been tempted to look at a woman's face" (126). She is lovely to the narrator because of her connection to two phallic emblems, the dagger and the lizard. Calling her "an apparition of dreams—the girl with the lizard, the girl with the dagger" (126), Kemp enjoys the knife-point of her touch: he thrills to the soft warmth of her hand because it is "as if she had slipped into my palm a weapon of extraordinary and inspiring potency" (204). As a purveyor of masculinity, she brings the narrator closer to Romance; however, she is not integrated into the novel, and was absent altogether from the first draft, which Ford composed himself. In the final version, she remains overshadowed by pirates, a "band of brothers, each loving the other" (383). One pirate makes it explicit that, in this world of Romance, male combat has more value than heterosexual play: threatening Kemp, this pirate says, "Don't you dream of tricks. I've cut more throats than you've kissed gals in your little life" (383). Another pirate draws out an "immense pointed knife," which he kisses "rapturously," exclaiming "Aha! . . .bear this kiss into his ribs at the back" (383). Although Conrad and Ford describe Seraphina's and Kemp's affair as a "romance of persecuted lovers" (84), the pirates—who kiss the knives they shove into each other's backs—are emblems of lovers more urgently persecuted in the England of 1898.

Appropriately, Conrad and Ford end their novel back in an English courtroom, where Kemp is on trial as a pirate. Romance, as a literary mode and as a sexual style, is being judged: to save his life, Kemp must tell it grippingly. In this situation of extremity, he discovers for himself the literary method Conrad and Ford have been using all along: Kemp realizes that if "there were to be any possibility of saving my life, I had to tell what I had been through—and to tell it vividly— I had to narrate the story of my life." But he must do so with a thrusting firmness: "I rammed all that into my story." Telling the story, he feels an odd separation from the "I"; his voice splits between "the one 'I'" who is narrating, and a second "I" who stays detached, conscious of "raving in front of a lot of open-eyed idiots, three old judges, and a young girl." His story consists in the counterpoint between two narrating "I"s: "in a queer way, the thoughts of the one 'I' floated through into the words of the other, that seemed to be waving its hands in its final struggle, a little way in front of me" (421–22). Though he finds this self-division "queer," he makes good use of it: Kemp on the witness stand, trying to save his life, discovers the utility of double speaking.

Kemp tries to defend his romance against England's laws; in another courtroom scene, three years before Conrad and Ford began collaborating, Oscar Wilde had also been forced to defend his romance. But Kemp wears no green carnation. In fact, he pits his ramming Romance against the aesthete—embodied in a witness for the prosecution whom Kemp describes as a "mincing swell": "A tiny, fair man, with pale hair oiled and rather long for those days, and with green and red signet rings on fingers that he was forever running through that hair, came mincingly into the witness-box" (414). Conrad's and Ford's *Romance*, despite its interest in naked pirates, ultimately does battle with the specter of Wilde. Because Kemp's final speech of vindication, which defines the homosexual witness as its enemy, didactically asserts itself as the entire work's microcosm and climax, Conrad's and Ford's *Romance* takes place in a courtroom where the writers stand trial for effeminate double writing, a charge they must refute by, paradoxically, composing a powerful Romance.

Conrad's and Ford's other two novels are soberer tales, rooted in England, without exotic touches; and yet, by dwelling on sensations of ambiguity or queerness, these works resume the themes of *Romance*. In *The Inheritors*, the narrator Etherington Granger (about whom a stranger asks, "Is he queer?") collaborates with an important man of letters and considers it "a tremendous—an incredibly tremendous—opportunity".[122] But he denies that his desire for literary force is sexual. Reading an article by another man, he admiringly thinks that "the touch was light, in places even gay," and admits that the man's writing "set me tingling with desire, with the desire that transcends the sexual; the desire for the fine phrase, for the right word—for all the other intangibles" (109–10). *The Inheritors*, which takes place in modern, post-Wilde England, felt pressured to deny the sexual nature of its narrator's desire for another man's gay linguistic touch. In Conrad's and Ford's last novel, *The Nature of a Crime*, wishing to naturalize the crime of collaboration, they use the novel's heterosexual plot as a mask for their own writerly marriage. The narrator notes, "For the union with you that I seek is a queer sort of thing; hardly at all, I think, a union of the body, but a sort of consciousness of our thoughts proceeding onwards together" (69). The union that the narrator seeks is queer indeed, for he observes, "She is alarmed and possibly fascinated because she feels that I am not 'straight'—that I might, in fact, be a woman or a poet" (47–48). The narrator further exposes himself as not straight when he describes the bundle of letters he is writing as a faggot: he gives the "little fagot" of letters to a sleepy girl, who will deliver the packet to his beloved. Conrad's and Ford's story, *The Nature of a Crime*, is a sequence of letters that its narrator brands a "little fagot" (86). It seems questionable to poise an entire book on male collaboration, soon to end, on a word like "fagot" whose sense has notoriously shifted. Collaboration fertilizes a work with double meanings that can never be justified and that sustain a dreamy half-life, impossible to dismiss and impossible to prove.

Afterworlds

Ford described his partnership with Conrad as a "conspiracy against the sleeping world"; the sleeping world female collaborators conspire against is patriarchy. When women enter the force field of male collaboration, they are subsumed as mediums and mediators; but when women collaborate, they create their own force field, which men may strive to break, but in which men have no place.[123]

No collaborative team in the fin de siècle aroused more touristic curiosity than "Michael Field," pseudonym of Katharine Bradley and Edith Cooper, aunt and niece, who inhabited their male pen-name so completely that friends called them "Michael" and "Henry." Prolific poets and playwrights (together they completed 27 plays), they were respected by such contemporaries as Oscar Wilde and Robert Browning. Though they moved in mainstream literary circles, their alias gave them a seclusion in which they could freely unfold their "natures set a little way apart."[124] Calling themselves "poets and lovers evermore," they wrote explicitly lesbian poetry: their completions of Sapphic fragments prompted Browning to call the poets "my two dear Greek women!"[125] Piety kept their audaciously Sapphic affinities in check; eager to remain united in the afterworld, crushed by the death of their dog, they converted to Roman Catholicism. The man who received Michael into the church was John Gray, Marc-André Raffalovich's lover; the two women thrived in that religious demimonde that protected gay and lesbian writers from disclosure.

Because Michael and Henry wrote together to ward off the crippling criticism of men, they wished to keep their gender and their collaborative practice secret from male readers. To prying Havelock Ellis, Michael Field had responded, "As to our work, let no man think he can put asunder what God has joined";[126] when Browning tried to ferret out their secrets, Michael insisted that "I do not care to speak to you again of our relations to our work."[127] Offended by men's voyeuristic peeping, Michael wrote to Browning an impassioned defense of collaboration, insisting that she and Edith together "make a *veritable Michael*," and that Browning, by letting the public know their gender, was "destroying this philosophic truth." They received a distressed letter from Raffalovich, who complained that "he thought he was writing to a boy—a young man," but that he had "learnt on the best authority it is not so." Michael asserts that revealing their double authorship "would indeed be utter ruin to us," and that exposing their gender would "dwarf and enfeeble our work at every turn. Like the poet Gray we shall never 'speak out.' And we have many things to say that the world will not tolerate from a woman's lips."[128] By speaking out as women and as collaborators, they risk admitting perverse sexual attachment: Symonds, after all, had used the same phrase—speaking out—to mean confessing homosexuality. Michael and Henry were right to keep their nature secret: when it was disclosed that "Michael Field" was actually two women, critical interest in their work waned. As their biographer Mary Sturgeon hypothesizes, "something in the fact of a collaboration was obscurely repellent."[129]

Michael Field's lesbian poems, when known to be collaborative work, might have repelled readers interested in keeping subject and object, writer and reader, distinct. In an early poem, "A Girl," with a palette drawn from the decadent poets and from Sappho, they describe their erotic cooperation on the collaborative page. The poem was published as Michael Field's, but who is speaking, Michael or Henry? Michael Field frees the love lyric, long a genre of possession, into an ownerless, borderless "field" without master or serf. One woman sees and desires "a mouth, the lips apart," a soul like "a deep-wave pearl." The speaker leaves the page half-empty so her lover can complete it:

> . . . and our souls so knit,
> I leave a page half-writ—
> The work begun
> Will be to heaven's conception done
> If she come to it.[130]

Happy to leave the work unfinished, Michael (or Henry) invites her partner to "come" onto a page where they might conceive a poem together. Michael and Henry relished the extremity of their commitment, priding themselves on a union more complete than the redoubt-able Brownings: "those two poets, man and wife, wrote alone; each wrote, but did not bless or quicken one another at their work; *we are closer married.*"[131]

Michael Field was not the only pair of "married" women in the fin de siècle. "Pansy," pseudonym of Isabella M. Alden, wrote several novels in collaboration, including *Divers Women* (1880) with Mrs. C. M. Livingston, and *From Different Standpoints* (1878) with Faye Huntington (pseudonym of Theodosia M. Foster). Pansy also com-mandeered *A Sevenfold Trouble* (1889), a collection of stories com-posed by seven women but organized by Pansy, who agreed to "mother the whole thing."[132] The sisters Emily and Dorothea Gerard collaborated on several novels under the name E. D. Gerard, including *Beggar My Neighbor* (1882) and *A Sensitive Plant* (1891). More prominent than Pansy or the Gerard sisters, however, were Edith Œ. Somerville and Martin Ross (whose real name was Violet Martin), distant cousins who lived and wrote together. On the bindings and copyright pages of their novels appeared an insignia woven from threads of the letters S and R uniting so fluently that it is difficult to see where one letter ends and the other begins.[133]

Unlike Michael Field, Somerville and Ross wrote to make money, and these financial demands curtailed their literary ambitions; their most popular work, *Some Experiences of an Irish R.M.* (1889), is a cheerful story of hunting in the Irish countryside.[134] The enigmatic, erudite Michael Field was part of a coterie; though Somerville and Ross were detached from the literary world, they had to contend with virulent male critics. After the publication of their first book, Violet Martin had a "hideous dream" about a review "written by a kind of intellectual Jack the Ripper."[135] Male readers were eager to rip open the hermetic workings of female collaboration. Andrew Lang, evi-dently disappointed with the results of his own effort with Haggard, cynically inquired into Somerville's and Ross's methods, as if he were vexed by their greater success. Martin reported:

> To me then with a kind of offhand fling he said "I suppose you are the one who did the writing." I explained with some care that it was not so. He said that he didn't know how any two people could equally evolve characters etc., that he had tried, and it was always he or the other who did it all. I said I didn't know how we managed, but anyhow I knew little of book making as a science. He said I must know a great deal, on which I had nothing to say.[136]

By pretending humbly to know little about books, Martin bars Lang's entrance into their privacy. An important part of their secret was what others might have called lesbianism. However, Edith and Violet were not strictly lovers, for after Violet died, Edith resisted the sexual advances of her new companion, composer Ethel Smyth. Ethel wrote to Edith, apparently after a rebuffed pass: "I don't mind you feeling as you do—you and V.M. It goes with your type . . . I have more experience of life stored in my little finger than you in your whole body. I mean of a certain kind of experience."[137] Apparently, Somerville and Ross deferred that sort of pleasure to the afterworld.

After Martin's death in 1915, Somerville lived to write 15 more books, which she claimed the dead Martin had co-authored: both women's names appear on the title pages. The search for a collaborator prompted Edith to call on Martin in séances; transcriptions of these sessions capture double writing at its most extreme. Edith asks, "Can I ever write alone?" and the late Martin responds, "Yes, some day. Jem [the medium] can help you now." In need of more specific guidance, Edith inquires, "When shall I try to write again?" Martin answers affectionately: "When you feel impelled, my dear." But she does not encourage Edith to write alone "just yet." Edith confesses, "I shouldn't know which were my own thoughts and which yours." Martin says "that would not matter." Edith sighs, "I don't feel any desire to write." Martin is enigmatic: "Not now, but perhaps you may."[138]

Men, too, have conferred with the dead. James Merrill, using his lover David Jackson as medium and implicit collaborator, cajoled spirits of the air to fill a poetic trilogy, *The Changing Light at Sandover* (1982). A séance text, Merrill's poem follows in the tradition of Yeats's *A Vision* (1925), which began when, a mere four days after the wedding, Yeats's bride began to perform automatic writing. He admits that his wife took to the servitude unhappily: "my wife bored and fatigued by her almost daily task and I thinking and talking of little else."[139] Although the system might be, Yeats admits, "the creation of my wife's Daimon and of mine,"[140] he framed the second printing with a dedicatory address to Ezra Pound. As in the history of *The Waste Land*, Pound could be trusted to straighten out male texts that depended too much on female mediums.

Yeats tapped his wife's unconscious in order to place her visions in his own name, and to repay a debt to Pound, who had helped him become a modernist. *A Vision*, with its urge to map universal cycles, recalls the work of Fliess and Freud, who collaborated to calculate and control menstrual and cosmic periods. Freud and Fliess and Yeats and Pound enjoyed dividing history into waves that echo a woman's bodily rhythms, but they finally wanted a symbolic system to transcend women. I began with Freud and Fliess and I end, glancingly, with Yeats and Pound: both pairs of men—the founders of psycho-analysis and the founders of modernism—borrowed language of female procreation to describe their own ambiguous conceptions.

Despite my attention to misogyny, I have, throughout this study, portrayed male sexuality as if it were an unambiguous, Arcadian balm. Believing in the baptismally purifying powers of acknowledged desire, I have indicted double talk as a detour, diluting lusts better fulfilled in the flesh. Although I profess faith in a buried sexuality worth bringing to light, my readings have shown, in fact, that collaborative texts do not bear such a simple relation to hidden desire. Double writing is not mere sublimation; in the case of such perhapsers as Pound, Eliot, Freud, and Fliess, homosexual desire is as much the consequence as it is the cause of double talk. Desire is a mist, only partially decipherable, that rises from the collaborative page, and that cannot be scrutinized apart from the words themselves.

Male collaboration becomes a hothouse luxury, an evasion and a delight, in a society where homo- and heterosexuality pose as warring styles. Upholding that wall between the two preferences (while tearing it down), I have savored double talk as a revolt against monolithic male authority, and yet I have, meanwhile, quietly bowed to the cult of the individual genius, atomistic and apolitical; I have listened carefully to texts—whether medical, poetic, or fictional—that strive for single-handed prestige. Although my subject has been men's use of texts to express and deny sexual community, I have isolated myself from the very word—"gay"—that signifies community, and have chosen, instead, to write about seemingly heterosexual men whom I could not accurately call gay. Thus I have fallen into the word "homosexual," and the dichotomies and duplicities it implies. When I think of my book's separation from the clamor of our own fin de siècle's crisis, I grow impatient with the bounds of what I have said, and long to include, in this last sentence, words like "AIDS" that have no logical place in *Double Talk*, missing words that make me regret the discursive limits I have so willingly embraced.

NOTES

Interpreting Double Talk: An Introduction

1. André Gide, *The Counterfeiters*, trans. Dorothy Bussy (New York: Modern Library, 1931), 351.

2. Quoted in Leonard Tancock's introduction to Edmond and Jules de Goncourt, *Germinie Lacerteux*, trans. Tancock (Harmondsworth: Penguin Books, 1984), 8.

3. H. Rider Haggard, *She* (Harmondsworth: Penguin Books, 1982), 291.

4. Whether men or maleness has a place in feminism is a charged issue. See Alice Jardine and Paul Smith, eds., *Men in Feminism* (New York: Methuen, 1987). Elaine Showalter speaks of the need to defamiliarize masculinity: see Showalter, "The Other Bostonians: Gender and Literary Study," *The Yale Journal of Criticism* 1 (1987): 179–87.

5. For general theory on the construction of homosexuality in the 19th century, see Michel Foucault, *The History of Sexuality, Volume I: An Introduction* (New York: Vintage Books, 1980). For specific historical discussion, see Jeffrey Weeks, *Coming Out: Homosexual Politics in Britain, from the 19th Century to the Present* (London: Quartet Books, 1977). The Labouchère Amendment was appended to the Criminal Law Amendment Bill, which raised the age of consent from 13 to 16—a measure for which the social purity movement had lobbied. For background, see H. Montgomery Hyde, *The Love That Dared Not Speak Its Name: A Candid History of Homosexuality in Britain* (Boston: Little Brown, 1970); F. B. Smith, "Labouchère's Amendment to the Criminal Law Amendment Bill," *Historical Studies* 17, no. 67 (Oct. 1976): 165–75; and Weeks, *Coming Out*. Two documents of the Labouchère Amendment's influence have recently occupied American consciousness: E. M. Forster's *Maurice*, written in 1913 but not published until 1971 (made in 1987 into a popular motion picture by the male team of Ivory and Merchant), and Hugh Whitemore's *Breaking the Code*, a West End-to-Broadway play about Alan Turing, a gay mathematician driven to suicide by police hounding.

6. See Eve Kosofsky Sedgwick, *Between Men: English Literature and Male Homosocial Desire* (New York: Columbia University Press, 1985).

7. See Claude Lévi-Strauss, *The Elementary Structures of Kinship* (Boston: Beacon Press, 1969); René Girard, *Deceit, Desire, and the Novel: Self and Other in Literary Structure*, trans. Yvonne Freccero (Baltimore: Johns Hopkins University Press, 1972); Luce Irigaray, *This Sex Which Is Not One*, trans. Catherine Porter (Ithaca: Cornell University Press, 1985); Gayle Rubin, "The Traffic in Women: Notes Towards a Political Economy of Sex," in *Toward an Anthropology of Women*, ed. Rayna Reiter (New York: Monthly Review Press, 1975), 157–210; and Sedgwick, *Between Men*.

8. See Peter Gay, *The Bourgeois Experience, Victoria to Freud: Education of the Senses* (New York: Oxford University Press, 1984).

9. In contrast, Luce Irigaray argues that homosexuality represents patriarchy's *status quo*. See Irigaray, *This Sex Which Is Not One*.

10. For a discussion of patriarchal poetics, see Sandra M. Gilbert and Susan Gubar, *The Madwoman in the Attic: The Woman Writer and the Nineteenth-Century Literary Imagination* (New Haven: Yale University Press, 1979), 3–106. See also Gilbert and Gubar, *No Man's Land: The Place of the Woman Writer in the Twentieth Century, Volume I: The War of the Words* (New Haven: Yale University Press, 1988). In a forthcoming book, Elaine Showalter describes the fin de siècle male revolt against female authority.

11. Sigmund Freud, *Three Essays on the Theory of Sexuality*, trans. James Strachey (New York: Basic Books, 1962).

12. See M. M. Bakhtin, *The Dialogic Imagination: Four Essays*, ed. Michael Holquist, trans. Caryl Emerson and Michael Holquist (Austin: University of Texas Press, 1981).

13. See Georges Bataille, *Visions of Excess: Selected Writings, 1927–1939*, trans. Allan Stoekl (Minneapolis: University of Minnesota Press, 1985).

14. Roland Barthes, *Writing Degree Zero*, trans. Annette Lavers and Colin Smith (New York: Hill and Wang, 1984), 78.

15. Roland Barthes, *A Lover's Discourse: Fragments*, trans. Richard Howard (New York: Hill and Wang, 1985), 150–51.

16. See Harold Bloom, *The Anxiety of Influence: A Theory of Poetry* (Oxford: Oxford University Press, 1973); and Bloom, *A Map of Misreading* (Oxford: Oxford University Press, 1975).

17. Leonard J. Leff, *Hitchcock and Selznick: The Rich and Strange Collaboration of Alfred Hitchcock and David O. Selznick in Hollywood* (New York: Weidenfeld & Nicolson, 1987).

18. See J. D. McClatchy, "On the Quay Brothers," forthcoming in *Connoisseur*. The (identical) Starn Twins, photographers, are another contemporary example of fraternal collaboration.

19. See Grace Glueck, "Artist and Model: Why the Tradition Endures," *The New York Times*, 8 June 1986.

20. Diego Cortez, Interview with David McDermott and Peter McGough, "AIDS: The Advent of the Infinite Divine Spirit," *Flash Art* (July/August 1986): 58–61.

21. I am grateful to Gerald Fitzgerald for calling my attention to the collaborative nature of Platonic dialogues.

22. Earl Roy Miner, *Japanese Linked Poetry: An Account with Translations of Renga and Haikai Sequences* (Princeton: Princeton University Press, 1979).

23. G. E. Bentley, *The Profession of Dramatist in Shakespeare's Time, 1590–1642* (Princeton: Princeton University Press, 1971), 199. See Francis Beaumont and John Fletcher, *Works*, The Mermaid Series, ed. by J. St. Loe Strachey (London: T. Fisher Unwin, 1949), vii.

24. See G. S. Rousseau, "The Pursuit of Homosexuality in the Eighteenth Century: 'Utterly Confused Category' and/or Rich Repository?", in Robert Purks Maccubbin, ed., *'Tis Nature's Fault: Unauthorized Sexuality during the Enlightenment* (Cambridge: Cambridge University Press, 1987), 135.

25. I am grateful to U. C. Knoepflmacher for helping me understand the range of implicit collaborations that resemble double writing. See U. C. Knoepflmacher, "On Exile and Fiction: The Lewes and the Shelleys," in Ruth Perry and Martine Watson Brownley, eds., *Mothering the Mind: Twelve Studies of Writers and Their Silent Partners* (New York: Holmes and Meier, 1984), 102–21. See also Knoepflmacher, "Avenging Alice: Christina Rossetti and Lewis Carroll," *Nineteenth Century Fiction* 41, no. 3 (December 1986): 299–328.

For an account of collaborative bonds between Victorian husbands and wives, see Phyllis Rose, *Parallel Lives: Five Victorian Marriages* (New York: Vintage Books, 1983).

26. See "*Les Stupra*," in *Rimbaud: Complete Works, Selected Letters*, trans. Wallace Fowlie (Chicago: University of Chicago Press, 1966), 152.

27. See *Locus Solus*, "A Special Issue of Collaborations," 2 (Summer 1961). I am grateful to David Shapiro for this reference.

28. For a droll history of the work of Cage, Rauschenberg, and Cunningham, see Calvin Tomkins, *The Bride and the Bachelors: Five Masters of the Avant Garde* (Harmondsworth: Penguin Books, 1976). On Frank O'Hara's collaborations, see Bill Berkson and Joe LeSueur, *Homage to Frank O'Hara* (Berkeley: Creative Arts Book Company, 1980), 58–63, 105–11.

29. John Ashbery and James Schuyler, *A Nest of Ninnies* (Calais, Vermont: Z Press, 1983); Marcel Allain and Pierre Souvestre, *Fantômas* (New York: William Morrow and Company, 1986). *The Boy Hairdresser* was never published; see John Lahr, *Prick Up Your Ears: The Biography of Joe Orton* (New York: Knopf, 1975), 7–10.

30. W. H. Auden and Christopher Isherwood, *The Ascent of F6* (New York: Random House, 1937); Auden and Isherwood, *The Dog Beneath the Skin; or, Where is Francis?* (London: Faber and Faber, 1935); Auden and Isherwood, *Journey to a War* (London: Faber and Faber, 1939); Auden and Isherwood, *On the Frontier* (New York: Random House, 1938); Auden and Louis MacNiece, *Letters from Iceland* (London: Faber and Faber, 1937); Hans Werner Henze, *The Bassarids*, libretto by Auden and Chester Kallman (New York: Associated Music Publishers, 1966); and Igor Stravinsky, *The Rake's Progress*, libretto by Auden and Kallman (London: Boosey and Hawkes, 1951).

31. Susan Gubar, "Sapphistries," in Estelle B. Freedman and others, eds., *The Lesbian Issue: Essays from SIGNS* (Chicago: University of Chicago Press, 1985), 91–110.

32. Olga Broumas and Jane Miller, *Black Holes, Black Stockings* (Middleton: Wesleyan University Press, 1985); Hélène Cixous and Catherine Clément, *The Newly Born Woman*, trans. Betty Wing (Minneapolis: University of Minnesota Press, 1986).

33. See Marxist-Feminist Literature Collective, "Women's Writing," *Ideology and Consciousness* 3 (Spring 1978): 27–48.

34. Marjorie Wallace, *The Silent Twins* (New York: Ballantine Books, 1986).

35. See Linda Wagner-Martin, *Sylvia Plath: A Biography* (New York: Simon and Schuster, 1987).

1 Privileging the Anus: Anna O. and the Collaborative Origin of Psychoanalysis

1. Ernest Jones describes this scene in *The Life and Work of Sigmund Freud*, vol. 1 (New York: Basic Books, 1953), 224–25. For Freud's own account, see his letter to Stefan Zweig, 2 June 1932, in *The Letters of Sigmund Freud*, ed. Ernst L. Freud, trans. Tania and James Stern (New York: Basic Books, 1960), 413. Henceforth, I will refer to this volume as *Letters of Freud*.

2. For the story of Bertha Pappenheim, see Max Rosenbaum and Melvin Muroff, *Anna O.: Fourteen Contemporary Reinterpretations* (New York: The Free Press, 1984), particularly essays by Anne Steinmann and Max Rosenbaum; Dora Edinger, *Bertha Pappenheim: Freud's Anna O.* (Highland Park, Ill.: Congregation Solel, 1968); Lucy Freeman, *The Story of Anna O.* (New York: Walker and Company, 1972); and Yolande Tisseron, *Du deuil à la réparation: "Anna O." restituée à Bertha Pappenheim: naissance d'une vocation sociale* (Paris: des femmes, 1986). To my knowledge, the only work of Bertha Pappenheim's in print is *Le travail de Sisyphe*, trans. Jacques Legrand (Paris: des femmes, 1986).

Feminist theory on hysteria underlies this chapter. I am indebted to Elaine Showalter's discussion of Anna O.'s hysterical childbirth as the birth of psychoanalysis. See Elaine Showalter, *The Female Malady: Women, Madness, and English Culture, 1830–1980* (New York: Pantheon, 1985), 155–59. My account of the case of Anna O. dovetails with the reading of Mary Jacobus, who calls the case "a trial of strength between men" and argues that Anna O. screens the question of male psychoanalytic priority. See Mary Jacobus, *Reading Woman: Essays in Feminist Criticism* (New York: Columbia University Press, 1986), 197–228. The other crucial feminist analysis of the case is Dianne Hunter, "Hysteria, Psychoanalysis, and Feminism: The Case of Anna O.," *Feminist Studies* 9 (1983): 465–88. The case of Dora has elicited a richer feminist commentary than has the case of Anna O.: see Charles Bernheimer and Claire Kahane, eds., *In Dora's Case: Freud—Hysteria—Feminism* (New York: Columbia University Press, 1985). Other important theoretical feminist explorations of Freud and hysteria include Jane Gallop, *The Daughter's Seduction: Feminism and Psychoanalysis* (Ithaca: Cornell University Press, 1982); Cixous and Clément, *The Newly Born Woman*; and Irigaray, *This Sex Which Is Not One*. An important historical discussion of female hysteria is Carroll Smith-Rosenberg, *Disorderly Conduct: Visions of Gender in Victorian America* (New York: Knopf, 1985).

There are several provocative, though traditionally Freudian, accounts of the Breuer-Freud collaboration and the Anna O. case. See Hannah Decker, "The Choice of a Name: 'Dora' and Freud's Relationship with Breuer," *Journal of the American Psychoanalytic Association* 30, no. 1 (1982): 113–36; Henri F. Ellenberger, "The Story of Anna O.: A Critical Review with New Data," *Journal of the History of the Behavioral Sciences* 8, no. 3 (July 1972): 267–279; Paul F. Cranefield, "Josef Breuer's Evaluation of His Contribution to Psycho-Analysis," *International Journal of Psychoanalysis* 39 (Sept.-Oct. 1958): 319–22; George H. Pollock, "The Possible Significance of Childhood Object-Loss in the Josef Breuer-Bertha Pappenheim (Anna O.)-Sigmund Freud Relationship," *Journal of the American Psychoanalytic Association* 16 (1968): 711–39; C. P. Oberndorf, "Autobiography of Josef Breuer," *International Journal of Psychoanalysis* 34 (1953); and Marc Hollender, "The Case of Anna O.: A Reformulation," *American Journal of Psychiatry* 137 (1980): 797–800. Peter Gay acknowledges the centrality of the Fliess friendship but devotes little space to a discussion of homosexuality. See Peter Gay, *Freud: A Life for Our Time* (New York: W. W. Norton, 1988).

3. "Some Neurotic Manifestations in Jealousy, Paranoia and Homosexuality," in *The Standard Edition of the Complete Psychological Works of Sigmund Freud*, vol. 18, trans. James Strachey (London: Hogarth Press, 1955), 232.

4. Sigmund Freud, *Leonardo da Vinci and a Memory of His Childhood*, trans. Alan Tyson (New York: W. W. Norton, 1964), 13. Subsequent references appear in my text.

5. My analysis of Freud's relation to men clearly follows the model set forth by Sedgwick. See Sedgwick, *Between Men*.

6. See Norman O. Brown, *Life Against Death: The Psychoanalytic Meaning of History*, 2nd ed. (Middletown: Wesleyan University Press, 1985).

7. Sigmund Freud, *Three Essays on the Theory of Sexuality*, trans. James Strachey (New York: Basic Books, 1962).

8. See William J. McGrath, *Freud's Discovery of Psychoanalysis: The Politics of Hysteria* (Ithaca: Cornell University Press, 1986).

9. Freud to Fliess, 7 Aug. 1901, in *The Complete Letters of Sigmund Freud to Wilhelm Fliess*, trans. and ed. Jeffrey Moussaieff Masson (Cambridge: Harvard University Press, 1985), 447. All subsequent references to Freud's letters to Fliess come from this volume; in my notes, I will give date and page number of letter.

10. Freud to Ferenczi, 7 Oct. 1910, quoted in Jeffrey Moussaieff Masson, *The Assault on*

Truth: Freud's Suppression of the Seduction Theory (New York: Viking Penguin, 1985), 216, n. 15.

11. Sándor Ferenczi, *First Contributions to Psycho-Analysis*, trans. Ernest Jones (London: Hogarth Press, 1952), 317.

12. Quoted in Jones, *Life and Work*, 28–29.

13. Quoted in Jones, *Life and Work*, 185.

14. Freud to Minna Bernays, 3 Dec. 1885, in *Letters of Freud*, 188.

15. Jones, *Life and Work*, 228.

16. Freud wrote that Breuer "cannot be influenced, and it is not possible to break with him." Freud to Fliess, 14 Oct. 1900, 426.

17. Freud to Fliess, 22 June 1894, 85.

18. Sigmund Freud, *An Autobiographical Study*, trans. James Strachey (New York: W. W. Norton, 1963), 32.

19. Quoted in *Letters to Fliess*, 19, n. 2.

20. Freud to Martha Bernays, 2 Feb. 1886, in *Letters of Freud*, 202.

21. Freud to Emmeline and Minna Bernays, 21 Oct. 1887, in *Letters of Freud*, 224.

22. Freud to Martha Bernays, 28 Jan. 1884, in *Letters of Freud*, 93.

23. Freud to Mathilde Breuer, 13 May 1926, in *Letters of Freud*, 369–70.

24. Freud to Emmeline and Minna Bernays, 21 Oct. 1887, in *Letters of Freud*, 226.

25. Freud to Martha Bernays, 10 Feb. 1886, in *Letters of Freud*, 208.

26. Jones, *Life and Work*, 143–44, 160.

27. Freud to Breuer, 7 Jan. 1898, in *Letters of Freud*, 234.

28. "On Transformations of Instinct as Exemplified in Anal Erotism," *Standard Edition*, vol. 17, 128.

29. Sigmund Freud, "From the History of an Infantile Neurosis," in *The Wolf Man*, ed. Muriel Gardiner (New York: Basic Books, 1971), 224.

30. "On Transformations," 133.

31. Freud to Martha Bernays, 24 Nov. 1885 and 19 March 1886, in *Letters of Freud*, 187, 214.

32. Breuer to Auguste Forel, 21 Nov. 1907, quoted in Cranefield, "Josef Breuer's Evaluation," 320.

33. See Max Rosenbaum, "Anna O. (Bertha Pappenheim): Her History," in Rosenbaum and Muroff, *Anna O.*, 5–8.

34. Quoted in Rosenbaum and Muroff, *Anna O.*, 8.

35. Freud to Martha Bernays, 13 July 1883, in *Letters of Freud*, 41.

36. Sigmund Freud, "On the History of the Psychoanalytic Movement," in *The History of the Psychoanalytic Movement*, ed. Philip Rieff (New York: Collier Books, 1963), 46.

37. *An Autobiographical Study*, 34.

38. Freud to Stefan Zweig, 2 June 1932, in *Letters of Freud*, 413.

39. "Josef Breuer," *Standard Edition*, vol. 19, 279–80.

40. Jones, *Life and Work*, 224–25; footnotes appear on 405, 412.

41. Josef Breuer and Sigmund Freud, *Studies on Hysteria*, trans. and ed. James Strachey in

collaboration with Anna Freud (London: Hogarth Press, 1952; reprinted, New York: Basic Books), 291. Subsequent page references will appear in my text. Curiously, this edition omits the date of publication, as if to permit the belated paperback to coexist with the more authoritative and disciple-sanctioned 1952 Standard Edition. The caption to the frontispiece photograph, "Sigmund Freud in 1891," provides the only date in sight: Freud alone occupies a definitive place in time. (Anna Freud, whose relation to Anna O. I discuss below, herself lent a hand to the translation.)

42. Anna O.'s case was omitted from the 1925 and 1952 German editions of the *Studies* (see *Studies*, 285, n. 2). The excision of Anna O. concealed the true origin of the text and made Freud seem more profoundly original.

43. Sigmund Freud, "Fragment of an Analysis of a Case of Hysteria," in *Dora: An Analysis of a Case of Hysteria*, ed. Philip Rieff (New York: Collier Books, 1963).

44. Her full name was Anna von Lieben. See Janet Malcolm, "J'appelle un chat un chat," *The New Yorker*, 20 April 1987, 91.

45. Sarah Kofman, *The Enigma of Woman: Woman in Freud's Writings*, trans. Catherine Porter (Ithaca: Cornell University Press, 1985), 45.

46. Freud to Fliess, 30 June 1896, 193.

47. Freud to Fliess, 17 Dec. 1896, 215.

48. Freud to Fliess, 27 July 1904, 466–68.

49. Freud to Fliess, 12 Jan. 1897, 223.

50. Freud to Fliess, 9 Oct. 1898, 330–31.

51. Freud to Fliess, 22 Dec. 1897, 289.

52. Freud to Fliess, 22 Dec. 1897, 288.

53. Freud to Fliess, 22 Dec. 1897, 288.

54. "From the History of an Infantile Neurosis," 224.

55. Freud to Fliess, 28 May 1899 and 23 March 1900, 353, 405.

56. Freud to Fliess, 14 Nov. 1897, 278.

57. Freud to Fliess, 9 Feb. 1898, 298.

58. Freud to Fliess, 29 Dec. 1899, 394.

59. See Masson, *The Assault on Truth*.

60. Freud to Fliess, 8 March 1895, 117.

61. Freud to Fliess, 1 March 1896, 175.

62. Freud to Fliess, 6 Nov. 1898, 333.

63. Freud to Fliess, 12 June 1895, 131.

64. Freud to Fliess, 20 Oct. 1895, 147.

65. Jones, *Life and Work*, 223.

66. *The History of the Psychoanalytic Movement*, 49.

67. Freud to Ernst Simmel, 11 Nov. 1928, in *Letters of Freud*, 382–83.

68. See Mircea Eliade, *The Sacred and the Profane: The Nature of Religion*, trans. Willard R. Trask (New York: Harcourt, Brace & World, 1959), and Eliade, *The Myth of the Eternal Return, or, Cosmos and History*, trans. Willard R. Trask (Princeton: Princeton University Press, 1971).

69. Quoted in Edinger, *Bertha Pappenheim*, 69.

70. See Freeman, *Story of Anna O.*, 245.
71. Quoted in Edinger, *Bertha Pappenheim*, 40.

2 Unlocking Symonds: Sexual Inversion

1. See Milton Dank, *The French against the French: Collaboration and Resistance* (New York: J. B. Lippincott Co., 1974), 286 (photograph); and Peter Novick, *The Resistance Versus Vichy: The Purge of Collaborators in Liberated France* (New York: Columbia University Press, 1968), 68–69.

2. For background on Symonds and Ellis, and on the history of *Sexual Inversion*, see Phyllis Grosskurth, *The Woeful Victorian: A Biography of John Addington Symonds* (New York: Holt, Rinehart and Winston, 1964); Phyllis Grosskurth, *Havelock Ellis: A Biography* (New York: Alfred A. Knopf, 1980); Havelock Ellis, *My Life* (London: Neville Spearman, 1967); Havelock Ellis, "A Note on the Bedborough Trial" (Watford: University Press, 1898; privately reprinted, D. C. McMurtie, 1925); Sheila Rowbatham and Jeffrey Weeks, *Socialism and the New Life: The Personal and Sexual Politics of Edward Carpenter and Havelock Ellis* (London: Pluto Press, 1977); and Vincent Brome, *Havelock Ellis, Philosopher of Sex: A Biography* (London: Routledge & Kegan Paul, 1979).
The second edition of *Sexual Inversion*, without Symonds's name, proved most damaging to Ellis. In 1898, George Bedborough, a London bookseller, was brought to trial for selling it. Though Ellis himself was not charged, the court took for granted that the volume was "obscene," a "filthy work," a document of "free love and Anarchism." See Grosskurth, *Havelock Ellis*, 193–201.

3. Symonds to Ellis, July 1891. In Herbert M. Schueller and Robert L. Peters, eds., *The Letters of John Addington Symonds*, vol. 3 (Detroit: Wayne State University Press, 1969), 587. Henceforth, I will refer to this volume as *Letters of Symonds*.

4. On sexology, see Jeffrey Weeks, *Sex, Politics, and Society: The Regulation of Sexuality Since 1800* (London: Longman, 1981); Sheila Jeffreys, *The Spinster and Her Enemies: Feminism and Sexuality 1880–1930* (London: Pandora Press, 1985); Lillian Faderman, *Surpassing the Love of Men: Romantic Friendship and Love between Women from the Renaissance to the Present* (New York: William Morrow and Company, 1981); and Foucault, *The History of Sexuality*.

5. Xavier Mayne [Edward Irenaeus Prime Stevenson], *The Intersexes: A History of Simisexualism as a Problem in Social Life* (1908; reprint, New York: Arno Press, 1975), 621.

6. See Timothy d'Arch Smith, *Love in Earnest: Some Notes on the Lives and Writings of English 'Uranian' Poets from 1889 to 1930* (London: Routledge & Kegan Paul, 1970), 75.

7. For an account of this homosexual literary subculture, see d'Arch Smith; and Brian Reade, *Sexual Heretics: Male Homosexuality in English Literature from 1850–1900* (London: Routledge & Kegan Paul, 1970).

8. Symonds to Carpenter, 29 Dec. 1892, *Letters of Symonds*, 797.

9. See Symonds to Ellis, 21 Sept. 1892, *Letters of Symonds*, 749. This letter bears no signature, but breaks off after "I am yours very sincerely." Symonds was adept at self-erasure.

10. Symonds to Sayle, 29 Nov. 1895, *Letters of Symonds*, 95.

11. Symonds to Ellis, 7 July 1892, in *Letters of Symonds*, 709.

12. Symonds to Ellis, 20 June 1892, *Letters of Symonds*, 694.

13. Symonds to Carpenter, 29 Dec. 1892, *Letters of Symonds*, 798.

14. Symonds to Carpenter, 29 Jan. 1893, *Letters of Symonds*, 810–11.

15. John Addington Symonds, "A Problem in Modern Ethics" (1891; reprinted as *Sexual Inversion*, New York: Bell Publishing, 1984), 168.

16. Havelock Ellis and John Addington Symonds, *Sexual Inversion* (London: Wilson and Macmillan, 1897; reprinted, New York: Arno Press, 1975), v. All subsequent references will appear in my text.

17. John Addington Symonds and Margaret Symonds, *Our Life in the Swiss Highlands* (London: Adams and Charles Black, 1892), 119.

18. Symonds to Symons, 13 June 1892, *Letters of Symonds*, 691.

19. Symonds to Carpenter, 29 Dec. 1892, *Letters of Symonds*, 799.

20. J. A. Symonds to Margaret Symonds, 16 June 1892, *Letters of Symonds*, 692.

21. Symonds to Whitman, 3 Aug. 1890, *Letters of Symonds*, 482.

22. Symonds to Symons, 13 June 1892, *Letters of Symonds*, 691.

23. Symonds to Ellis, 1 Dec. 1892, *Letters of Symonds*, 789.

24. Symonds to Ellis, 22 Feb. 1893, *Letters of Symonds*, 821.

25. Symonds to Ellis, 22 Feb. 1893, *Letters of Symonds*, 821.

26. Symonds to Ellis, 1 Dec. 1892, *Letters of Symonds*, 789.

27. Symonds to Ellis, 7 Dec. 1885, *Letters of Symonds*, 98–99.

28. See Edward Carpenter, *Selected Writings* (London: GMP, 1984).

29. Michael Field to Ellis, May 1886, quoted in Mary Sturgeon, *Michael Field* (London: George G. Harrap & Co. Ltd., 1922), 47. Also quoted in Faderman, *Surpassing the Love of Men*, 210.

30. See Grosskurth, *Havelock Ellis*, 173.

31. Ellis to Symonds, 1 July 1892, quoted in Grosskurth, *Havelock Ellis*, 178.

32. See Grosskurth, *Havelock Ellis*, 179.

33. Grosskurth, *Havelock Ellis*, 179.

34. Symonds to Carpenter, 21 Jan. 1893, *Letters of Symonds*, 808.

35. Symonds to Ellis, 12 Feb. 1893, *Letters of Symonds*, 817.

36. Wallace Stevens, "The Noble Rider and the Sound of Words," *The Necessary Angel* (New York: Random House, 1951), 36.

37. *The Memoirs of John Addington Symonds*, ed. Phyllis Grosskurth (Chicago: University of Chicago Press, 1984), 61.

38. *Memoirs*, 62.

39. See Ellis, *My Life*, 68.

40. Symonds to Carpenter, 21 Jan. 1893, *Letters of Symonds*, 808.

41. Symonds to Ellis, 16 Dec. 1885, *Letters of Symonds*, 104.

42. Quoted in Havelock Ellis, "A Note on the Bedborough Trial," 16–26.

43. Symonds to Henry Graham Dakyns, 23 Jan. 1891, *Letters of Symonds*, 548.

44. "A Problem in Modern Ethics," 157.

45. "A Problem in Modern Ethics," 114, 107.

46. "A Problem in Modern Ethics," 122.

47. *Memoirs*, 168, 166.

48. *Memoirs*, 61.

49. "A Problem in Modern Ethics," 182.

50. See Oscar Wilde, "The Decay of Lying," in *De Profundis and Other Writings*, ed. Hesketh Pearson (Harmondsworth: Penguin Books, 1986), 55–87; and André Gide, *Corydon*, trans. Richard Howard (New York: Farrar, Straus and Giroux, 1983).

51. *Memoirs*, 266.

52. Horatio Forbes Brown, *John Addington Symonds: A Biography* (London: Smith, Elder & Co., 1903, 2nd ed.), xii.

53. Brown, *John Addington Symonds*, xii.

54. Symonds to Horace Traubel, 27 Feb. 1892, *Letters of Symonds*, 667.

55. Symonds to Horace Traubel, 27 Feb. 1892, *Letters of Symonds*, 667.

56. Symonds to Carpenter, 13 Feb. 1893, *Letters of Symonds*, 819.

57. *Our Life in the Swiss Highlands*, 303.

58. *Our Life in the Swiss Highlands*, 305–6.

59. "You know also that I regard 'L'Amour de l'Impossible' with terror." Symonds to Charles Edward Sayle, 29 Nov. 1885, *Letters of Symonds*, 95. See Symonds's sonnet sequence, "L'Amour de l'Impossible," in *Animi Figura* (London: Smith, Elder & Co., 1882), 36–49.

60. *Our Life in the Swiss Highlands*, 359.

61. See Eve Kosofsky Sedgwick, "Privilege of Unknowing," *Genders* 1 (1988): 102–24.

62. *Our Life in the Swiss Highlands*, 360.

3 The Marinere Hath his Will(iam): Wordsworth's and Coleridge's Lyrical Ballads

1. Coleridge to Southey, 13 Nov. 1795, *Collected Letters of Samuel Taylor Coleridge*, vol. 1, ed. Earl Leslie Griggs (Oxford: Clarendon Press, 1956), 173. Henceforth, *Letters of STC*.

2. Stephen Maxfield Parrish, *The Art of the Lyrical Ballads* (Cambridge: Harvard University Press, 1973), 62.

3. Coleridge to Poole, 6 May 1799, *Letters of STC*, 490.

4. Coleridge to Poole, 24 Sept. 1796, *Letters of STC*, 235.

5. Coleridge to Poole, 5 Nov. 1796, *Letters of STC*, 249.

6. Coleridge to Poole, 26 Oct. 1798, *Letters of STC*, 430.

7. *The Notebooks of Samuel Taylor Coleridge*, vol. 2, ed. Kathleen Coburn (New York: Pantheon Books, 1961), entry 3148.

8. Coleridge to Sir George Beaumont, 2 Feb. 1804, *Letters of STC*, vol. 2, 1054–55.

9. For background on the *Lyrical Ballads* project, see A. M. Buchan, "The Influence of Wordsworth on Coleridge, 1795–1800," in Alun R. Jones and William Tydeman, eds., *The Ancient Mariner and Other Poems: A Casebook* (London: Macmillan, 1973), 136–59; Mark L. Reed, "Wordsworth, Coleridge, and the 'Plan' of the *Lyrical Ballads*," in Jones and Tydeman, *Ancient Mariner*, 117–35; John E. Jordan, *Why the Lyrical Ballads?* (Berkeley: University

of California Press, 1976), 19; Parrish, *Art*; Mary Jacobus, *Tradition and Experiment in Wordsworth's Lyrical Ballads (1798)* (Oxford: Clarendon Press, 1976).

10. Samuel Taylor Coleridge, *Complete Poetical Works*, ed. Ernest Hartley Coleridge (Oxford: Clarendon Press, 1912), 286–87.

11. Quoted in David Perkins, ed., *English Romantic Writers* (New York: Harcourt Brace Jovanovich, 1967), 404.

12. W. Wordsworth to William Mathews, 24 Dec. 1794, *The Letters of William and Dorothy Wordsworth, Volume 1, The Early Years 1787–1805*, ed. Ernest de Selincourt, rev. Chester L. Shaver (Oxford: Clarendon Press, 1967), 137. Henceforth, *Letters of W*.

13. D. Wordsworth to Mary Hutchinson, 5 March 1798, *Letters of W*, 200.

14. See D. Wordsworth to Richard Wordsworth, 30 April 1798, *Letters of W*, 216.

15. Coleridge to Joseph Cottle, 28 May 1798, *Letters of STC*, 412.

16. Review, *British Critic* 14 (October 1799), quoted in Jones and Tydeman, *Ancient Mariner*, 45.

17. "Note to the Ancient Mariner," from *Lyrical Ballads*, 1800 edition, in Wordsworth and Coleridge, *Lyrical Ballads*, ed. R. L. Brett and A. R. Jones (New York: Barnes and Noble, 1963), 276–77.

18. Coleridge to James Webbe Tobin, 17 Sept. 1800, *Letters of STC*, 623.

19. The full extent of Wordsworth's and Coleridge's fraternal intertextuality has been richly documented in Paul Magnuson, *Coleridge and Wordsworth: A Lyrical Dialogue* (Princeton: Princeton University Press, 1988). His dialogic reading understands the separate works of the two poets to form one interdependent sequence. However, Magnuson does not consider the 1798 *Lyrical Ballads* to be of "major significance in the dialogue," except for "Tintern Abbey" and the "Ancient Mariner" (21). My reading of the *Lyrical Ballads* attempts a dialogic interpretation similar to Magnuson's. However, the interpenetration of voices enacted in the *Lyrical Ballads* can tell us much about the relationship of male sexuality to male poetry. I do not want my reading to be a formalist account of poetic interdependence that ignores the gender of the poets, and the sexual implications of their amalgamation.

20. "Ancient Mariner," l. 409. All references to poems in the *Lyrical Ballads* are to the following reprint of the original 1798 edition: *Lyrical Ballads 1798*, ed. W. J. B. Owen (Oxford: Oxford University Press, 1969). In my text, I will give line numbers, not page numbers.

21. Samuel Taylor Coleridge, chapter 14, *Biographia Literaria*, ed. J. Shawcross (London: Oxford University Press, 1968).

22. See A. W. Brian Simpson, *Cannibalism and the Common Law* (Chicago: University of Chicago Press, 1984), 45.

23. According to G. S. Rousseau, it was common knowledge in 18th century Britain that sodomy was rampant on the high seas. See Rousseau, "The Pursuit of Homosexuality," in Maccubbin, *'Tis Nature's Fault*, 146.

24. Quoted in John Livingston Lowes, *The Road to Xanadu: A Study in the Ways of the Imagination* (Boston: Houghton Mifflin, 1927), 133.

25. In his comments to Reverend Alexander Dyce, Wordsworth claimed the entire stanza; in the note to "We are Seven" that he dictated to Isabella Fenwick, he specifically claimed only the last two lines of the stanza. Note to "We are Seven," quoted in Owen, *Lyrical Ballads*, 135–36.

26. See Lowes, *Road to Xanadu*, 253–54.

27. David Bergman is writing on the connection between maritime cannibalism and homo-

eroticism. On the drinking of urine as a step taken *before* cannibalism, see Simpson, *Cannibalism.*

28. Note to "The Thorn," appended to the 1800 Preface to the *Lyrical Ballads,* quoted in Owen, *Lyrical Ballads,* 140.

29. Owen, *Lyrical Ballads,* 140–41.

30. Owen, *Lyrical Ballads,* 139.

31. Owen, *Lyrical Ballads,* 140. Emphasis mine.

32. For a discussion of Wordsworth's depiction of Nature as feminine, and the consequences for Dorothy Wordsworth of this imagined equivalence, see Margaret Homans, *Woman Writers and Poetic Identity: Dorothy Wordsworth, Emily Brontë, and Emily Dickinson* (Princeton: Princeton University Press, 1980).

33. Coleridge to Joseph Cottle, 8 June 1797, *Letters of STC,* 325.

34. W. Wordsworth to Joseph Cottle, 12 April 1798, *Letters of W,* 215.

35. "Lewti," in Brett and Jones, *Lyrical Ballads,* 311–13.

36. Coleridge to Wordsworth, 10 May 1798, *Letters of STC,* 406.

37. Wordsworth's note to "We are Seven," dictated by Isabella Fenwick. Quoted in Owen, *Lyrical Ballads,* 136.

38. Coleridge, *Biographia Literaria,* vol. 2, chapter 14, 6. Emphasis mine.

39. Wordsworth's note to "Lines written upon a Seat in a Yew-tree," dictated to Isabella Fenwick, quoted in Owen, *Lyrical Ballads,* 126.

40. Owen, *Lyrical Ballads,* 127.

41. Wordsworth's note to "Tintern Abbey," dictated to Isabella Fenwick. Quoted in Owen, *Lyrical Ballads,* 149.

42. Coleridge to Southey, 13 Nov. 1795, *Letters of STC,* 173.

43. See Brett and Jones, *Lyrical Ballads,* 273.

4 The Waste Land: *T. S. Eliot's and Ezra Pound's Collaboration on Hysteria*

1. T. S. Eliot, "Ezra Pound," reprinted in Walter Sutton, ed., *Ezra Pound: A Collection of Critical Essays* (Englewood Cliffs: Prentice-Hall, 1963), 19. Also quoted in Ronald Bush, *T. S. Eliot: A Study in Character and Style* (New York: Oxford University Press, 1983), 70.

2. The statement is attributed to Joyce by Richard Ellmann, "The First Waste Land," in A. Walton Litz, ed., *Eliot in His Time* (Princeton: Princeton University Press, 1973), 51. Pound's statement occurs in his letter to Felix E. Schelling, 8 July 1922, in D. D. Paige, *The Letters of Ezra Pound 1907–1941* (New York: Harcourt, Brace and Company, 1950), no. 189.

3. I. A. Richards, "The Poetry of T. S. Eliot," in Jay Martin, ed., *A Collection of Critical Essays on "The Waste Land"* (Englewood Cliffs: Prentice-Hall, 1968), 44–45.

4. Delmore Schwartz, "T. S. Eliot as International Hero," in Martin, *Critical Essays,* 97. D. C. Fowler, excerpt from "*The Waste Land*: Mr. Eliot's 'Fragments,'" in Martin, *Critical Essays,* 35.

5. John Crowe Ransom, excerpt from "Gerontion," in Martin, *Critical Essays,* 15.

6. See Hunter, "Hysteria, Psychoanalysis, and Feminism: The Case of Anna O.," 474–75, and Showalter, *The Female Malady,* 157.

190 / Notes to Chapter 4

7. Julia Kristeva, "Oscillation between 'power' and 'denial'," in Elaine Marks and Isabelle de Courtivron, eds., *New French Feminisms: An Anthology* (New York: Schocken Books, 1981), 165, 167.

8. Breuer and Freud, *Studies*, 25.

9. Breuer and Freud, *Studies*, 276. Emphasis mine. On the sibyl, see Nina Auerbach, *Woman and the Demon: The Life of a Victorian Myth* (Cambridge: Harvard University Press, 1982).

10. Breuer and Freud, *Studies*, 291.

11. Breuer and Freud, *Studies*, 282.

12. My account of Eliot's personal life largely depends on Peter Ackroyd, *T. S. Eliot: A Life* (New York: Simon and Schuster, 1984). *The Letters of T. S. Eliot, Volume 1 1898–1922*, edited by Valerie Eliot, was published after the completion of my book. I regret not having the chance to use this new evidence.

13. See Showalter, *Female Malady*, 167–94; Sandra M. Gilbert, "Soldier's Heart: Literary Men, Literary Women, and the Great War," *Signs* 8 (1983), 422–50.

14. T. S. Eliot, *The Complete Poems and Plays, 1909–1950* (New York: Harcourt Brace Jovanovich, 1971), 25–26.

15. Eliot, *Complete Poems*, 19.

16. Breuer and Freud, *Studies*, 48–49.

17. Valerie Eliot, "Introduction," in T. S. Eliot, *The Waste Land: A Facsimile and Transcript of the Original Drafts Including the Annotations of Ezra Pound*, ed. Valerie Eliot (New York: Harcourt Brace Jovanovich, 1971), xviii.

18. Interview with T. S. Eliot, in *Writers at Work: The Paris Review Interviews*, Second Series, introduced by Van Wyck Brooks (New York: The Viking Press, 1963), 98.

19. Conrad Aiken, "An Anatomy of Melancholy," in Allen Tate, ed., *T. S. Eliot: The Man and His Works* (New York: Dell Publishing Co., 1966), 195. Quoted in Bush, *T. S. Eliot*, 56.

20. Pound to Quinn, 27 Dec. 1918, quoted in Eliot, *Facsimile*, xv; Eliot to Richard Aldington, undated, quoted in Eliot, *Facsimile*, xxi. See Harry Trosman, "T. S. Eliot and *The Waste Land*: Psychopathological Antecedents and Transformations," *Archives of General Psychiatry* 30.5 (May 1974): 709–17. Trosman compares the Pound/Eliot relationship to Freud's friendship with Fliess.

21. Eliot to his mother, 13 Nov. 1918, quoted in Eliot, *Facsimile*, xv.

22. Eliot to Richard Aldington, 6 Nov. 1921, quoted in Eliot, *Facsimile*, xxii.

23. Aiken, "Anatomy of Melancholy," 195.

24. For an account of Dr. Vittoz's methods, see Trosman, "T. S. Eliot."

25. Breuer and Freud, *Studies*, 277.

26. Eliot, *Facsimile*, 129.

27. T. S. Eliot, "The *Pensées* of Pascal," in *Essays, Ancient and Modern* (London: Faber and Faber, 1936), 142.

28. Breuer and Freud, *Studies*, 45.

29. T. S. Eliot, *The Use of Poetry and the Use of Criticism* (London: Faber and Faber, 1967), 144–45.

30. T. S. Eliot, "The Three Voices of Poetry," *On Poetry and Poets* (London: Faber and Faber, 1957; reprinted, New York: Noonday–Farrar, Straus and Giroux, 1961), 107. Quoted

in James E. Miller, Jr., *T. S. Eliot's Personal Waste Land: Exorcism of the Demons* (University Park: Penn. State University Press, 1977), 43.

31. Ackroyd, *T. S. Eliot*, 94.

32. Ackroyd, *T. S. Eliot*, 62, 66.

33. Aiken to Robert N. Linscott, 4 Jan. 1926, in *Selected Letters of Conrad Aiken*, ed. Joseph Killorin (New Haven: Yale University Press, 1978), no. 70. See Bush, *T. S. Eliot*, 8.

34. Ackroyd, *T. S. Eliot*, 114.

35. T. S. Eliot to Henry Ware Eliot, Sr., quoted in Eliot, *Facsimile*, xxii.

36. Ackroyd, *T. S. Eliot*, 129; Vivien Eliot to "Jack" [Hutchinson], placed in her diary entry for 8 Dec. 1935, in Bodleian Library, quoted in Ackroyd, *T. S. Eliot*, 150.

37. Donald Gallup, *T. S. Eliot and Ezra Pound: Collaborators in Letters* (New Haven: H. W. Wenning/C. A. Stonehill, 1970), 5. Eliot, *Facsimile*, ix.

38. Pound to Henry Ware Eliot, Sr., 28 June 1915, typescript at Beinecke Library, Yale University.

39. Ackroyd, *T. S. Eliot*, 66.

40. Eliot, *The Use of Poetry*, 70. Obliquely referring to his indebtedness to Pound, Eliot writes, "I doubt whether the impulse in Coleridge would have been strong enough to have worked its way out, but for the example and encouragement of Wordsworth" (75).

41. Eliot to Pound, 2 Feb. 1915, xerox at Beinecke Library, Yale University.

42. These undated letters of Vivien Eliot are in the Beinecke Library, Yale University.

43. Eliot, *Facsimile*, xxii. Richard Ellmann argues that in Paris, November 1921, Eliot discussed *The Waste Land* with Pound, and sent revisions to Pound and Vivien from Lausanne. See Ellmann, "First Waste Land," 62. Helen Gardner suggests that Eliot showed Pound the poem even before Margate. See Helen Gardner, "The Waste Land: Paris 1922," in Litz, *Eliot in His Time*, 73–74.

44. Eliot to Pound, 15 April 1915; Eliot to Pound, 23 Sept. 1917; Eliot to Pound, 31 Oct. 1917. Xeroxes of all three letters are in the Beinecke Library, Yale University.

45. Quinn to Pound, 16 Oct. 1920, in the Beinecke Library, Yale University. I have excerpted these passages from a longer letter.

46. Ackroyd, *T. S. Eliot*, 52.

47. Pound to Eliot, 24 Saturnus, An l, in D. D. Paige, *Letters of Pound*, no. 181.

48. Eliot to Pound, 24 Saturnus, An 1, from Paige transcription in the Beinecke Library, Yale University.

49. Ezra Pound, "Postscript," in Rémy de Gourmont, *The Natural Philosophy of Love*, trans. Ezra Pound (London: Neville Spearman, 1957), vii-xvii. I am grateful to A. Walton Litz for suggesting this source.

50. Pound to Eliot, 24 Saturnus, An l, in Paige, *Letters*, no. 181. In a letter to John Quinn, Pound restated his fear of artistic decadence: "I don't want to go soft, or get to producing merely 'objets d'art' instead of 'oeuvres.'" Quoted in B. L. Reid, *The Man from New York: John Quinn and His Friends* (New York: Oxford University Press, 1968), 437.

51. Pound to his mother, 18 Sept. 1921, in Beinecke Library, Yale University.

52. Pound to Eliot, 24 Saturnus, An l, Paige transcription in the Beinecke Library, Yale University.

53. Aiken to Robert N. Linscott, 4 Jan. 1926, in *Selected Letters*, ed. Killorin, no. 70.

192 / Notes to Chapter 5

54. Freud and Breuer, *Studies*, 7.

55. See Miller, *Personal Waste Land*.

56. In a 1922 letter to Pound, Eliot described the original epigraph to the poem as "somewhat elucidative." Unnumbered letter in Paige, *Letters*, 171.

57. Pound to Eliot, approx. Jan. 1922, no. 182 in Paige, *Letters*. Unexpurgated Paige transcription is in the Beinecke Library, Yale University.

58. Eliot, "Ezra Pound," in Sutton, *Ezra Pound*, 19. Quoted in Bush, *T. S. Eliot*, 70.

59. Pound to Eliot, approx. Jan. 1922, unexpurgated Paige transcription in the Beinecke Library, Yale University.

60. Eliot, *Facsimile*, 7. To keep my text relatively unencumbered by numbers, I will not give line or page references for quotations from the final, familiar version of *The Waste Land*, but will give page references to the labyrinthian fascimile when discussing Pound's comments or omitted passages.
See Barbara Everett, "Eliot's Marianne: *The Waste Land* and Its Poetry of Europe," *Review of English Studies*, New Series, vol. 31, no. 121 (1980): 41–53. I am grateful to Christopher Ricks for this reference.

61. "Bel Esprit" proposal, enclosed in Pound's letter to William Carlos Williams, 18 March 1922, in Paige, *Letters*, no. 184.

62. Pound to Eliot, approx. Jan. 1922, in Paige, *Letters*, no. 182.

63. Coleridge to Robert Southey, 26 Sept. 1794, in *Collected Letters of STC*, 109. I thank Christopher Ricks for this reference.

64. George Moore, *Celibate Lives* (London: Chatto and Windus, 1922), 80. See also George Moore, *Celibates* (New York: Macmillan, 1895). I am grateful to Elaine Showalter for this reference.

65. Eliot, *Facsimile*, vii.

66. Breuer and Freud, *Studies*, 26.

67. Sigmund Freud, "Medusa's Head," *Standard Edition*, vol. 18, 273.

68. Eliot, *Facsimile*, 125.

69. Breuer and Freud, *Studies*, 24–25.

70. Breuer and Freud, *Studies*, 25.

71. See Showalter, *Female Malady*, 150–54. Quotation from George Frederick Drinka, *The Birth of Neurosis: Myth, Malady, and the Victorians* (New York: Simon and Schuster, 1984), 95–96.

72. Pound to Eliot, 24 Saturnus, An 1, in Paige, *Letters*, no. 181. Emphasis mine.

73. Aiken, "Anatomy of Melancholy," 202.

5 Manuscript Affairs: Collaborative Romances of the Fin de Siècle

1. See Nicholas Delbanco, *Group Portrait* (New York: William Morrow, 1982), 145–47.

2. Henry James, *The Wheel of Time; Collaboration; Owen Wingrave* (New York: Harper and Brothers Publishers, 1893). I will give page references in my text. I am grateful to Elaine Showalter for calling this story to my attention.

3. See Richard Ellmann, *Oscar Wilde* (New York: Alfred A. Knopf, 1988), 179, 367, 493, 505.

4. I owe to Elaine Showalter my understanding of the fin de siècle as a time of instability in gender roles and sexual preference. Her forthcoming book on the fin de siècle describes the social and cultural change that, I would argue, encouraged double writing. I owe to Sandra M. Gilbert my understanding of modernism as a dialectical struggle between male and female writers: I would suggest that modernism emerged as a struggle between homosexual and homophobic energies as well. See Gilbert and Gubar, *No Man's Land.*

5. See W. G. Lockett, *Robert Louis Stevenson at Davos* (London: Hurst & Blackett, Ltd., 1934), 158, 243.

6. Symonds to Herbert Harlakenden Gilchrist, 14 Sept. 1885, in *Letters of Symonds*, 77.

7. Andrew Lang, "Recollections of Robert Louis Stevenson," *Adventures Among Books* (London: Longmans, Green, and Co., 1905), 51. Lang wrote that Stevenson looked "more like a lass than a lad."

8. [Andrew Lang], *Saturday Review*, 61 (9 January 1886): 55–56.

9. Henry James, *Partial Portraits* (London: Macmillan, 1888), 146, 141, 139.

10. Alice Brown, "Study of Stevenson," (Boston: Copeland and Day, 1895); quoted in J. A. Hammerton, *Stevensoniana* (Edinburgh: John Grant, 1907), 187.

11. See Robert Louis Stevenson and William Ernest Henley, *Deacon Brodie, or, The Double Life: a melodrama, founded on facts, in four acts and ten tableaux* (Edinburgh: T. E. Constable, 1880).

12. Fanny Osborne-Stevenson, "Prefatory Note," in Robert Louis Stevenson, *The Strange Case of Dr. Jekyll & Mr. Hyde, Other Stories & Fragments* (London: William Heinemann, 1924), xvii.

13. See David Daiches, *Robert Louis Stevenson and His World* (London: Thames and Hudson, 1973), 58. See also Lockett, *Stevenson at Davos*, 157.

14. Stevenson to Henley, Spring 1887, quoted in Malcolm Elwin, *The Strange Case of Robert Louis Stevenson* (London: Macdonald, 1950), 198–99.

15. Lloyd Osborne, *An Intimate Portrait of R. L. S.* (New York: Scribner's, 1924), 22.

16. Lloyd Osborne, "Stevenson at Thirty-two," in Robert Louis Stevenson, *Treasure Island* (New York: Charles Scribner's Sons, 1925), xvi-xvii.

17. Osborne, *Intimate Portrait*, 139–40.

18. Robert Louis Stevenson and Lloyd Osborne, *The Ebb-Tide: A Trio and Quartette* (New York: Charles Scribner's Sons, 1908), 1. Page numbers will appear in my text.

19. See Lord Alfred Douglas, "Two Loves," in Karl Beckson, ed., *Aesthetes and Decadents of the 1890s: An Anthology of British Poetry and Prose* (Chicago: Academy Chicago, 1981), 82. "He lieth, for his name is Shame, / And I am Love."

20. Robert Louis Stevenson, *The Strange Case of Dr. Jekyll and Mr. Hyde* (1885; reprint, Harmondsworth: Penguin Books, 1981), 29. Page numbers will appear in my text.

21. See Ellmann, *Oscar Wilde*, 426.

22. Tzvetan Todorov, *The Fantastic: A Structural Approach to a Literary Genre*, trans. Richard Howard (Cleveland: Press of Case Western Reserve University, 1973).

23. Robert Louis Stevenson and Lloyd Osborne, *The Wrecker* (New York: Charles Scribner's Sons, 1895), 16.

24. Quoted in Elwin, *Strange Case*, 198.

25. Stevenson to Sidney Colvin, 16–23 May 1893, quoted in Paul Maixner, ed., *Robert Louis Stevenson: The Critical Heritage* (London: Routledge & Kegan Paul, 1981), 451.

26. Richard Le Gallienne, review in the *Star*, 27 September 1894; quoted in Maixner, *Critical Heritage*, 457.

27. Unsigned review in *Speaker* 10 (29 September 1894): 362–63; quoted in Maixner, *Critical Heritage*, 458.

28. Robert Louis Stevenson, *Virginibus Puerisque and Other Essays in Belles Lettres* (London: William Heinemann, 1924), 9.

29. Quoted in Elwin, *Strange Case*, 198.

30. See Fanny Osborne-Stevenson, "Prefatory Note," xvii–iii.

31. See Fanny Osborne-Stevenson, "Prefatory Note," xvii–iii. See also Lloyd Osborne, *Intimate Portrait*, 64–65.

32. "A Chapter on Dreams," in *The Essays of Robert Louis Stevenson*, ed. Malcolm Elwin (London: Macdonald, 1950), 440.

33. Quoted in Jenni Calder, *Robert Louis Stevenson: A Life Study* (New York: Oxford University Press, 1980), 118.

34. H. Rider Haggard, *The Private Diaries of H. Rider Haggard*, ed. D. S. Higgins (London: Cassell, 1980), 183, 190–91.

35. Lang, *Adventures*, 24.

36. Lang, *Adventures*, 5.

37. Lang, *Adventures*, 23–24.

38. Andrew Lang, *In the Wrong Paradise, and Other Stories* (New York: Harper & Brothers, 1887).

39. H. Rider Haggard, *King Solomon's Mines* (London: Cassell & Company, 1885).

40. H. Rider Haggard, *Allan Quatermain* (London: Longmans, Green, and Co., 1887).

41. See John Boswell, *Christianity, Social Tolerance, and Homosexuality: Gay People in Western Europe from the Beginning of the Christian Era to the Fourteenth Century* (Chicago: University of Chicago Press, 1980), 29–30.

42. George Saintsbury, "The Present State of the Novel," quoted in Morton N. Cohen, *Rider Haggard: His Life and Works* (New York: Walker and Company, 1960), 116.

43. Quoted in Cohen, *Rider Haggard*, 116.

44. See Cohen, *Rider Haggard*, 122, 184.

45. H. Montgomery Hyde, *Oscar Wilde* (New York: Farrar, Straus and Giroux, 1975), 112.

46. Quoted in John Gross, *The Rise and Fall of the Man of Letters* (London: Weidenfeld and Nicolson, 1969), 152.

47. Roger Lancelyn Green, *Andrew Lang: A Critical Biography* (Leicester: Edmund Ward, 1946), ix.

48. H. Rider Haggard, *The Days of My Life*, vol. 2 (London: Longmans, 1926), 78.

49. Haggard, *Days of My Life*, 82. See photograph 1 in Peter Berresford Ellis, *H. Rider Haggard: A Voice from the Infinite* (London: Routledge & Kegan Paul, 1978).

50. Quoted in D. S. Higgins, *Rider Haggard: A Biography* (New York: Stein and Day, 1981), 118.

51. Quoted in Cohen, *Rider Haggard*, 187.

52. Green, *Andrew Lang*, 123.

53. Green, *Andrew Lang*, 123. Hyder Ragged [Sir Henry Chartres Biron], *King Solomon's Wives* (London: Vizetelly & Co., 1887). Biron later renounced his sympathy for gender ambiguity: he was the Chief Magistrate for the British obscenity trial of Radclyffe Hall's lesbian novel, *The Well of Loneliness*. See Walter Kendrick, *The Secret Museum: Pornography in Modern Culture* (Harmondsworth: Penguin Books, 1987), 181.

54. *Punch* (24 May 1890): 250.

55. [Andrew Lang and Walter H. Pollock], *He* (London: Longmans, Green, and Co., 1887). Page numbers will appear in my text. Walter H. Pollock collaborated as well with Guy C. Pollock (his brother?) on *Hay Fever* (London: Longmans, Green, and Co., 1905), and with Sir Walter Besant on *The Charm, and Other Drawing-Room Plays* (New York: Frederick A. Stokes Co., 1897). In "The Charm," one of Besant's and Pollock's characters seems to reveal the motive of the authors' collaboration: "Let us leave this cursed salon. Let us retreat to our own rooms, where we will rail at women" (45). See also James Brander Matthews, *With my friends; tales told in partnership; with an introductory essay on the art and mystery of collaboration* (New York: Longmans, Green, and Co., 1891), on which W. H. Pollock collaborated.

Other men shared Lang's desire to undo She's power: John De Morgan wrote a parody of *She*, also entitled *He*, that same year. John De Morgan was also responsible for a second *King Solomon's Wives*, and for *Bess*, a gender-reversed parody of Haggard's *Jess*. These parodists enjoyed changing one letter of a name to switch the gender.

56. Quoted in Norman Etherington, *Rider Haggard* (Boston: Twayne Publishers, 1984), 9.

57. Quoted in Higgins, *Rider Haggard*, 65.

58. Quoted in Cohen, *Rider Haggard*, 188.

59. Quoted in Cohen, *Rider Haggard*, 187.

60. Quoted in Green, *Andrew Lang*, 96.

61. *Recreations of the Rabelais Club, 1885–1888* (Guilford: Billing and Sons, 1888), 68.

62. Ella Haggard, *Life and Its Author* (London: Longmans, Green, and Co., 1890).

63. Quoted in Lilias Rider Haggard, *The Cloak That I Left* (London: Hodder and Stoughton, 1951), 135.

64. Quoted in Lilias Rider Haggard, *The Cloak That I Left*, 206–7.

65. Quoted in Higgins, *Rider Haggard*, 127.

66. Quoted in Green, *Andrew Lang*, 128.

67. Cohen, *Rider Haggard*, 187; Higgins, *Rider Haggard*, 124.

68. Quoted in Green, *Andrew Lang*, 128.

69. Boswell, *Christianity, Social Tolerance, and Homosexuality*, 29–30.

70. Quoted in Green, *Andrew Lang*, 129.

71. Quoted in Ellis, *Voice from the Infinite*, 135.

72. H. Rider Haggard and Andrew Lang, *The World's Desire* (London: Longmans, Green, and Co., 1890; reprint, 1929). Page numbers will appear in my text.

73. H. G. Wells, *The Time Machine* (1895; reprint, New York: Bantam Books, 1982), 5.

74. The prologue, not published with the novel, appears as an appendix in Green, *Andrew Lang*, 235.

75. "Clevedon Church, In Memoriam H. B.," and "Almae Matres." Quoted in Green, *Andrew Lang*, 24–25.

76. I am grateful to U. C. Knoepflmacher for uncovering these puns.

77. James Barrie, review in *British Weekly* 9 (20 Nov. 1890): 54.

78. *The English Catalogue of Books*, vol. 5, January 1890–December 1897 (reprint, New York: Kraus Reprint Corp., 1963).

79. William Ferrero and Cesar Lombroso, *The Female Offender* (London: T. F. Unwin, 1895).

80. See Ellmann, *Oscar Wilde*, 415.

81. Arthur Christopher Benson and Herbert Francis William Tatham, *Men of Might: Studies of Great Characters* (London: E. Arnold, 1902).

82. Sir Walter Besant, *Autobiography of Sir Walter Besant* (New York: Dodd, Mead, and Co., 1902), 186.

83. Walter Besant and James Rice, *The Case of Mr. Lacroft and Other Tales* (New York: Dodd, Mead, and Co., 1888), vi.

84. Besant, *Autobiography*, 187.

85. Quoted in Miriam J. Benkowitz, *Frederick Rolfe: Baron Corvo* (New York: G. P. Putnam's Sons, 1977), 80. For accounts of Corvo's collaborations, see Benkowitz.

86. [Frederick Rolfe and C. H. C. Pirie-Gordon], *Hubert's Arthur; being certain curious documents found among the literary remains of Mr. N. C., here produced by Prospero and Caliban* (London: Cassell and Company, Ltd., 1935). [Rolfe and Pirie-Gordon], *The Weird of the Wanderer, being the papyrus records of some incidents in one of the previous lives of Mr. Nicholas Crabbe, here produced by Prospero and Caliban* (London: W. Rider and Son, Ltd., 1912).

87. Quoted in Benkowitz, *Frederick Rolfe*, 130.

88. Quoted in Benkowitz, *Frederick Rolfe*, 131.

89. See Ellmann, *Oscar Wilde*, 402–3.

90. See Brocard Sewell, *In the Dorian Mode: A Life of John Gray* (Cornwall: Tabb House, 1983), 34; Brocard Sewell, *Footnote to the Nineties: A Memoir of John Gray and André Raffalovich* (London: Cecil and Amelia Woolf, 1968), 33.

91. Robinson K. Leather and Richard Le Gallienne, *The Student and the Body-Snatcher and Other Trifles* (London: Elkin Mathews, 1890). Robinson K. Leather also collaborated with Norman Rowland Gale on a volume of poetry aptly titled *On Two Strings* (privately printed by George E. Over, Rugby Press, 1894). Richard Le Gallienne, Norman Rowland Gale, and Alfred Hayes collaborated on a similar volume of poetry, *A Fellowship in Song* (London: Elkin Mathews and John Lane, 1893).

92. The classic specimen of Romish homoeroticism is Jack Bloxam, "The Priest and the Acolyte," *The Chameleon* (December 1894).

93. Dowson to Plarr, 2 March and 5 March 1891, in *The Letters of Ernest Dowson*, Desmond Flower and Henry Maas, eds. (London: Cassell & Company Ltd., 1967), 185–88.

94. Quoted in Mark Longaker, *Ernest Dowson* (Philadelphia: University of Pennsylvania Press, 1944), 237.

95. Dowson to Moore, 23 June 1889, in *Letters of Dowson*, 85–86.

96. Dowson to Moore, 16–17 Sept. 1890, in *Letters of Dowson*, 167.

97. Dowson to Moore, 27 Aug. 1893, in *Letters of Dowson*, 288; Dowson to Moore, 26 May 1889, in *Letters of Dowson*, 81.

98. Dowson to Moore, 27 Aug. 1890, in *Letters of Dowson*, 162.

99. Dowson to Moore, 5 March 1889, in *Letters of Dowson*, 45.

100. Dowson to Moore, 3 Jan. 1889, in *Letters of Dowson*, 23.

101. Quoted in John D. Gordan, " 'The Ghost' at Brede Place" (New York: New York Public Library, 1953), 4. See also Delbanco, *Group Portrait*, 41–46.

102. Quoted in John McRae, "Introduction" to Oscar Wilde [?] and others, *Teleny* (London: GMP, 1986), 10. Page numbers will appear in my text. For background on *Teleny*, see Reade, *Sexual Heretics*, 50.

103. Ford Madox Ford, "Working with Conrad," *The Yale Review*, Summer 1929; reprinted Autumn 1985, 13–28. H. L. Mencken remembers Mrs. Conrad denouncing Ford in these terms: see Bernard C. Meyer, *Joseph Conrad: A Psychoanalytic Biography* (Princeton: Princeton University Press, 1967), 152n. For background on Conrad's and Ford's collaboration, see Raymond Brebach, *Joseph Conrad, Ford Madox Ford, and the Making of "Romance"* (Ann Arbor: UMI Research Press, 1985); Delbanco, *Group Portrait*; Frederick Karl, *Joseph Conrad: The Three Lives* (New York: Farrar, Straus and Giroux, 1979); Meyer, *Joseph Conrad*; and Arthur Mizener, *The Saddest Story: A Biography of Ford Madox Ford* (New York: World Publishing Co., 1971).

104. Joseph Conrad and Ford Madox Ford, *The Nature of a Crime* (Garden City, New York: Doubleday, Page, and Co., 1924), ix. Page numbers will appear in my text.

105. Quoted in Meyer, *Joseph Conrad*, 152.

106. Conrad to Edward Garnett, 26 March 1900, in *Letters from Joseph Conrad 1895–1924*, ed. Edward Garnett (Indianapolis: Bobbs-Merrill Co., 1928), 168.

107. Ford Madox Ford, *Joseph Conrad: A Personal Remembrance* (London: Duckworth & Co., 1924), 73–74.

108. Ford, *Joseph Conrad*, 135.

109. Conrad to Henley, 18 Oct. 1898, in *The Collected Letters of Joseph Conrad*, vol. 2, ed. Frederick R. Karl and Laurence Davies (New York: Cambridge University Press, 1983), 107.

110. Quoted in Karl, *Joseph Conrad*, 549.

111. Ford, "Working with Conrad," 23. Ford, *Joseph Conrad*, 134.

112. Quoted in Mizener, *Saddest Story*, 49.

113. Ford, *Joseph Conrad*, 129–30.

114. Ford, *Joseph Conrad*, 118.

115. Joseph Conrad, *The Mirror of the Sea: Memories and Impressions* (London: Methuen and Co., 1907), 83. Quoted in Meyer, *Joseph Conrad*, 55.

116. Ford, "Working with Conrad," 19.

117. See Thomas Moser, *The Life in the Fiction of Ford Madox Ford* (Princeton: Princeton University Press, 1980), 56.

118. Ford, *Joseph Conrad*, 51.

119. Conrad's comment is quoted in Karl, *Joseph Conrad*, 521. Ford makes his observation in Ford, *Joseph Conrad*, 29.

120. Ford, *Joseph Conrad*, 38.

121. Joseph Conrad and Ford Madox Ford, *Romance* (1903; reprint, New York: Carroll and Graf Publishers, 1985), 112, 5. Page numbers will appear in my text.

122. Joseph Conrad and Ford Madox Ford, *The Inheritors* (1901; reprint, New York: Carroll and Graf Publishers, 1985), 195, 73. Page numbers will appear in my text.

123. See Faderman, *Surpassing the Love of Men*, 204–13. Discussing Michael Field and Somerville and Ross, Faderman describes female collaboration as an outgrowth of romantic friendship, and a way to create professional lives apart from male interference.

124. Sturgeon, *Michael Field*, 23.

125. Sturgeon, *Michael Field*, 79, 40. For an account of other women writers who have turned to Sappho as an imaginary collaborator, see Gubar, "Sapphistries."

126. Sturgeon, *Michael Field*, 47.

127. T. and D. C. Sturge Moore, eds., *Works and Days, from the Journal of Michael Field* (London: John Murray, 1933), 7.

128. Sturge Moore, *Works and Days*, 6.

129. Sturgeon, *Michael Field*, 80.

130. Quoted in Sturgeon, *Michael Field*, 79–80.

131. Quoted in Sturge Moore, *Works and Days*, 16.

132. Pansy and her friends, *A Sevenfold Trouble* (Boston: D. Lothrop Co., 1889), 2.

133. See, for example, the copyright page of Somerville and Ross, *The Real Charlotte* (Ward & Downey, 1894; reprinted, London: Longmans, Green, & Co., 1911).

134. E. Œ. Somerville and Martin Ross [Violet Martin], *Some Experiences of an Irish R.M.* (London: Longmans, Green, and Co., 1899).

135. Quoted in Maurice Collins, *Somerville and Ross: A Biography* (London: Faber and Faber, 1968), 72.

136. Quoted in Collins, *Somerville and Ross*, 104.

137. Quoted in Collins, *Somerville and Ross*, 72.

138. Quoted in Collins, *Somerville and Ross*, 178, 181.

139. W. B. Yeats, *A Vision* (London: Macmillan and Co., Ltd., 1962), 9.

140. Yeats, *A Vision*, 22.

Bibliography

Ackroyd, Peter. *T. S. Eliot: A Life.* New York: Simon and Schuster, 1984.

Aiken, Conrad. "An Anatomy of Melancholy." In Allen Tate, ed., *T. S. Eliot: The Man and His Works.* New York: Dell Publishing Co., 1966.

———. *Selected Letters of Conrad Aiken.* Ed. Joseph Killorin. New Haven: Yale University Press, 1978.

Allain, Marcel, and Pierre Souvestre. *Fantômas.* New York: William Morrow and Company, 1986.

Ashbery, John, and James Schuyler. *A Nest of Ninnies.* Calais, Vermont: Z Press, 1983.

Auden, W. H., and Christopher Isherwood. *The Ascent of F6.* New York: Random House, 1937.

———. *The Dog Beneath the Skin; or, Where is Francis?* London: Faber and Faber, 1935.

———. *Journey to a War.* London: Faber and Faber, 1939.

———. *On the Frontier.* New York: Random House, 1938.

Auden, W. H., and Louis MacNiece. *Letters from Iceland.* London: Faber and Faber, 1937.

Auerbach, Nina. *Woman and the Demon: The Life of a Victorian Myth.* Cambridge: Harvard University Press, 1982.

Bakhtin, M. M. *The Dialogic Imagination: Four Essays.* Ed. Michael Holquist, trans. Caryl Emerson and Michael Holquist. Austin: University of Texas Press, 1981.

Barrie, James. "Review." *British Weekly* 9 (20 Nov. 1890): 54.

Barthes, Roland. *A Lover's Discourse: Fragments.* Trans. Richard Howard. New York: Hill and Wang, 1984.

———. *The Pleasure of the Text.* Trans. Richard Miller. New York: Hill and Wang, 1985.

———. *Writing Degree Zero.* Trans. Annette Lavers and Colin Smith. New York: Hill and Wang, 1984.

Bataille, Georges. *Visions of Excess: Selected Writings, 1927–1939.* Trans. Allan Stoekl. Minneapolis: University of Minnesota Press, 1985.

Beaumont, Francis, and John Fletcher. *Works.* The Mermaid Series, ed. J. St. Loe Strachey. London: T. Fisher Unwin Ltd., 1949.

Beckson, Karl, ed. *Aesthetes and Decadents of the 1890s: An Anthology of British Poetry and Prose.* Chicago: Academy Chicago, 1981.

Benkowitz, Miriam J. *Frederick Rolfe: Baron Corvo.* New York: G. P. Putnam's Sons, 1977.

Benson, Arthur Christopher, and Herbert Francis William Tatham. *Men of Might: Studies of Great Characters.* London: E. Arnold, 1902.

Bentley, G. E. *The Profession of Dramatist in Shakespeare's Time, 1590–1642.* Princeton: Princeton University Press, 1971.

Berkson, Bill, and Joe LeSueur. *Homage to Frank O'Hara.* Berkeley: Creative Arts Book Company, 1980.

Bernheimer, Charles, and Claire Kahane, eds. *In Dora's Case: Freud—Hysteria—Feminism.* New York: Columbia University Press, 1985.

Besant, Sir Walter. *Autobiography of Sir Walter Besant.* New York: Dodd, Mead, and Co., 1902.

Besant, Walter, and James Rice. *The Case of Mr. Lacroft and Other Tales*. New York: Dodd, Mead, and Co., 1888.

Biron, Sir Henry Chartres [Hyder Ragged, pseud.]. *King Solomon's Wives*. London: Vizetelly & Co., 1887.

Bloom, Harold. *The Anxiety of Influence: A Theory of Poetry*. Oxford: Oxford University Press, 1973.

———. *A Map of Misreading*. Oxford: Oxford University Press, 1975.

Bloxam, Jack. "The Priest and the Acolyte." In *The Chameleon* (December 1894).

Boswell, John. *Christianity, Social Tolerance, and Homosexuality: Gay People in Western Europe from the Beginning of the Christian Era to the Fourteenth Century*. Chicago: University of Chicago Press, 1980.

Brebach, Raymond. *Joseph Conrad, Ford Madox Ford, and the Making of "Romance."* Ann Arbor: UMI Research Press, 1985.

Breuer, Josef, and Sigmund Freud. *Studies on Hysteria*. Trans. and ed. James Strachey with collaboration of Anna Freud. New York: Basic Books.

Brome, Vincent. *Havelock Ellis, Philosopher of Sex: A Biography*. London: Routledge & Kegan Paul, 1979.

Broumas, Olga, and Jane Miller. *Black Holes, Black Stockings*. Middletown: Wesleyan University Press, 1985.

Brown, Alice. "Study of Stevenson." Boston: Copeland and Day, 1895. In J. A. Hammerton. *Stevensoniana*. Edinburgh: John Grant, 1907.

Brown, Horatio Forbes. *John Addington Symonds: A Biography*. Second ed. London: Smith, Elder & Co., 1903.

Brown, Norman O. *Life Against Death: The Psychoanalytic Meaning of History*. Second ed. Middletown: Wesleyan University Press, 1985.

Bush, Ronald. *T. S. Eliot: A Study in Character and Style*. New York: Oxford University Press, 1983.

Calder, Jenni. *Robert Louis Stevenson: A Life Study*. New York: Oxford University Press, 1980.

Caldwell, Elsie Noble. *Last Witness for Robert Louis Stevenson*. Norman: University of Oklahoma Press, 1960.

Carpenter, Edward. *Selected Writings*. London: GMP, 1984.

Cixous, Hélène, and Catherine Clément. *The Newly Born Woman*. Trans. Betty Wing. Minneapolis: University of Minnesota Press, 1986.

Cohen, Morton N. *Rider Haggard: His Life and Works*. New York: Walker and Company, 1960.

Coleridge, Samuel Taylor. *Biographia Literaria*. Ed. J. Shawcross. London: Oxford University Press, 1968.

———. *Collected Letters of Samuel Taylor Coleridge*. Ed. Earl Leslie Griggs. Oxford: Clarendon Press, 1956.

———. *Complete Poetical Works*. Ed. Ernest Hartley Coleridge. Oxford: Clarendon Press, 1912.

———. *The Notebooks of Samuel Taylor Coleridge*. Ed. Kathleen Coburn. New York: Pantheon Books, 1961.

Coleridge, Samuel Taylor, and William Wordsworth. *Lyrical Ballads*. Ed. R. L. Brett and A. R. Jones. New York: Barnes and Noble, Inc., 1963.

———. *Lyrical Ballads 1798*. Ed. W. J. B. Owen. Oxford: Oxford University Press, 1969.

Collins, Maurice. *Somerville and Ross: A Biography*. London: Faber and Faber, 1968.

Conrad, Joseph. *The Collected Letters of Joseph Conrad*, vol. 2. Ed. Frederick R. Karl and Laurence Davies. New York: Cambridge University Press, 1983.

————. *Letters from Joseph Conrad 1895–1924*. Ed. Edward Garnett. Indianapolis: Bobbs-Merrill Co., 1928.
————. *The Mirror of the Sea: Memories and Impressions*. London: Methuen and Co., 1907.
Conrad, Joseph, and Ford Madox Ford. *The Inheritors*. New York: Carroll and Graf Publishers, 1985.
————. *The Nature of a Crime*. Garden City: Doubleday, Page, and Co., 1924.
————. *Romance*. New York: Carroll and Graf Publishers, 1985.
Cortez, Diego. "AIDS: The Advent of the Infinite Divine Spirit." *Flash Art* (July/August 1986): 58–61.
Cranefield, Paul F. "Josef Breuer's Evaluation of His Contribution to Psycho-Analysis." *International Journal of Psychoanalysis* 39 (Sept.–Oct. 1958): 319–22.
Daiches, David. *Robert Louis Stevenson and His World*. London: Thames and Hudson, 1973.
Dank, Milton. *The French against the French: Collaboration and Resistance*. New York: J. B. Lippincott Co., 1974.
d'Arch Smith, Timothy. *Love in Earnest: Some Notes on the Lives and Writings of English 'Uranian' Poets from 1889–1930*. London: Routledge & Kegan Paul, 1970.
Decker, Hannah. "The Choice of a Name: 'Dora' and Freud's Relationship with Breuer." *Journal of the American Psychoanalytic Association* 30, no. 1 (1982): 113–36.
Delbanco, Nicholas. *Group Portrait*. New York: William Morrow, 1982.
Dowson, Ernest. *The Letters of Ernest Dowson*. Ed. Desmond Flower and Henry Maas. London: Cassell & Company, Ltd., 1967.
Dowson, Ernest, and Arthur Moore. *Adrian Rome*. London: Methuen & Co., 1899.
————. *A Comedy of Masks*. London: William Heinemann, 1896.
Drinka, George Frederick. *The Birth of Neurosis: Myth, Malady, and the Victorians*. New York: Simon and Schuster, 1984.
Edinger, Dora. *Bertha Pappenheim: Freud's Anna O*. Highland Park, Illinois: Congregation Solel, 1968.
Eliade, Mircea. *The Myth of the Eternal Return, or, Cosmos and History*. Trans. Willard R. Trask. Princeton: Princeton University Press, 1971.
————. *The Sacred and the Profane: The Nature of Religion*. Trans. Willard R. Trask. New York: Harcourt, Brace & World, 1959.
Eliot, T. S. *The Complete Poems and Plays, 1919–1950*. New York: Harcourt Brace Jovanovich, 1971.
————. *Essays, Ancient and Modern*. London: Faber and Faber, 1936.
————. "Ezra Pound." Reprinted in *Ezra Pound: A Collection of Critical Essays*, ed. Walter Sutton. Englewood Cliffs: Prentice-Hall, 1963.
————. Unpublished letters. Collection of American Literature, Beinecke Rare Book and Manuscript Library, Yale University.
————. *On Poetry and Poets*. London: Faber and Faber, 1957.
————. *The Use of Poetry and the Use of Criticism*. London: Faber and Faber, 1967.
————. *The Waste Land: A Facsimile and Transcript of the Original Drafts Including the Annotations of Ezra Pound*. Ed. Valerie Eliot. New York: Harcourt Brace Jovanovich, 1971.
————. "Interview." In *Writers at Work: The Paris Review Interviews*. Second Series. New York: The Viking Press, 1963.
Eliot, Vivien Haigh-Wood. Unpublished letters. Collection of American Literature, Beinecke Rare Book and Manuscript Library, Yale University.
Ellenberger, Henri F. "The Study of Anna O.: A Critical Review with New Data." *Journal of the History of the Behavioral Sciences* 8, no. 3 (July 1972): 267–79.
Ellis, Havelock. *My Life*. London: Neville Spearman, 1967.

———. "A Note on the Bedborough Trial." Watford: University Press, 1898. Privately reprinted, D. C. McMurtie, 1925.

Ellis, Havelock, and John Addington Symonds. *Sexual Inversion.* London: Wilson and Macmillan, 1897. Reprinted, New York: Arno Press, 1975.

Ellis, Peter Berresford. *H. Rider Haggard: A Voice from the Infinite.* London: Routledge & Kegan Paul, 1978.

Ellmann, Richard. *Oscar Wilde.* New York: Alfred A. Knopf, 1988.

Elwin, Malcolm. *The Strange Case of Robert Louis Stevenson.* London: Macdonald, 1950.

The English Catalogue of Books. Vol. 5, January 1890–December 1897. New York: Kraus Reprint Corp., 1963.

Etherington, Norman. *Rider Haggard.* Boston: Twayne Publishers, 1984.

Everett, Barbara. "Eliot's Marianne: *The Waste Land* and Its Poetry of Europe." *Review of English Studies,* New Series, vol. 31, no. 121 (1980): 41–53.

Faderman, Lillian. *Surpassing the Love of Men: Romantic Friendship and Love between Women from the Renaissance to the Present.* New York: William Morrow and Company, 1981.

Ferenczi, Sándor. *First Contributions to Psycho-Analysis.* Trans. Ernest Jones. London: Hogarth Press, 1952.

Ferrero, William, and Cesar Lombroso. *The Female Offender.* London: T. F. Unwin, 1895.

Ford, Ford Madox. *Joseph Conrad: A Personal Remembrance.* London: Duckworth & Co., 1924.

———. "Working with Conrad." *The Yale Review* (Autumn 1985): 13–28. Originally published, Summer 1929.

Forster, E. M. *Maurice.* New York: W. W. Norton, 1987.

Foucault, Michel. *The History of Sexuality, Vol. 1: An Introduction.* New York: Vintage Books, 1980.

Freeman, Lucy. *The Story of Anna O.* New York: Walker and Company, 1972.

Freud, Sigmund. *An Autobiographical Study.* New York: W. W. Norton, 1963.

———. *The Complete Letters of Sigmund Freud to Wilhelm Fliess.* Trans. and ed. Jeffrey Moussaieff Masson. Cambridge: Harvard University Press, 1985.

———. "Fragment of an Analysis of a Case of Hysteria." In *Dora: An Analysis of a Case of Hysteria,* ed. Philip Rieff. New York: Collier Books, 1963.

———. "From the History of an Infantile Neurosis." In *The Wolf Man,* ed. Muriel Gardiner. New York: Basic Books, 1971.

———. "Josef Breuer." *The Standard Edition of the Complete Psychological Works of Sigmund Freud,* vol. 19. London: Hogarth Press, 1955.

———. *Leonardo da Vinci and a Memory of His Childhood.* Trans. Alan Tyson. New York: W. W. Norton, 1964.

———. *The Letters of Sigmund Freud.* Ed. Ernst L. Freud, trans. Tania and James Stern. New York: Basic Books, 1960.

———. "Medusa's Head." *Standard Edition,* vol. 18.

———. "On the History of the Psychoanalytic Movement." In *The History of the Psychoanalytic Movement,* ed. Philip Rieff. New York: Collier Books, 1963.

———. "On Transformations of Instinct as Exemplified in Anal Erotism." *Standard Edition,* vol. 17.

———. "Some Neurotic Manifestations in Jealousy, Paranoia and Homosexuality." *Standard Edition,* vol. 18.

———. *Three Essays on the Theory of Sexuality.* Trans. James Strachey. New York: Basic Books, 1962.

Furnas, J. G. *Voyage to Windward: The Life of Robert Louis Stevenson.* New York: William Sloane Associates, 1951.

Gallop, Jane. *The Daughter's Seduction: Feminism and Psychoanalysis.* Ithaca: Cornell University Press, 1982.

Gallup, Donald. *T. S. Eliot and Ezra Pound: Collaborators in Letters.* New Haven: H. W. Wenning/C. A. Stonehill, 1970.

Gay, Peter. *The Bourgeois Experience, Victoria to Freud: Education of the Senses.* New York: Oxford University Press, 1984.

———. *Freud: A Life for Our Time.* New York: W. W. Norton, 1988.

Gide, André. *Corydon.* Trans. Richard Howard. New York: Farrar, Straus and Giroux, 1983.

———. *The Counterfeiters.* Trans. Dorothy Bussy. New York: Modern Library, 1931.

Gilbert, Sandra M. "Soldier's Heart: Literary Men, Literary Women, and the Great War." *Signs* 8 (1983): 422–50.

Gilbert, Sandra M., and Susan Gubar. *The Madwoman in the Attic: The Woman Writer and the Nineteenth-Century Literary Imagination.* New Haven: Yale University Press, 1979.

———. *No Man's Land: The Place of the Woman Writer in the Twentieth Century, Volume 1: The War of the Words.* New Haven: Yale University Press, 1988.

Girard, René. *Deceit, Desire, and the Novel: Self and Other in Literary Structure.* Trans. Yvonne Freccero. Baltimore: Johns Hopkins University Press, 1972.

Glueck, Grace. "Artist and Model: Why the Tradition Endures." *The New York Times,* 8 June 1986.

———. "Singular Artists Who Work in the First Person Plural." *The New York Times,* 10 May 1987.

Goncourt, Edmond and Jules de. *Germinie Lacerteux.* Trans. Leonard Tancock. Harmondsworth: Penguin Books, 1984.

Gordan, John D. "'The Ghost' at Brede Place." New York: New York Public Library, 1953.

Green, Roger Lancelyn. *Andrew Lang: A Critical Biography.* Leicester: Edmund Ward, 1946.

Gross, John. *The Rise and Fall of the Man of Letters.* London: Weidenfeld and Nicolson, 1969.

Grosskurth, Phyllis. *Havelock Ellis: A Biography.* New York: Alfred A. Knopf, 1980.

———. *The Woeful Victorian: A Biography of John Addington Symonds.* New York: Holt, Rinehart and Winston, 1964.

Gubar, Susan. "Sapphistries." In Estelle B. Freedman and others, eds. *The Lesbian Issue: Essays from SIGNS.* Chicago: University of Chicago Press, 1985.

Haggard, Ella. *Life and Its Author.* London: Longmans, Green, and Co., 1890.

Haggard, H. Rider. *Allan Quatermain.* London: Longmans, Green, and Co., 1887.

———. *Cleopatra.* London: Longmans, Green, and Co., 1889.

———. *The Days of My Life.* London: Longmans, 1926.

———. *King Solomon's Mines.* London: Cassell & Company, 1885.

———. *The Private Diaries of H. Rider Haggard.* Ed. D. S. Higgins. London: Cassell, 1980.

———. *She.* 1886; Harmondsworth: Penguin Books, 1982.

Haggard, H. Rider, and Andrew Lang. *The World's Desire.* 1890; London: Longmans, Green, and Co., 1929.

Haggard, Lilias Rider. *The Cloak That I Left.* London: Hodder and Stoughton, 1951.

Hayes, Alfred, Richard Le Gallienne, and Norman Rowland Gale. *A Fellowship in Song.* London: Elkin Mathews and John Lane, 1893.

Henze, Hans Werner. *The Bassarids.* Libretto by W. H. Auden and Chester Kallman. New York: Associated Music Publishers, 1966.

Higgins, D. S. *Rider Haggard: A Biography.* New York: Stein and Day, 1981.

Hollender, Marc. "The Case of Anna O.: A Reformulation." *American Journal of Psychiatry* 137 (1980): 797–800.

Homans, Margaret. *Woman Writers and Poetic Identity: Dorothy Wordsworth, Emily Brontë, and Emily Dickinson.* Princeton: Princeton University Press, 1980.

Hunter, Dianne. "Hysteria, Psychoanalysis, and Feminism: The Case of Anna O." *Feminist Studies* 9 (1983): 465–88.

Hyde, H. Montgomery. *The Love That Dared Not Speak Its Name: A Candid History of Homosexuality in Britain.* Boston: Little Brown, 1970.

———. *Oscar Wilde.* New York: Farrar, Straus and Giroux, 1975.

Irigaray, Luce. *This Sex Which Is Not One.* Trans. Catherine Porter. Ithaca: Cornell University Press, 1985.

Jacobus, Mary. *Reading Woman: Essays in Feminist Criticism.* New York: Columbia University Press, 1986.

———. *Tradition and Experiment in Wordsworth's Lyrical Ballads (1798).* Oxford: Clarendon Press, 1976.

James, Henry. *Partial Portraits.* London: Macmillan, 1888.

———. *The Wheel of Time; Collaboration; Owen Wingrave.* New York: Harper and Brothers Publishers, 1893.

Jardine, Alice, and Paul Smith, eds. *Men in Feminism.* New York: Methuen, 1987.

Jeffreys, Sheila. *The Spinster and Her Enemies: Feminism and Sexuality 1880–1930.* London: Pandora Press, 1985.

Jones, Alun R., and William Tydeman, eds. *The Ancient Mariner and Other Poems: A Casebook.* London: Macmillan, 1973.

Jones, Ernest. *The Life and Work of Sigmund Freud.* New York: Basic Books, 1953.

Jordan, John E. *Why the Lyrical Ballads?* Berkeley: University of California Press, 1976.

Karl, Frederick. *Joseph Conrad: The Three Lives.* New York: Farrar, Straus and Giroux, 1979.

Kendrick, Walter. *The Secret Museum: Pornography in Modern Culture.* Harmondsworth: Penguin Books, 1987.

Knoepflmacher, U. C. "Avenging Alice: Christina Rossetti and Lewis Carroll." *Nineteenth Century Fiction* 41, no. 3 (December 1986): 299–328.

———. "On Exile and Fiction: The Lewes and the Shelleys." In Ruth Perry and Martine Watson Brownley, eds. *Mothering the Mind: Twelve Studies of Writers and Their Silent Partners.* New York: Holmes and Meier, 1984.

Koestenbaum, Wayne. "The Shadow on the Bed: Dr. Jekyll, Mr. Hyde, and the Labouchère Amendment." *Critical Matrix: Princeton Working Papers in Women's Studies,* Special Issue No. 1 (Spring 1988): 31–55.

Kofman, Sarah. *The Enigma of Woman: Woman in Freud's Writings.* Trans. Catherine Porter. Ithaca: Cornell University Press, 1985.

Kristeva, Julia. "Oscillation between 'power' and 'denial.'" In Elaine Marks and Isabelle de Courtrivron, eds. *New French Feminisms: An Anthology.* New York: Schocken Books, 1981.

Lahr, John. *Prick Up Your Ears: The Biography of Joe Orton.* New York: Knopf, 1975.

Lang, Andrew. *Adventures Among Books.* London: Longmans, Green and Co., 1905.

———. *In the Wrong Paradise, and Other Stories.* New York: Harper & Brothers, 1887.

Lang, Andrew, and Walter H. Pollock. *He.* London: Longmans, Green, and Co., 1887.

Le Gallienne, Richard, and Robinson K. Leather. *The Student and the Body-Snatcher and Other Trifles.* London: Elkin Mathews, 1890.

Leather, Robinson K., and Norman Rowland Gale. *On Two Strings.* Privately printed by George E. Over at the Rugby Press, 1894.

Leff, Leonard J. *Hitchcock and Selznick: The Rich and Strange Collaboration of Alfred Hitchcock and David O. Selznick in Hollywood.* New York: Weidenfeld & Nicolson, 1987.

Lévi-Strauss, Claude. *The Elementary Structures of Kinship.* Boston: Beacon Press, 1969.

Litz, A. Walton, ed. *Eliot in His Time.* Princeton: Princeton University Press, 1973.

Lockett, W. G. *Robert Louis Stevenson at Davos.* London: Hurst & Blackett, Ltd., 1934.

Locus Solus. "A Special Issue of Collaborations." Vol. 2 (Summer 1961).

Longaker, Mark. *Ernest Dowson.* Philadelphia: University of Pennsylvania Press, 1944.

Lowes, John Livingston. *The Road to Xanadu: A Study in the Ways of the Imagination.* Boston: Houghton Mifflin, 1927.

MacShane, Frank, ed. *Ford Madox Ford: The Critical Heritage.* London: Routledge & Kegan Paul, 1972.

Magnuson, Paul. *Coleridge and Wordsworth: A Lyrical Dialogue.* Princeton: Princeton University Press, 1988.

Maixner, Paul, ed. *Robert Louis Stevenson: The Critical Heritage.* London: Routledge & Kegan Paul, 1981.

Malcolm, Janet. "J'appelle un chat un chat." *The New Yorker,* 20 April 1987, 84–92.

Martin, Jay, ed. *A Collection of Critical Essays on "The Waste Land."* Englewood Cliffs: Prentice-Hall, 1968.

Marxist-Feminist Literature Collective. "Women's Writing." *Ideology and Consciousness* 3 (Spring 1978): 27–48.

Masson, Jeffrey Moussaieff. *The Assault on Truth: Freud's Suppression of the Seduction Theory.* New York: Viking Penguin, 1985.

Matthews, James Brander, and others. *With my friends; tales told in partnership; with an introductory essay on the art and mystery of collaboration.* New York: Longmans, Green, and Co., 1891.

Mayne, Xavier [Edward Irenaeus Prime Stevenson]. *The Intersexes: A History of Simisexualism as a Problem in Social Life.* Reprint of edition privately printed in 1908. New York: Arno Press, 1975.

McClatchy, J. D. "On the Quay Brothers." Forthcoming in *Connoisseur.*

McGrath, William J. *Freud's Discovery of Psychoanalysis: The Politics of Hysteria.* Ithaca: Cornell University Press, 1986.

Meyer, Bernard C. *Joseph Conrad: A Psychoanalytic Biography.* Princeton: Princeton University Press, 1967.

Miller, James E., Jr. *T. S. Eliot's Personal Waste Land: Exorcism of the Demons.* University Park: Penn. State University Press, 1977.

Miner, Earl Roy. *Japanese Linked Poetry: An Account with Translations of Renga and Haikai Sequences.* Princeton: Princeton University Press, 1979.

Mizener, Arthur. *The Saddest Story: A Biography of Ford Madox Ford.* New York: World Publishing Co., 1971.

Moon, Michael. "'The Gentle Boy from the Dangerous Classes': Pederasty, Domesticity, and Capitalism in Horatio Alger." *Representations* 19 (Summer 1987): 87–110.

Moore, George. *Celibate Lives.* London: Chatto and Windus, 1922.

———. *Celibates.* New York: Macmillan, 1895.

Moser, Thomas. *The Life in the Fiction of Ford Madox Ford.* Princeton: Princeton University Press, 1980.

Novick, Peter. *The Resistance Versus Vichy: The Purge of Collaborators in Liberated France.* New York: Columbia University Press, 1968.

Oberndorf, C. P. "Autobiography of Josef Breuer." *International Journal of Psychoanalysis* 34 (1953).

Osborne, Lloyd. *An Intimate Portrait of R. L. S.* New York: Scribner's, 1924.

———. "Stevenson at Thirty-two." In Robert Louis Stevenson. *Treasure Island.* New York: Charles Scribner's Sons, 1925.

Osborne-Stevenson, Fanny. "Prefatory Note." In Robert Louis Stevenson. *The Strange Case of Dr. Jekyll & Mr. Hyde, Fables, Other Stories & Fragments.* London: William Heinemann, Ltd., 1924.

Pansy and her friends. *A Sevenfold Trouble*. Boston: D. Lothrop Co., 1889.
Pappenheim, Bertha. *Le travail de Sisyphe*. Trans. Jacques Legrand. Paris: des femmes, 1986.
Parrish, Stephen Maxfield. *The Art of the Lyrical Ballads*. Cambridge: Harvard University Press, 1973.
Perkins, David, ed. *English Romantic Writers*. New York: Harcourt Brace Jovanovich, Inc., 1967.
Pollock, George H. "The Possible Significance of Childhood Object-Loss in the Josef Breuer-Bertha Pappenheim (Anna O.)-Sigmund Freud Relationship." *Journal of the American Psychoanalytic Association* 16 (1968): 711–39.
Pollock, Walter H., and Sir Walter Besant. *The Charm, and Other Drawing-Room Plays*. New York: Frederick A. Stokes Co., 1897.
Pollock, Walter H., and Guy C. Pollock. *Hay Fever*. London: Longmans, Green, and Co., 1905.
Pound, Ezra. Unpublished letters. Collection of American Literature, Beinecke Rare Book and Manuscript Library, Yale University.
———. *The Letters of Ezra Pound 1907–1941*. Ed. D. D. Paige. New York: Harcourt, Brace and Company, 1950.
———. "Postscript." In Rémy de Gourmont. *The Natural Philosophy of Love*. Trans. Ezra Pound. London: Neville Spearman, 1957.
Quinn, John. Unpublished letters. Collection of American Literature, Beinecke Rare Book and Manuscript Library, Yale University.
Raffalovich, Marc-André. *Uranisme et unisexualité: étude sur différentes manifestations de l'instinct sexuel*, Bib. de Criminologie. Vol. 15. Lyon: A. Storck; Paris: Masson, 1896.
Reade, Brian. *Sexual Heretics: Male Homosexuality in English Literature from 1850–1900*. London: Routledge & Kegan Paul, 1970.
Recreations of the Rabelais Club, 1885–1888. Guilford: Billing and Sons, 1888.
Reid, B. L. *The Man from New York: John Quinn and His Friends*. New York: Oxford University Press, 1968.
Rimbaud, Arthur. *Complete Works, Selected Letters*. Trans. Wallace Fowlie. Chicago: University of Chicago Press, 1966.
Rolfe, Frederick [Baron Corvo, pseud.]. *The Desire and Pursuit of the Whole: A Romance of Modern Venice*. London: Cassell, 1934.
Rolfe, Frederick, and Sholto Douglas, trans. *The Songs of Meleager*. London: The First Edition Club, 1937.
[Rolfe, Frederick, and C. H. C. Pirie-Gordon.] *Hubert's Arthur; being certain curious documents found among the literary remains of Mr. N. C., here produced by Prospero and Caliban*. London: Cassell and Company, Ltd., 1935.
———. *The Weird of the Wanderer, being the papyrus records of some incidents in one of the previous lives of Mr. Nicholas Crabbe, here produced by Prospero and Caliban*. London: W. Rider and Son, Ltd., 1912.
Rose, Phyllis. *Parallel Lives: Five Victorian Marriages*. New York: Vintage Books, 1983.
Rosenbaum, Max, and Melvin Muroff. *Anna O.: Fourteen Contemporary Reinterpretations*. New York: The Free Press, 1984.
Rousseau, G. S. "The Pursuit of Homosexuality in the Eighteenth Century: 'Utterly Confused Category' and/or Rich Repository?" In Robert Purks Maccubbin, ed. *'Tis Nature's Fault: Unauthorized Sexuality during the Enlightenment*. Cambridge: Cambridge University Press, 1987.
Rowbatham, Sheila, and Jeffrey Weeks. *Socialism and the New Life: The Personal and Sexual Politics of Edward Carpenter and Havelock Ellis*. London: Pluto Press, 1977.
Rubin, Gayle. "The Traffic in Women: Notes Towards a Political Economy of Sex." In

Toward an Anthropology of Women. Ed. Rayna Reiter. New York: Monthly Review Press, 1975.

Sedgwick, Eve Kosofsky. *Between Men: English Literature and Male Homosocial Desire*. New York: Columbia University Press, 1985.

————. "Privilege of Unknowing." *Genders* 1 (1988): 102–24.

Sewell, Brocard. *Footnote to the Nineties: A Memoir of John Gray and André Raffalovich*. London: Cecil and Amelia Woolf, 1968.

————. *In the Dorian Mode: A Life of John Gray*. Cornwall: Tabb House, 1983.

Showalter, Elaine. *The Female Malady: Women, Madness, and English Culture, 1830–1980*. New York: Pantheon Books, 1985.

————, ed. *The New Feminist Criticism: Essays on Women, Literature, and Theory*. New York: Pantheon Books, 1985.

————. "The Other Bostonians: Gender and Literary Study." *The Yale Journal of Criticism* 1 (1987): 179–87.

Simpson, A. W. Brian. *Cannibalism and the Common Law*. Chicago: University of Chicago Press, 1984.

Smith, F. B. "Labouchère's Amendment to the Criminal Law Amendment Bill." *Historical Studies* 17, no. 67 (October 1976): 165–75.

Smith, Roberta. "Singular Artists Who Work in the First Person Plural." *The New York Times*, 10 May 1987.

Smith-Rosenberg, Carroll. *Disorderly Conduct: Visions of Gender in Victorian America*. New York: Knopf, 1985.

Somerville, Edith Œ., and Martin Ross [Violet Martin]. *The Real Charlotte*. Ward & Downey, 1894; reprinted, London: Longmans, Green, & Co., 1911.

————. *Some Experiences of an Irish R.M.* London: Longmans, Green, and Co., 1899.

Stevens, Wallace. *The Necessary Angel*. New York: Random House, 1951.

Stevenson, Robert Louis. *The Essays of Robert Louis Stevenson*. Ed. Malcolm Elwin. London: Macdonald, 1950.

————. *The Strange Case of Dr. Jekyll and Mr. Hyde*. 1885; Harmondsworth: Penguin Books, 1981.

————. *Virginibus Puerisque and Other Essays in Belles Lettres*. London: William Heinemann, 1924.

Stevenson, Robert Louis, and William Ernest Henley. *Deacon Brodie, or, The Double Life: a melodrama, founded on facts, in four acts and ten tableaux*. Edinburgh: T. E. Constable, 1880.

Stevenson, Robert Louis, and Lloyd Osborne. *The Ebb-Tide: A Trio and Quartette*. New York: Charles Scribner's Sons, 1908.

————. *The Wrecker*. New York: Charles Scribner's Sons, 1895.

————. *The Wrong Box*. London: Longmans, Green, and Co., 1889.

Stevenson, Robert Louis, and Fanny Van de Grift Stevenson. *More New Arabian Nights: The Dynamiter*. London: Longmans, Green, and Co., 1885.

Stravinsky, Igor. *The Rake's Progress*. Libretto by W. H. Auden and Chester Kallman. London: Boosey and Hawkes, 1951.

Sturge Moore, T. and D. C., eds. *Works and Days, from the Journal of Michael Field*. London: John Murray, 1933.

Sturgeon, Mary. *Michael Field*. London: George G. Harrap & Co., Ltd., 1922.

Symonds, John Addington. *Animi Figura*. London: Smith, Elder & Co., 1882.

————. *In the Key of Blue and Other Prose Essays*. London: Elkin Mathews, 1893.

————. *The Letters of John Addington Symonds*. Ed. Herbert M. Schueller and Robert L. Peters. Detroit: Wayne State University Press, 1969.

———. *The Memoirs of John Addington Symonds.* Ed. Phyllis Grosskurth. Chicago: University of Chicago Press, 1984.

———. "A Problem in Greek Ethics" and "A Problem in Modern Ethics." Reprinted as *Sexual Inversion.* New York: Bell Publishing Company, 1984.

Symonds, John Addington, and Margaret Symonds. *Our Life in the Swiss Highlands.* London: Adams and Charles Black, 1892.

Symonds, Margaret. *Out of the Past.* New York: Charles Scribner's Sons, 1925.

Tisseron, Yolande. *Du deuil à la réparation: "Anna O." restituée à Bertha Pappenheim: naissance d'une vocation sociale.* Paris: des femmes, 1986.

Todorov, Tzvetan. *The Fantastic: A Structural Approach to a Literary Genre.* Trans. Richard Howard. Cleveland: Press of Case Western Reserve University, 1973.

Tomkins, Calvin. *The Bride and the Bachelors: Five Masters of the Avant Garde.* Harmondsworth: Penguin Books, 1986.

Trosman, Harry. "T. S. Eliot and *The Waste Land*: Psychopathological Antecedents and Transformations." *Archives of General Psychiatry* 30.5 (May 1974): 709–17.

Wagner-Martin, Linda. *Sylvia Plath: A Biography.* New York: Simon and Schuster, 1987.

Wallace, Marjorie. *The Silent Twins.* New York: Ballantine Books, 1986.

Weeks, Jeffrey. *Coming Out: Homosexual Politics in Britain, from the 19th Century to the Present.* London: Quartet Books, 1977.

———. *Sex, Politics, and Society: The Regulation of Sexuality Since 1800.* London: Longman, 1981.

Wells, H. G. *The Time Machine.* 1895; reprinted, New York: Bantam Books, 1982.

Wilde, Oscar. *De Profundis and Other Writings.* Ed. Hesketh Pearson. Harmondsworth: Penguin Books, 1986.

Wilde, Oscar [?], and others. *Teleny.* Introduction by John MacRae. London: GMP, 1986.

Wordsworth, William, and Dorothy Wordsworth. *The Letters of William and Dorothy Wordsworth, Volume 1, The Early Years 1787–1805.* Ed. Ernest de Selincourt, rev. Chester L. Shaver. Oxford: Clarendon Press, 1967.

Yeats, W. B. *A Vision.* London: Macmillan and Co., Ltd., 1962.

Index

Addison, Joseph, 12
Adrian Rome (Dowson and Moore), 163
Allain, Marcel, 13
Aiken, Conrad, 115, 116, 117, 118, 123, 138
Allan Quatermain (H. R. Haggard), 152
Alden, Isabella M., 175
Allan's Wife (H. R. Haggard), 154
Alleyne, Leonora Blanche, 155
"Ambush of Young Days, The" (Gray and Raffalovich), 163
Andreas-Salomé, Lou, 23–24
"Anecdote for Fathers" (W. Wordsworth), 99–100
Anna O. [pseud. of Pappenheim], 116; career of, 18, 41–42; as collaborator, 34–35; hysterical childbirth of, 22, 25–26, 27–29, 38, 40; language disturbance of, 33–34, 113, 131, 135, 136; sharing of, 40–41; *Studies in Hysteria* dominated by, 17, 29–31, 32
Ashbery, John, 13
"Astrophel and Stella" (Sidney), 75
Auden, W. H., 13
Augustine, St., 136
Autobiographical Study, An (S. Freud), 27

Bakhtin, M. M., 8
Barrie, James M., 160
Barthes, Roland, 9, 58
Bataille, Georges, 8
Beatrice (H. R. Haggard), 154
Beaumont, Francis, 12
"Beauty and Moonlight" (W. Wordsworth), 96
Beckett, Thomas à, 162
Beggar My Neighbor (Gerard), 175
Benson, A. C., 161
Benson, E. F., 161
Benson, Robert Hugh, 162
Bernays, Martha, 12–22
Bernheim, Hippolyte, 32

Besant, Walter, 155, 161–62
Black Holes, Black Stockings (Miller and Broumas), 13
Blackmailers, The (Gray and Raffalovich), 163
Bloom, Harold, 10
"Body-Snatcher, The" (R. L. Stevenson), 163
Boswell, James, 12
Boy Hairdresser, The (Orton and Halliwell), 13
Bradley, Katharine, 53, 144
Breton, André, 13
Breuer, Josef, 13; S. Freud's collaboration with, 17–35, 40–41
Breuer, Mathilde, 22
Brontë sisters, 12
Broumas, Olga, 13
Brown, Alice, 145
Brown, Horatio Forbes, 44, 61–62
Brown, Norman O., 19
Browning, Elizabeth Barrett, 175
Browning, Robert, 158, 173, 174, 175
Brücke, Ernst, 20
Bryher, 13

Cäcilie M., 32–33
Cage, John, 13
Cain and Abel, 10, 72, 75
Carpenter, Edward, 46, 47, 49, 52, 56
Changing Light at Sandover, The (Merrill), 176
Char, René, 13
Charcot, J.-M., 20–21, 23, 129, 137
"Childe Roland to the Dark Tower Came" (R. Browning), 158
"Christabel" (Coleridge), 73–74
Cixous, Hélène, 9, 13
Clarissa (Richardson), 134
"Claude the Cabin Boy" (T. S. Eliot), 123, 124
Clément, Catherine, 13

Cleopatra (H. R. Haggard), 154, 156, 159
Coleridge, Samuel Taylor, 10, 14, 121; decline of, 73–74; T. S. Eliot on, 118; romanticism and, 4–5; unsuccessful collaborations of, 71–72; W. Wordsworth's collaboration with, 71–111
"Collaboration" (H. James), 143
Collins, William, 104
Comedy of Masks, A (Dowson and Moore), 163
Communist Manifesto (Marx and Engels), 13
"Complaint of a Forsaken Indian Woman, A" (W. Wordsworth), 88
Conrad, Joseph, 125, 144, 164, 165–73
"Convict, The" (W. Wordsworth), 95–96
Cooper, Edith, 53, 144
Corvo, Baron [pseud. of Rolfe], 162–63
Corydon (Gide), 63
Counterfeiters, The (Gide), 1
Crane, Stephen, 164–65
Critique scientifique, La (Hennequin), 65
Cronenberg, David, 11
Cruikshank, John, 72
Cunningham, Merce, 13

Da Vinci, Leonardo, 18, 19, 24–25
Deacon Brodie (R. L. Stevenson and Henley), 145
Dead Ringers (Cronenberg), 11
"Death of Saint Narcissus, The" (T. S. Eliot), 123
"Decay of Lying, The" (Wilde), 63
De Gourmont, Rémy, 121
Desire and Pursuit of the Whole, The (Corvo), 162
"Dirge" (T. S. Eliot), 213
Divers Women (Pansy and Livingston), 175
Dora, 32
Douglas, Lord Alfred, 161, 163
Douglas, Sholto, 162
Dowson, Ernest, 163–64
"Dungeon, The" (Coleridge), 95

Ebb-Tide, The (R. L. Stevenson and Osborne), 145, 148–49
Eckstein, Emma, 38, 40
Elektra (Strauss and Hofmannsthal), 10
Eliade, Mircea, 41
Eliot, George, 12, 153
Eliot, T. S., 4, 50, 75, 98, 110–11; on Coleridge and W. Wordsworth, 118; emotional

disturbances of, 112–17; misogyny of, 118–19; Pound's collaboration with, 117–39
Eliot, Vivien, 114, 117, 118, 123, 126, 133
Elisabeth von R., 32, 33
Ellis, Havelock, 173–74; J. A. Symonds's collaboration with, 4, 5, 43–61
Eluard, Paul, 13
Emmy von N., 32, 115, 116
Engels, Friedrich, 13
English Catalogue of Books, 161
Eric Brighteyes (H. R. Haggard), 154
Everett, Barbara, 125
Evolution of Modesty, The (Ellis), 47
"Exequy" (T. S. Eliot), 123
"Expostulation and Reply" (W. Wordsworth), 101–2

Fantômas (Allain and Souvestre), 13
Female Offender, The (Lombroso and Ferrero), 161
"Female Vagrant, The" (W. Wordsworth), 87, 88
Ferenczi, Sándor, 20
Ferrero, Guglielmo, 161
Field, Michael [pseud. of Bradley and Cooper], 53, 144, 173–75
Flaubert, Gustave, 168
Fletcher, John, 12
Fliess, Wilhelm, 7, 18, 35–41, 176–77
Ford, Ford Madox, 144, 165–73
Foster, Theodosia M. [pseud. Faye Huntington], 175
"Foster-Mother's Tale, The" (Coleridge), 95
Fowler, D. C., 113
Freud, Anna, 39–41
Freud, Sigmund, 4, 13, 131; Breuer's collaboration with, 17–35, 40–41; Fliess's collaboration with, 35–41; homosexuality viewed by, 5, 19, 77; on hysteria, 113–14, 123, 129; in mentor-disciple relationships, 21, 28, 31; Symonds contrasted with, 67
From Different Standpoints (Pansy and Huntington), 175
"Frost at Midnight" (Coleridge), 73, 96, 107, 109

Gerard, Emily and Dorothea [pseud. E. D. Gerard], 175
Ghost, The, 164–65

Gibbons, June and Jennifer, 13–14
Gide, André, 1, 63
Gilbert, Sandra M., 13
Gilbert, W. S., 10
Gilbert and George, 11
Gilman, Charlotte Perkins, 115
Girard, René, 3
"Girl, A" (Field), 174
Gissing, George, 164
Goncourt, Edmond and Jules de, 1, 13
"Goody Blake and Harry Gill" (W. Words-
    worth), 89, 90
Gozzi, Carlo, 66
Gray, John, 56, 145, 163, 173
"Green Carnation—1887, The," (McDer-
    mott and McGough), 11
Gubar, Susan, 13

Haggard, Arthur ("Jock"), 152
Haggard, Ella, 156, 159, 160
Haggard, H. Rider, 1, 2, 144, 151–61, 164,
    165, 175
Hallam, Arthur, 12, 158
Halliwell, Kenneth, 13
Hammerschlag, Anna, 40
H. D., 13
He (Lang and Pollock), 154
Heart of Darkness (Conrad), 125
Henley, W. E., 145, 146, 150, 153, 167
Hennequin, M. Emile, 65
*History and Techniques of Vaginal Radical
    Operation* (L. and T. Landau), 161
Hitchcock, Alfred, 10
Hofmannsthal, Hugo von, 10
Holden, John, 162
Homer, 151
Housman, A. E., 116
Hubert's Arthur (Prospero and Caliban),
    162
Hueffer, Elsie, 166
Hughes, Ted, 17
Huntington, Faye [pseud. of Foster], 175
"Hysteria" (T. S. Eliot), 115

"Idiot Boy, The" (W. Wordsworth), 82–85
Inheritors, The (Conrad and Ford), 166,
    167, 172
In Memoriam (Tennyson), 12, 158
Interpretation of Dreams, The (S. Freud),
    37
Intersexes, The (Mayne), 45
In the Key of Blue (J. A. Symonds), 49

In the Wrong Paradise (Andrew Lang), 152
Irigaray, Luce, 3
Isherwood, Christopher, 13

Jackson, D. C. and J. P., 161
Jackson, David, 176
James, Alice, 115
James, Henry, 143–44, 145, 153, 164, 168
James, William, 56
Jeune Née, La (Cixous and Clément), 13
John Addington Symonds (H. F. Brown),
    61–62, 63–64
Jones, Ernest, 21, 28
Joseph Conrad (Ford), 166
Joyce, James, 98, 122

Kallman, Chester, 13
Katharina—, 32, 33
"King Bolo and His Great Black Queen"
    (T. S. Eliot), 120
King Solomon's Mines (H. R. Haggard),
    151, 152
Kipling, Rudyard, 127
Kofman, Sarah, 35
Kristeva, Julia, 113
"Kubla Khan" (Coleridge), 73
Kurella, Hans, 47

Labouchère Amendment (1886), 3, 44, 50,
    157
Lacan, Jacques, 56
Landau, L. and T., 161
Lang, Andrew, 1, 2, 144, 145, 151–61, 165,
    175
"Last of the Flock, The" (W. Wordsworth),
    93–94
Leather, Robinson K., 163
Leçons du mardi (Charcot), 21
Leçons sur les maladies du système nerveux
    (Charcot), 21
Lees, Edith, 53
Leff, Leonard J., 10
Le Gallienne, Richard, 149, 163
"Leonardo da Vinci and a Memory of His
    Childhood" (S. Freud), 24–25
Lévi-Strauss, Claude, 3
Lewes, George Henry, 12
"Lewti" (Coleridge), 96
Life and Its Author (E. Haggard), 156
Life of Samuel Johnson (Boswell), 12
"Lines left upon a Seat in a Yew-Tree" (W.
    Wordsworth), 91, 103

"Lines written at a small distance from my House" (W. Wordsworth), 103
"Lines written in early spring" (W. Wordsworth), 103, 104
"Lines written near Richmond" (W. Wordsworth), 103, 104
Little Review, 119
Livingston, Mrs. C. M., 175
Lombroso, Cesare, 161
Longman, Charles, 156
"Love Song of J. Alfred Prufrock, The" (T. S. Eliot), 124, 127, 132
Lucy R., 32
Lyrical Ballads (W. Wordsworth and Coleridge), 4, 71–111; "Anecdote for Fathers," 99–100; authorship and editions of, 71–74; "Convict," 95–96; "Dungeon," 95; "Expostulation and Reply," 101–2; "Female Vagrant," 87, 88; "Foster-Mother's Tale," 95; "Goody Blake and Harry Gill," 89, 90; "Idiot Boy," 82–85; "Lewti," 96; "Last of the Flock," 93–94; "Lines left upon a Seat in a Yew-Tree," 91, 103; "Lines written at a small distance from my House," 103; "Lines written in early spring," 103, 104; "Lines written near Richmond," 103, 104; "Mad Mother," 81, 87, 88; "Nightingale," 96–99; "Old Man Travelling," 95; "Simon Lee," 90–92, 93, 97; "Tables Turned," 101–2; "Thorn," 81, 85–87, 88; "Tintern Abbey," 74, 82, 86, 88–89, 90, 96, 103, 105–10; Waste Land compared with, 5, 111; "We are Seven," 74, 100–101. See also "Rime of the Ancyent Marinere"

McDermott, David, 11
McGough, Peter, 11
MacNiece, Louis, 13
"Mad Mother, The" (W. Wordsworth), 81, 87, 88
Madwoman in the Attic, The (Gilbert and Gubar), 13
Marivaux, Pierre, 125
Marlowe, Christopher, 50
Martin, Violet [pseud. Martin Ross], 144, 176
Marx, Karl, 12
Marxist-Feminist Literature Collective, 13
Masson, Jeffrey Moussaieff, 38

Mayne, Xavier [pseud. of E. I. P. Stevenson], 45
Men of Might (Tatham and Benson), 161
Merrill, James, 176
"Michael" (W. Wordsworth), 90
Michelangelo Buonarroti, 161
Midwives' Gazette, 117, 118, 123
Miller, Jane, 13
Moffat, W. G., 161
Moore, Arthur, 163–64
More New Arabian Nights (R. L. Stevenson and F. Stevenson), 150
My Life (Ellis), 60

Nada the Lily (H. R. Haggard), 154
Natural Philosophy of Love, The (de Gourmont), 121
Nature of a Crime, The (Conrad and Ford), 166, 172
Nest of Ninnies, A (Ashbery and Schuyler), 13
"Nightingale, The" (Coleridge), 96–99
"No Arguments" (McDermott and McGough), 11, 12
"Northern Aspect, A" (Gray and Raffalovich), 163
"Note on the Bedborough Trial, A" (Ellis), 61

"Ode on the Death of Thomson" (Collins), 104
Odyssey (Homer), 151
"Of He and She" (Besant), 155
O'Hara, Frank, 13
"Old Man Travelling" (W. Wordsworth), 95
"On Transformations of Instinct as Exemplified in Anal Erotism" (S. Freud), 23
"On the History of the Psychoanalytic Movement" (S. Freud), 26–27
Orton, Joe, 13
Osborne, Lloyd, 144, 145–49, 150, 165
Osborne-Stevenson, Fanny, 150
Our Life in the Swiss Highlands (J. A. Symonds and M. Symonds), 48, 61, 64–67

Paige, D. D., 120, 123
Pansy [pseud. of Alden], 175
Pappenheim, Bertha. See Anna O.
Pater, Walter, 167
Patience (W. S. Gilbert and Sullivan), 10
Peret, Benjamin, 13
Peter Pan (Barrie), 160

Picture of Dorian Gray, The (Wilde), 33, 163
Pirie-Gordon, C. H. C., 162
Plarr, Victor, 163
Plath, Sylvia, 14
Plato, 63, 159
Pollock, W. H., 154
Poole, Thomas, 71–72
"Portrait of a Lady" (T. S. Eliot), 118
Pound, Ezra, 4, 50, 110-11; T. S. Eliot's collaboration with, 117–39; on *Waste Land*, 112; Yeats and, 166, 176–77
"Problem in Greek Ethics, A" (J. A. Symonds), 45, 47, 62, 151
"Problem in Modern Ethics, A" (J. A. Symonds), 45, 51, 62, 63
Prospero and Caliban, 162

Quay brothers, 10
Queensbury, Marquess of, 147
"Queer—1885" (McDermott and McGough), 11
Quinn, John, 119, 122

Rabelais Club, 155
Raffalovich, Marc-André, 45, 56, 145, 163
Ransom, John Crowe, 113
Rauschenberg, Robert, 13
Ready-Money Mortiboy (Besant and Rice), 161
Recreations of the Rabelais Club, 155
Reitler, R., 25
Renaissance in Italy (J. A. Symonds), 43
Reviews of Unwritten Books (Corvo and S. Douglas), 162–63
Revolt of Man, The (Besant), 162
Rice, James, 161–62
Richards, I. A., 112–13
Richardson, Samuel, 134
Rimbaud, Arthur, 13
"Rime of the Ancyent Marinere" (Coleridge), 72–73, 74–83; deletion from *Lyrical Ballads* of, 44; W. Wordsworth influenced by, 85, 87, 89, 95, 99, 100, 103, 107
Rolfe, Frederick [pseud. Baron Corvo], 162–63
Romance (Conrad and Ford), 144, 165–73
Ross, Martin [pseud. of Martin], 144, 176
Rubin, Gayle, 3

Saintsbury, George, 152–53
Salomé (Wilde), 163
"Sapphistries" (Gubar), 13

Savile Club, 153
Sayle, Charles Edward, 46
Schiller, Friedrich von, 18
Schuyler, James, 13
Schwartz, Delmore, 113
Seamy Side, The (Besant and Rice), 161
Sedgwick, Eve Kosofsky, 2, 18
Selected Letters of Ezra Pound (ed. Paige), 120
Selznick, David O., 10
Sensitive Plant, A (Gerard), 175
Sevenfold Trouble, A (Pansy and others), 175
Sexual Inversion (J. A. Symonds and Ellis), 4, 5, 43–61, 161
Shakespeare, William, 76–77
She (H. R. Haggard), 1, 151, 154
Sidney, Sir Philip, 75
"Simon Lee" (Wordsworth), 74, 90–92, 93, 97
Sitwell, Edith, 119
Smyth, Ethel, 176
Society of Authors, 162
Socrates, 12
Somerville, Edith, 144, 175, 176
Some Experiences of an Irish R. M. (Somerville and Ross), 175
"Song for the Opherion" (T. S. Eliot), 123
Songs of Meleager, The (trans. Corvo and S. Douglas), 162
Southey, Robert, 71, 75, 108
Souvestre, Pierre, 13
Spectator, 12
Steele, Sir Richard, 12
Stein, Gertrude, 13
Stevens, Wallace, 57
Stevenson, Edward Irenaeus Prime [pseud. Xavier Mayne], 45
Stevenson, Fanny Osborne, 150
Stevenson, Robert Louis, 45, 144, 145–51, 153, 157, 161, 165, 167, 169
Strachey, James, 29–30
Strange Case of Dr. Jekyll and Mr. Hyde, The (R. L. Stevenson), 33, 45, 147, 150–51
Strauss, Richard, 10
Student and the Body-Snatcher, The (Le Gallienne and Leather), 163
Studies in the Psychology of Sex (Ellis), 43, 47
Studies on Hysteria (S. Freud and J. Breuer), 17–18, 21, 29–35, 40, 56–57, 113, 161

Sturgeon, Mary, 174
Sullivan, Sir Arthur, 10
"Suppressed Complex" (T. S. Eliot), 118
"Sweeney Erect" (T. S. Eliot), 114
Swift, Jonathan, 19
Symonds, John Addington, 122, 145, 149, 174; Ellis's collaboration with, 4, 5, 43–61; Freud contrasted with, 67; various collaborators of, 61–67
Symonds, Margaret, 61, 64, 65, 66
Symons, Arthur, 50
Symposium (Plato), 63, 159

"Tables Turned, The" (W. Wordsworth), 101–2
Tatham, Herbert F. W., 161
Tatler, 12
Teleny (Wilde[?] and others), 165
Tennyson, Alfred, 12, 125, 158
Thirty Naughty Emperors (Corvo and S. Douglas), 162
"This Lime-Tree Bower My Prison" (Coleridge), 73
"Thorn, The" (W. Wordsworth), 81, 85–87, 88
Three Essays on the Theory of Sexuality (S. Freud), 7
Time Machine, The (Wells), 157
"Tintern Abbey" (Wordsworth), 74, 82, 86, 88–89, 90, 96, 102, 103, 105–10
Toklas, Alice B., 13
"To William Wordsworth" (Coleridge), 77
Traubel, Horace, 64
Treasure Island (R. L. Stevenson), 146
Two Men (Wells), 143

Ulrichs, Karl Heinrich, 63
Ulysses (Joyce), 122
"Ulysses" (Tennyson), 158
Uranisme et unisexualité (Raffalovich), 56
Use of Poetry and the Use of Criticism, The (T. S. Eliot), 116

Varieties of Religious Experience, The (W. James), 56
Venturi, Silvio, 47
Verdenal, Jean, 123, 133
Verlaine, Paul, 13, 49–50
Victoria, Queen, 153, 161
Vie de Marianne, La (Marivaux), 125
Vision, A (Yeats), 176

Vittoz, Dr., 116

"Wanderings of Cain, The" (W. Wordsworth and Coleridge), 72
Ward, Mrs. Humphry, 151
Waste Land, The (T. S. Eliot), 4, 7, 50, 75, 176; "Burial of the Dead," 129–31, 134; critical views of, 112–13; "Death by Water," 138; T. S. Eliot's emotional disturbances and, 112–17; "Fire Sermon," 119, 134–36; "Game of Chess," 131–34; as hysterical discourse, 112–14, 137–39; *Lyrical Ballads* compared with, 5, 111; Pound as editor of, 119–29; "What the Thunder Said," 136–37
"We are Seven" (W. Wordsworth), 74, 100–101
Weird of the Wanderer, The (Prospero and Caliban), 162
Weir of Hermiston, The (R. L. Stevenson), 146
Wells, H. G., 129, 157, 164
What's the World Coming To? (Moffat and White), 161
White, J., 161
Whitman, Walt, 49, 50, 51, 64–65, 67, 145
Wilde, Oscar, 10, 45, 144, 163–64, 165, 172, 173; prosecution of, 3, 147, 153
"Winter Nights at Davos" (J. A. Symonds), 66
Wolf Man case, 23, 37
Woolf, Virginia, 115
Wordsworth, Dorothy, 84, 118
Wordsworth, William, 10, 14; "Rime of Ancyent Marinere" deleted by, 44; ascendancy of, 72–74; Coleridge's collaboration with, 71–111; Eliot on, 118; illegitimate child of, 99; on repetition, 81–82; romanticism and, 4–5
"World is Too Much With Us, The" (W. Wordsworth), 110
World's Desire, The (Andrew Lang and H. R. Haggard), 2, 144, 151–61, 162
Wrecker, The (R. L. Stevenson and Osborne), 145, 147–48
Wrong Box, The (R. L. Stevenson and Osborne), 145

Yeats, William Butler, 90, 122, 166, 176–77
Young, Edward, 107